IMAGES
of America

TOWN OF AURORA
1818–1930

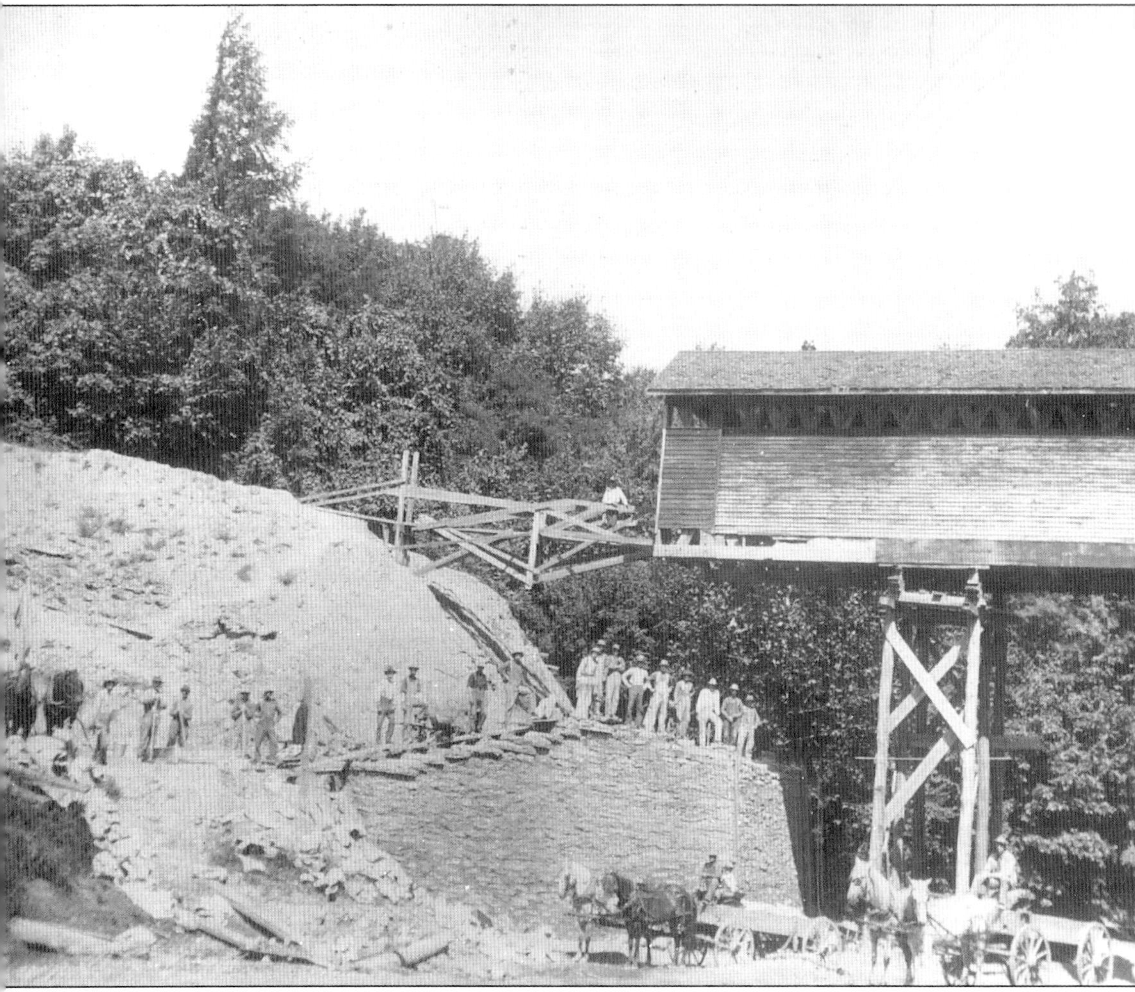

Through the hard work of these strong and resourceful early settlers, a thriving community developed. This high covered bridge over Cazenovia Creek is but one example of the combined efforts of men and their horses.

IMAGES
of America

TOWN OF AURORA
1818–1930

Donald H. Dayer, Harold L. Utts, and Janet R. Utts

ARCADIA
PUBLISHING

ISBN 978-0-7385-0445-2

Published by Arcadia Publishing
Charleston, South Carolina

Printed in the United States of America

Library of Congress Catalog Card Number: 00104083

For all general information contact Arcadia Publishing at:
Telephone 843-853-2070
Fax 843-853-0044
E-mail sales@arcadiapublishing.com
For customer service and orders:
Toll-Free 1-888-313-2665

Visit us on the Internet at www.arcadiapublishing.com

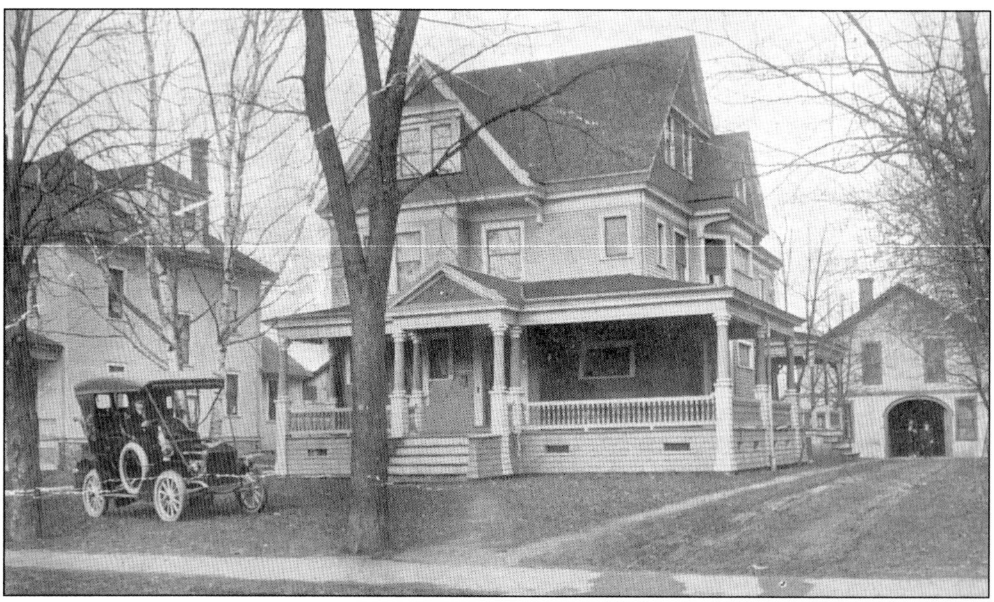

This picture of E.E. Henshaw's residence at 476 Main Street illustrates one of the many changes that have come to this community: the brand-new automobile in the front yard and the horse in the stable. This is currently 530 Main Street. Street numbers were changed in the 1920s.

Contents

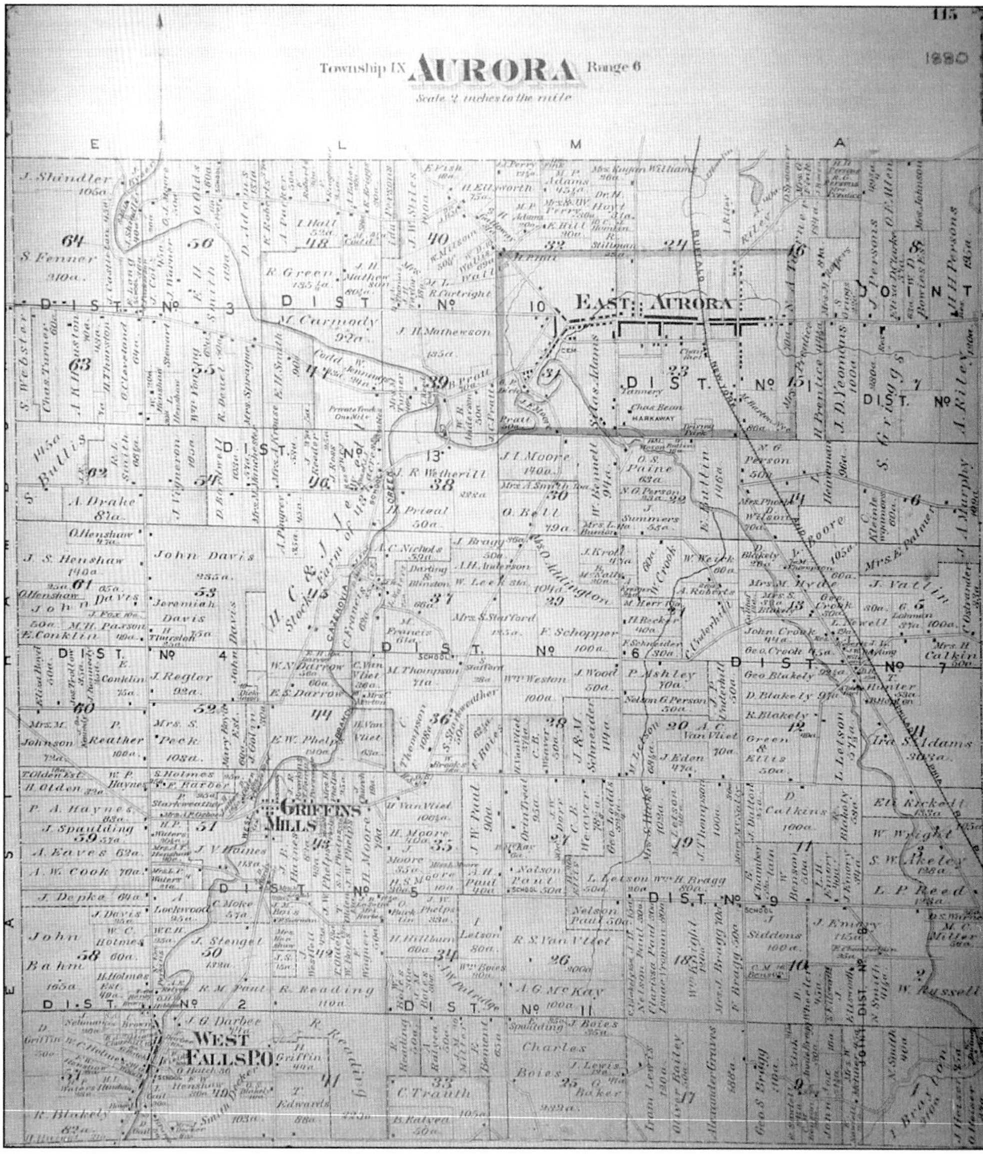

This 1880 map of the township of Aurora, New York, shows the village of East Aurora as well as the hamlets of Griffins Mills and West Falls.

INTRODUCTION

The word "aurora" refers to the morning twilight, the dawn, and new beginnings. In 1804, settler Jabez Warren came upon the land now known as the town of Aurora; he made a small opening in the forest and built a log home. It was the beginning of a new life for Warren and his family and the dawn of the town of Aurora, which over the years would come to include the village of East Aurora and the hamlets of West Falls, Griffins Mills, and South Wales.

Located 20 miles south of Buffalo, the land is rich with natural beauty. The town is situated between two lines of hills, which extend southward to form the Allegheny Mountains. The Cazenovia Creek, named for Holland Land Company agent Theophilus Cazenove, runs through the town. The west branch of the creek winds through West Falls, and the east branch meanders in just south of South Wales. Both branches join before crossing Route 20A just west of the village. The creeks furnished the early settlers with waterpower to run the mills, which allowed them to provide a living for their families.

Throughout the 1800s, settlers came to Aurora to build homes and establish roots. Some came after the British burned the settlement of Buffalo. Others came from New England and eastern New York communities. All came looking for the quality of life that the town of Aurora offers. The town became home to hundreds of families, who made a comfortable living from farms, business, and industry and who created the sense of community, which remains a cornerstone of the town of Aurora today.

Some of those settlers came to be recognized beyond Aurora for their distinguished good works. In 1823, the young Millard Fillmore settled in Aurora to study law, teach school, and build a home for his bride. He would later become the 13th president of the United States. His home has been restored and now houses the Millard Fillmore Museum.

Early on, Aurora's proximity to the growing city of Buffalo allowed the town to profit from its farm products. Dairy farmers in the area joined forces to produce cheeses from their surplus milk, which was then transported via one of the earliest toll roads to Buffalo. After many stops and starts, a railroad connection to the city of Buffalo was established in December 1867.

For a time, Aurora was nationally known as a mecca for the raising, breeding, and training of trotter horses. Several horse farms, most notably owned by the Jewett and Hamlin families, established the area as a horse-breeding center. The community still celebrates Racing Days each year with a horse race down Girard Avenue.

At the turn of the century, writer-philosopher-entrepreneur Elbert Hubbard founded the Roycroft community at Main and Grove Streets. The success of the arts community brought international fame to Hubbard and many dignitaries to the community. The Roycroft Campus, now a National Historic Landmark, continues to bring people from around the world to East Aurora.

While many Aurora residents commute to Buffalo and surrounding suburbs for their work, the main employer within the town was Fisher-Price Toys for many years. The plant closed in the early 1980s, but Fisher-Price headquarters remain on Girard Avenue.

The town of Aurora is deeply rooted in its history, with an active historical society and several annual festivals and events to recognize the area's rich past. A walk around the town and village is a veritable history lesson, with street names and markers paying tribute to the families that made the area what it is today: names like Godfrey, Peek, Fillmore, Riley, Persons, Warren, Price, Emery, Clement, Hamlin, Jewett, Knox, and many others. The photographs in this volume come from many of the families of early settlers, from the office of the town historian, and from the archives of the local newspaper, the *East Aurora Advertiser*.

The town of Aurora is recognized as "Toy Town, USA" for being home to Fisher-Price and is designated as a "Tree City, USA" for its tree-lined streets and beautification efforts. But for those who grew up in Aurora, it remains best known as an unparalleled Hometown, USA.

—Sara Foster

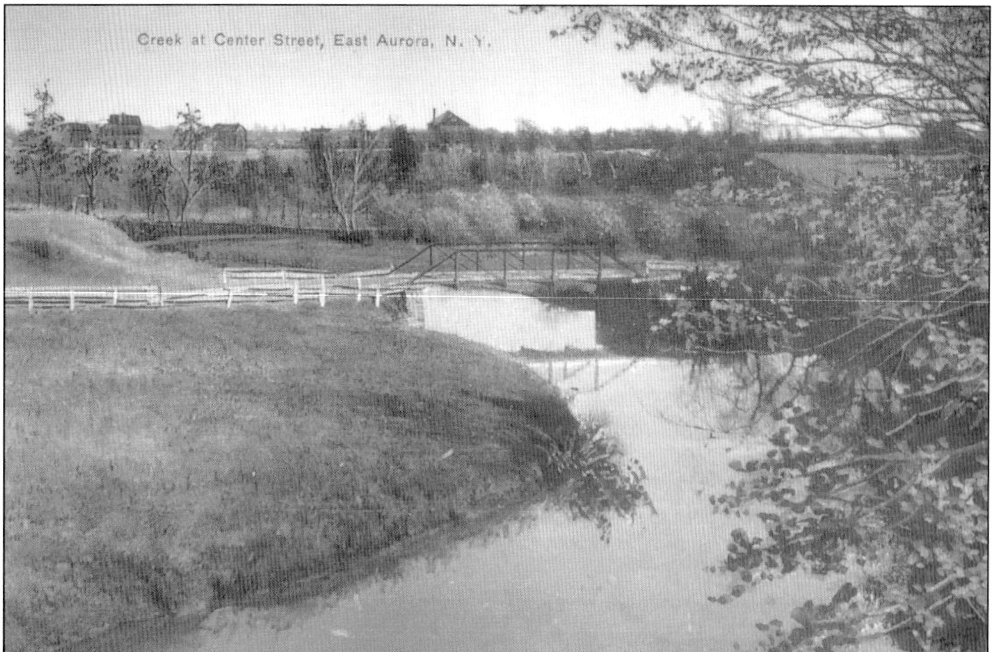

This familiar site is the Center Street bridge across Cazenovia Creek, south of the village, as it appeared in earlier times.

One

PEOPLE

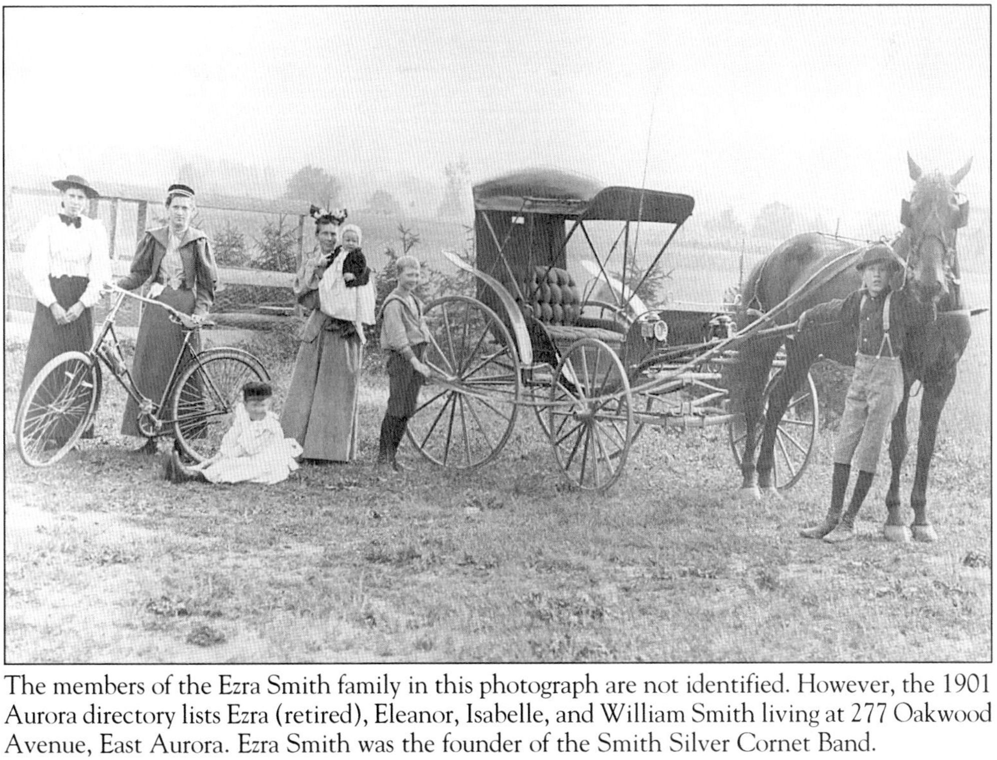

The members of the Ezra Smith family in this photograph are not identified. However, the 1901 Aurora directory lists Ezra (retired), Eleanor, Isabelle, and William Smith living at 277 Oakwood Avenue, East Aurora. Ezra Smith was the founder of the Smith Silver Cornet Band.

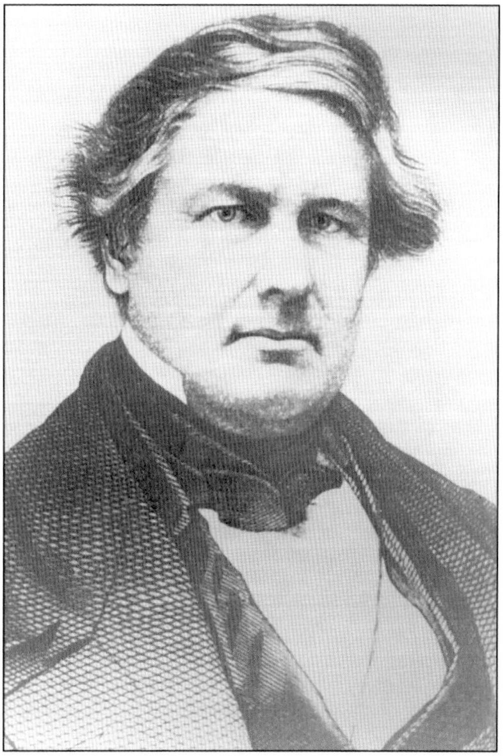

Millard Fillmore was the 13th president of the United States. As vice president, he took the higher office after the death of Pres. Zachary Taylor on July 9, 1850. Earlier in his career, Fillmore served as a congressman, a state assemblyman, and state comptroller. He was the only lawyer in East Aurora from 1823 until 1830, when he moved to Buffalo. He was born July 7, 1800 in a log cabin in Locke, Cayuga County, New York. President Fillmore died March 8, 1874, and is buried at Forest Lawn Cemetery in Buffalo.

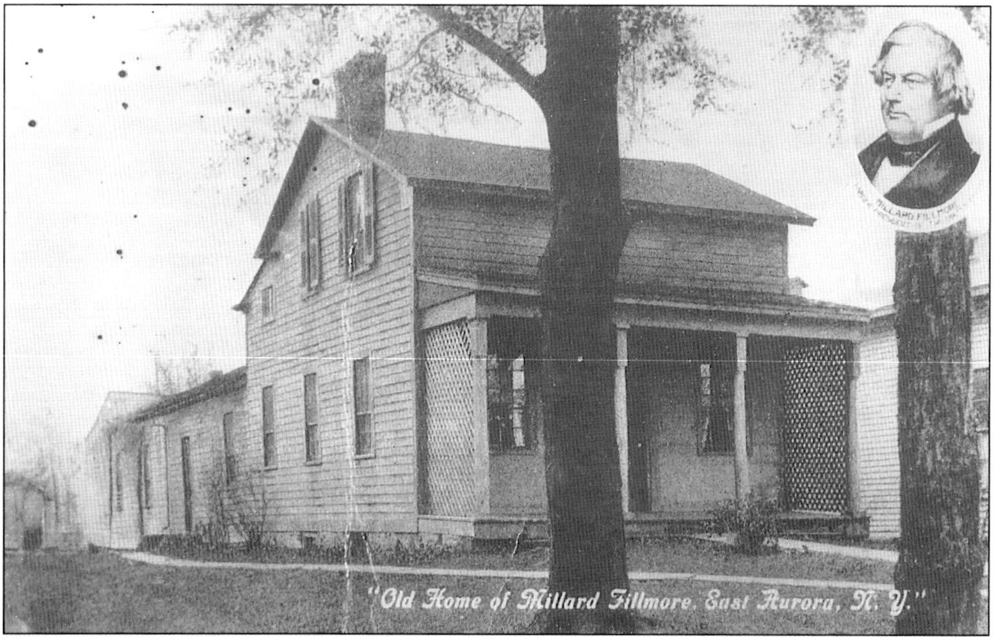

In 1826, Millard Fillmore brought his bride to this unpretentious house, which he built in East Aurora. Fillmore recorded in his diary, "With my own hands and the help of friends, I built a home for my bride-to-be, Miss Abigail." They lived in this home until 1830. Originally it was located about where the Aurora Theater is today. Sometime between 1916 and 1920, it was moved to the short street connecting Elm Street and Temple Place.

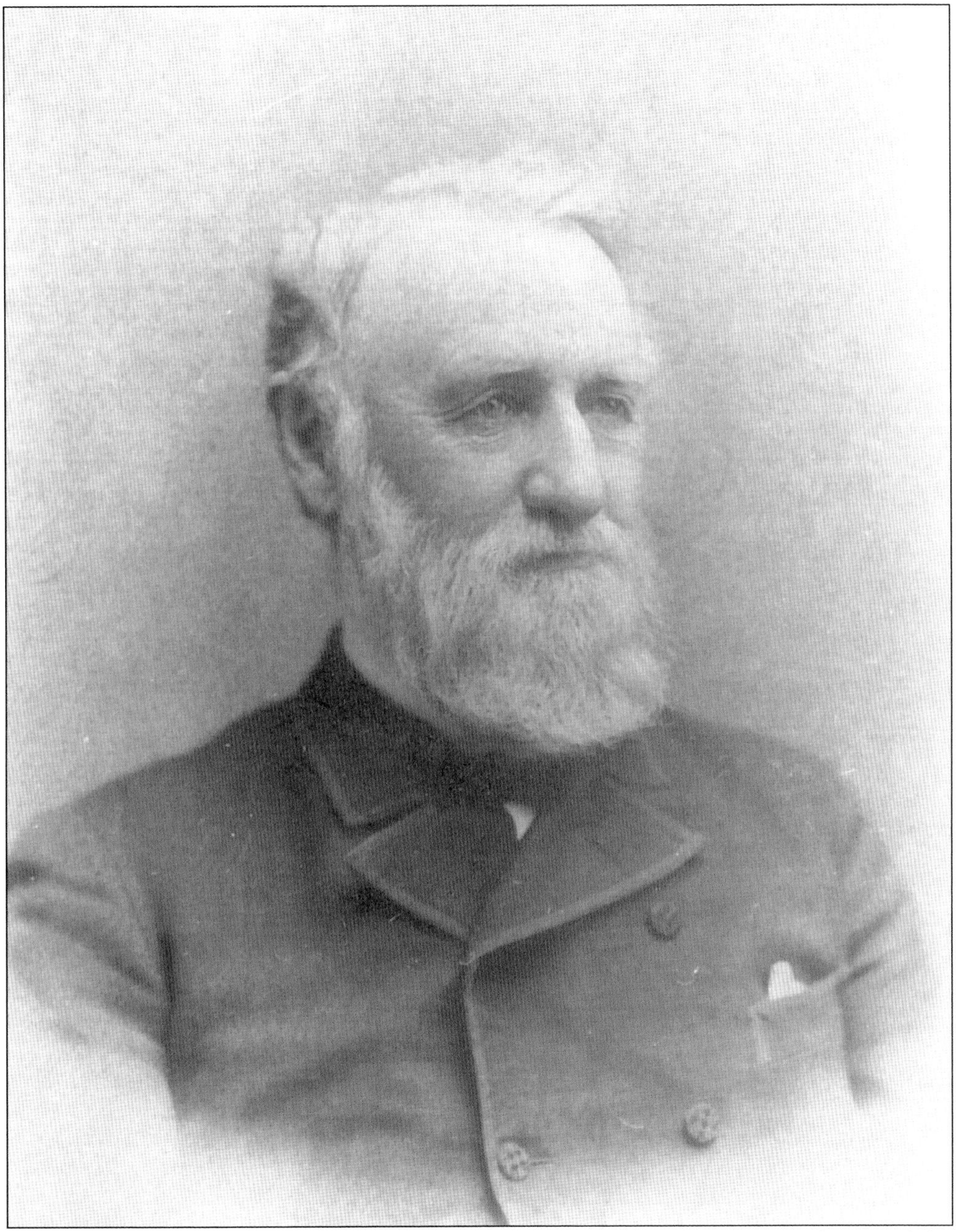

Cicero J. Hamlin was born in 1819 in Columbia County, New York. He was the son of the Reverend Jabez Hamlin and Esther Stow Hamlin. In 1836, he came to Willink, now East Aurora. He married Susan Ford on September 21, 1842. Hamlin owned a store on the north side of Main Street not far from Buffalo Road. He was an astute businessman and a superior judge of horses. On May 1, 1855, he purchased 60 acres of land on the north side of Main Street between Tannery Brook and Buffalo Road. That was the beginning of Village Farm. He immediately began the construction of many barns and eventually built stables for more than 700 horses. Village Farm was known as the "world's greatest trotting nursery." More 2:10 racers were bred here than at any other establishment. Hamlin died February 20, 1905, at 86 years of age.

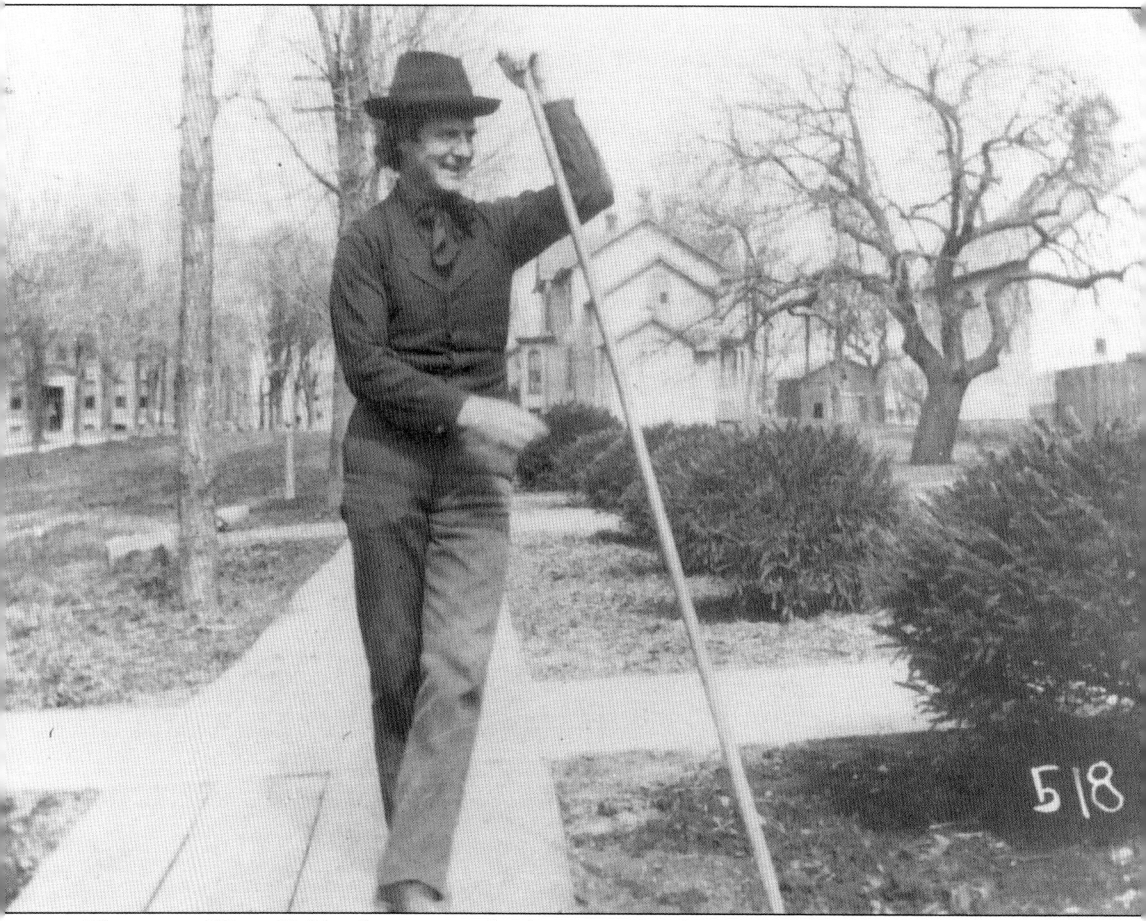

The young Elbert Hubbard poses near his home on South Grove Street, which was the site of the future Roycroft Inn, *c.* 1896. To the left, in the distance, is the East Aurora Academy. The building with the rounded tower on the right was a private home that later became a part of the inn, connected by the Peristyle. (Courtesy of the Roycroft Inn.)

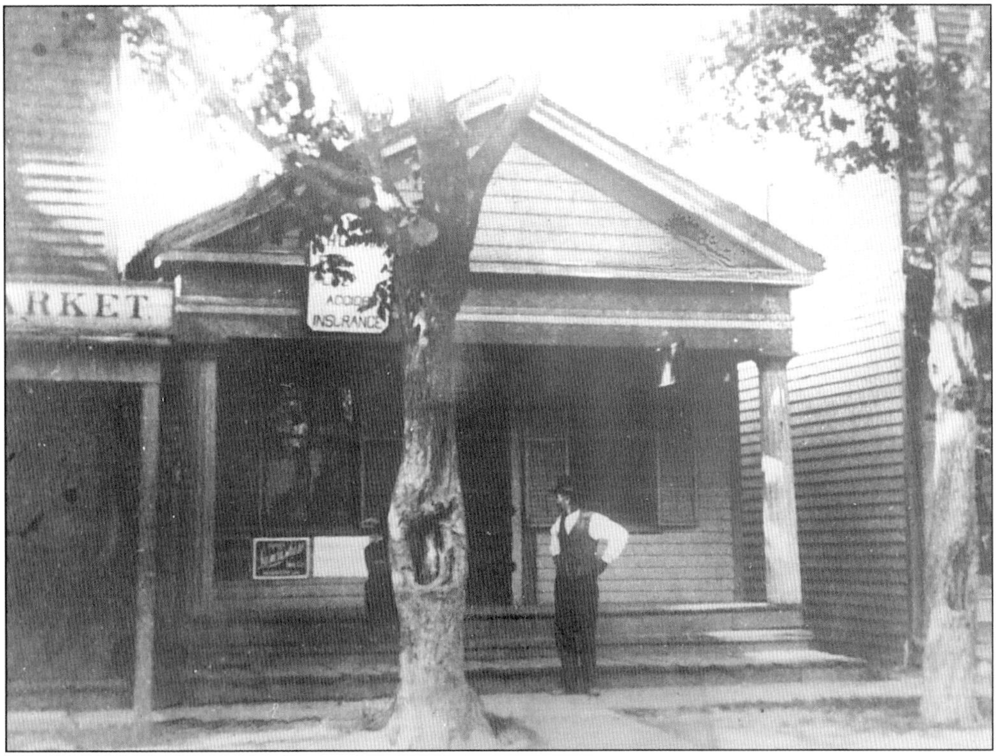

Millard Fillmore's law office was on Main Street. On summer evenings, Fillmore would sit in front of his law office and share anecdotes with his friends and neighbors. It was at one of these times when his partner, George Johnson, suggested that Fillmore run for Congress. What was said in jest was eventually realized and Fillmore was elected to the 23rd Congress in 1833.

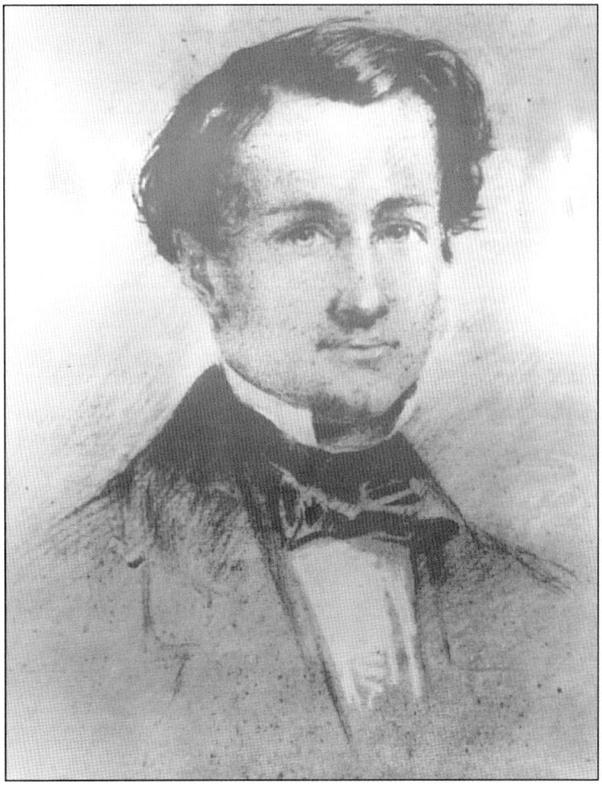

Millard Fillmore is shown at age 25, when he was a "country lawyer" in East Aurora. He was the only lawyer in East Aurora from 1823 to 1830.

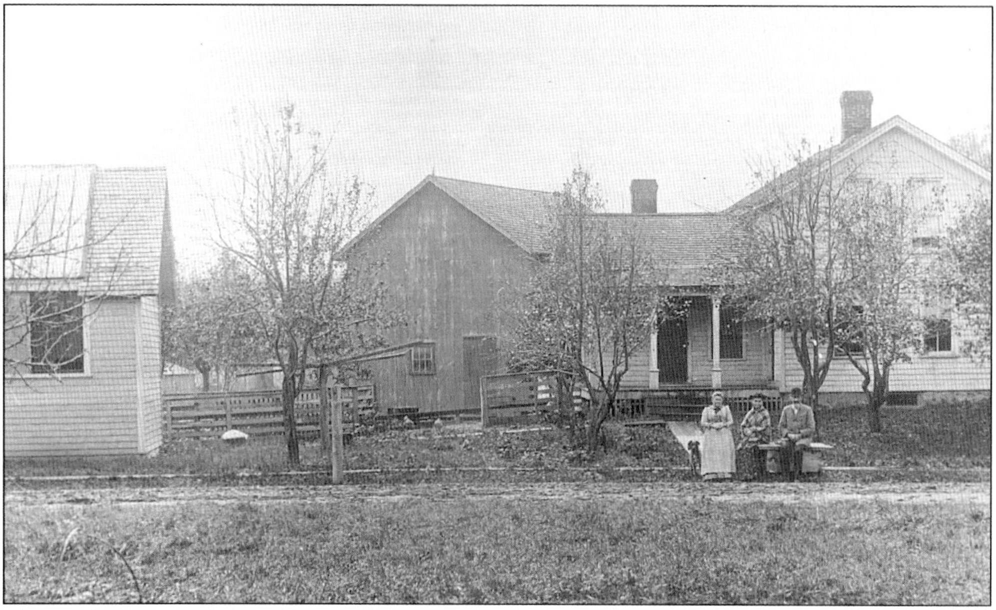

This is the home of Alfred F. Hitchcox, an attorney in the early 1890s. It was on the corner of Big Tree Road and Grey Street. The property today is 31 Grey Street at the corner of Knox Road. Celia Blood Hitchcox is seated in the center, on either side of her are Dr. and Mrs. Barry. At the left of the house is the photograph gallery of Mary Hitchcox, which was later moved across the street to Ernst Place and incorporated into the Hath property at 80 Hamburg Street.

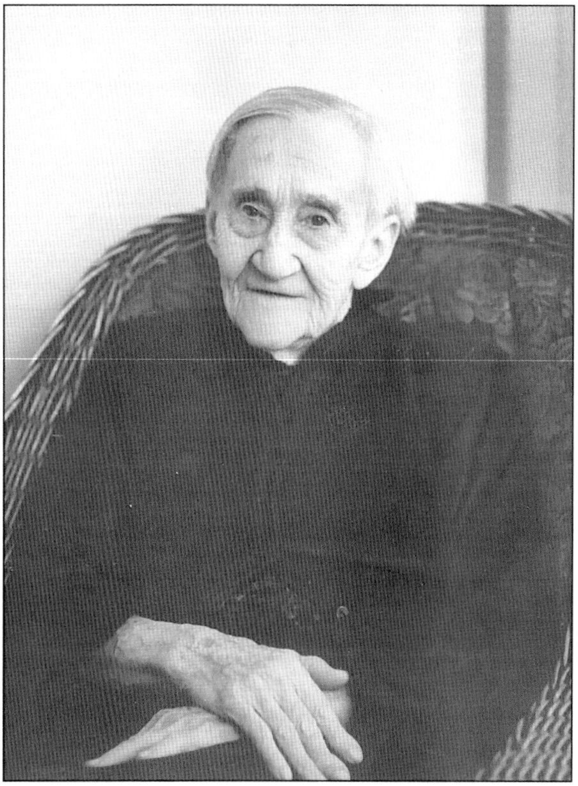

King Street, previously Mechanic Street, in East Aurora was named for Caroline Poulder King. She was the last surviving widow of the War of 1812 in the entire United States. She was 17 when she married Darius King, a veteran of that war. Born in 1795, Darius was 71 at the time of their marriage. Mrs. King was 89 years of age when she died on June 30, 1938. She was survived by one step-grandson and five step-granddaughters: Clara Bussingham, Mrs. Thomas Tasker, Fannie Smith, Ralph A. King, Mrs. Carl Wesp Armor, and Mrs. Arthur L. Wood.

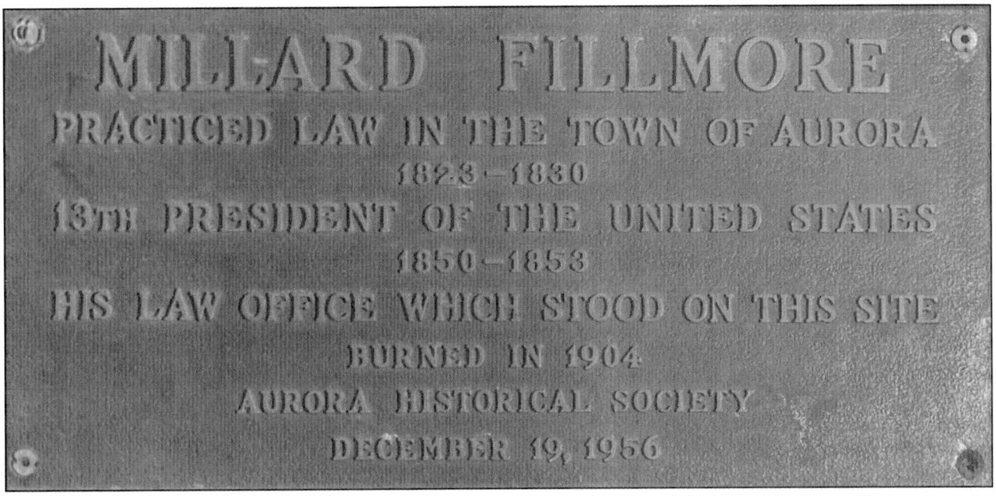

The Millard Fillmore historical plaque marks the site of Millard Fillmore's law office on Main Street from 1823 to 1830. The building was destroyed by fire many years ago. The plaque, marking this site at Vidler's Store, was placed there by the Aurora Historical Society in 1956.

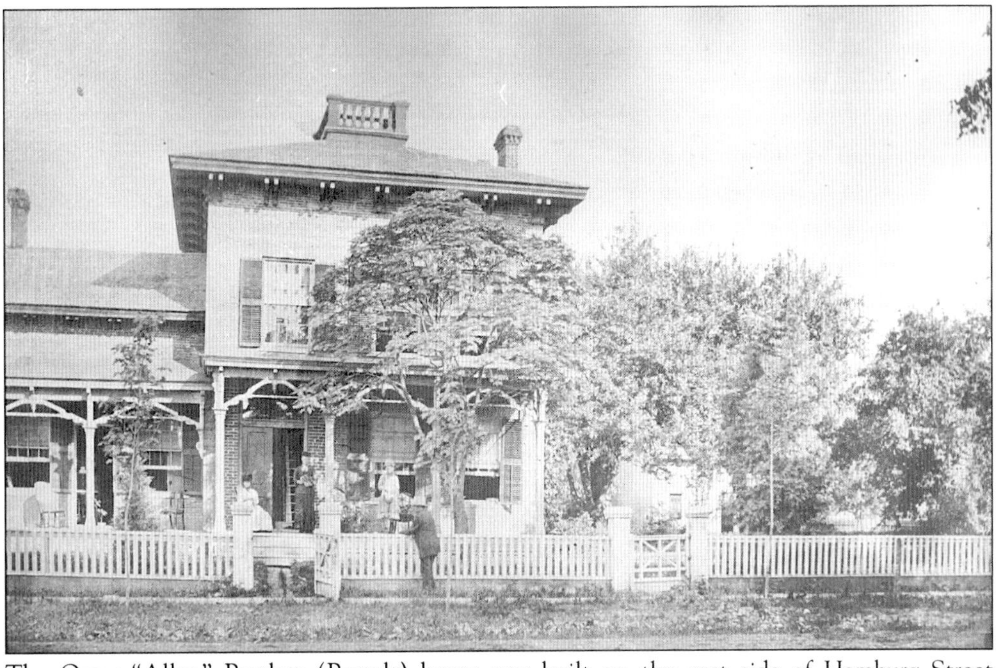

The Oscar "Allen" Bartlett (Bartelt) house was built on the east side of Hamburg Street between Main Streets and Oakwood Avenue. In 1877, O.A. Bartlett opposed the Methodist Church in their taking the "community bell" from Hamburg Street to their building on Main and Center Streets. Through his efforts, the Supreme Court awarded the bell to the fire company. In 1894, the bell cracked. The Bartlett Brothers bequeathed to the Fire Association "all their right, title, and interest in the bell to be disposed by the Fire Association as their best judgment may dictate." The bell was traded for a new one, which is now at the new firehouse on Oakwood Avenue.

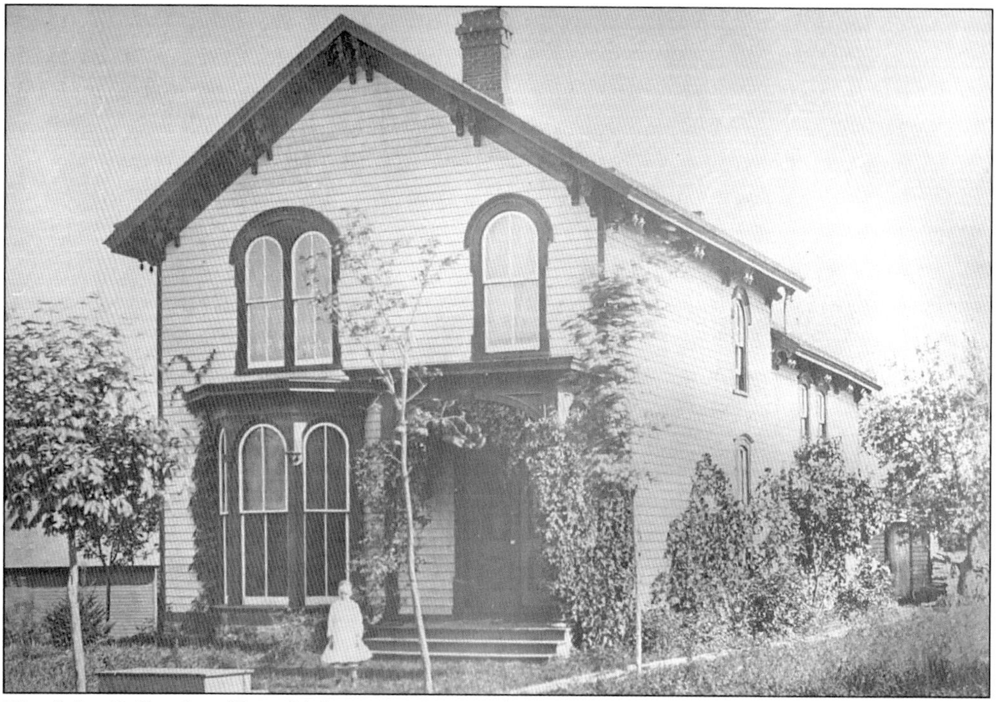

The John P. Bartlett (Bartelt) home at 34 Hamburg Street was built before 1866. Bartlett was the Aurora town supervisor from 1864 to 1865. He operated the Willink Post Office from 1885 to 1893. On May 11, 1848, he married Elizabeth Aldrich of Belmont, New York. Together they had four children: Frank S. Bartlett, Eugene E. Bartlett, Anna M. Bartlett, and Jennie E. Bartlett. Mrs. John Hosie was the daughter of Eugene, and Mrs. Stacy Mosser was his granddaughter.

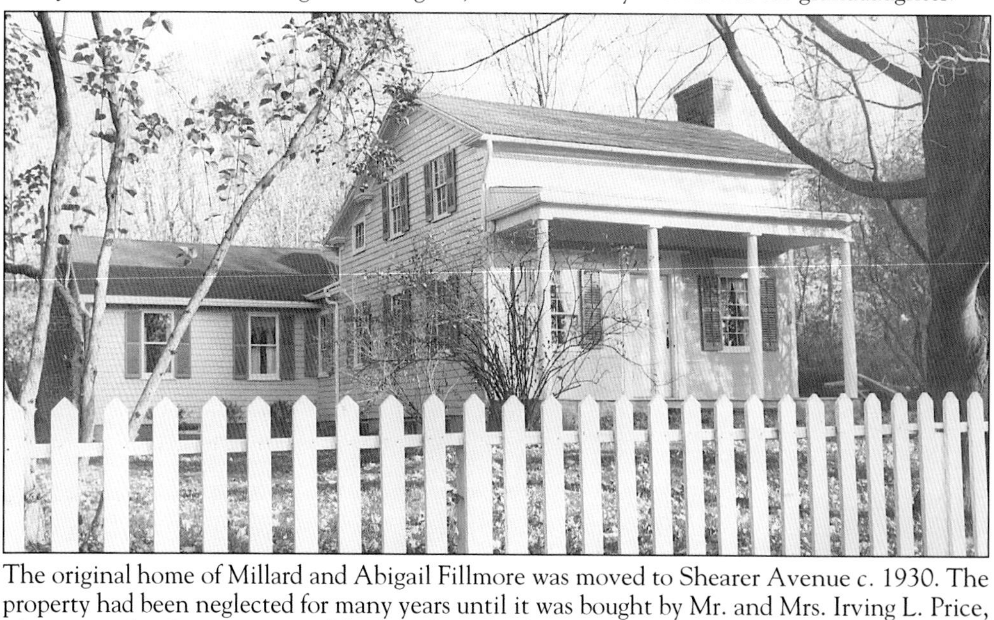

The original home of Millard and Abigail Fillmore was moved to Shearer Avenue c. 1930. The property had been neglected for many years until it was bought by Mr. and Mrs. Irving L. Price, who restored it. Price was one of the founders of Fisher-Price Toys. The building served as an art studio for Mrs. Price, a well-known artist, until it was sold to the East Aurora Historical Society in 1979. It is now a National Historic Landmark.

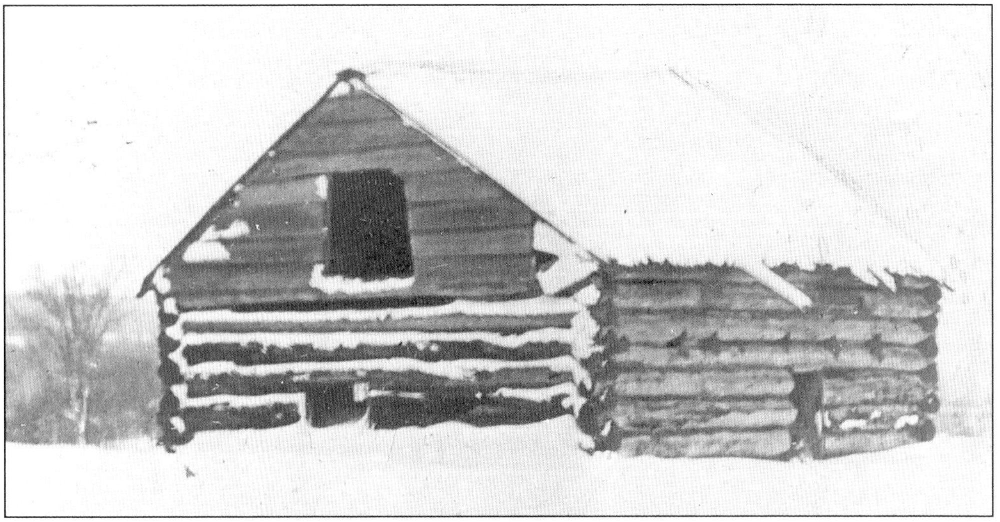

Abel Fuller's original log cabin was built in 1805 at the corner of Olean and South Streets. He was one of the first settlers in Aurora. Later, in 1807, he built a home on the south side of South Street. It is still standing and is one of the two oldest homes in the village.

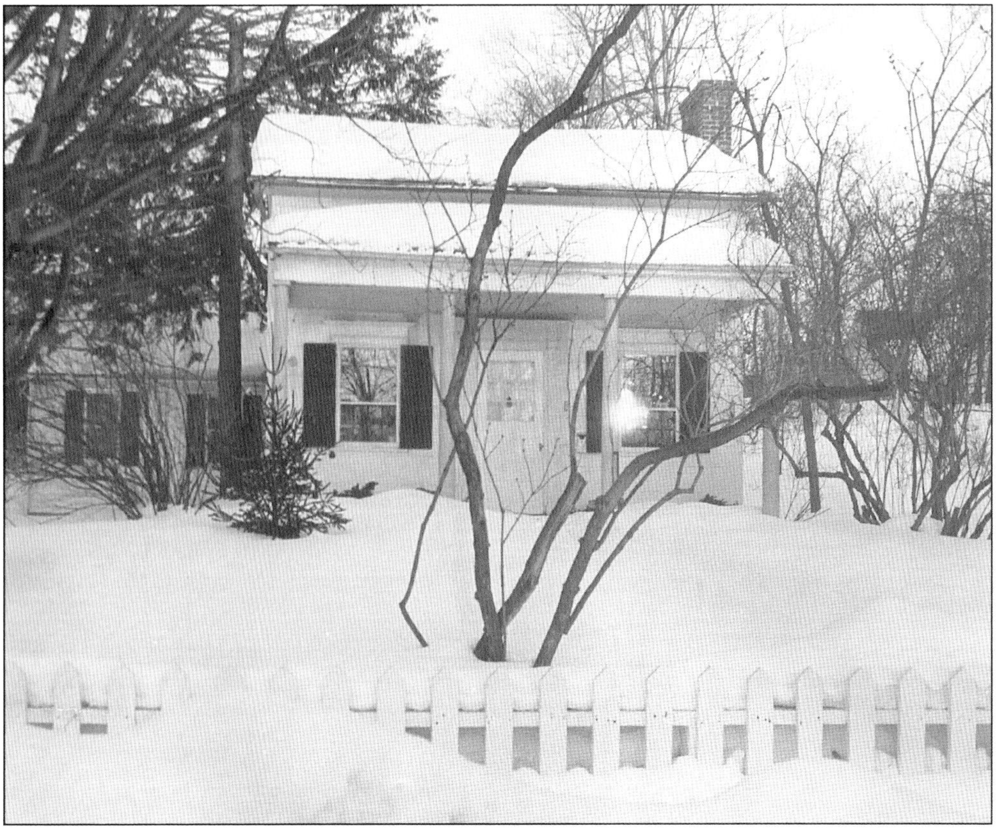

This house on Shearer Avenue, is a National Historic Landmark. It is the only existing U.S. president's home built by the president himself. This photograph captures a typical scene of winter in East Aurora.

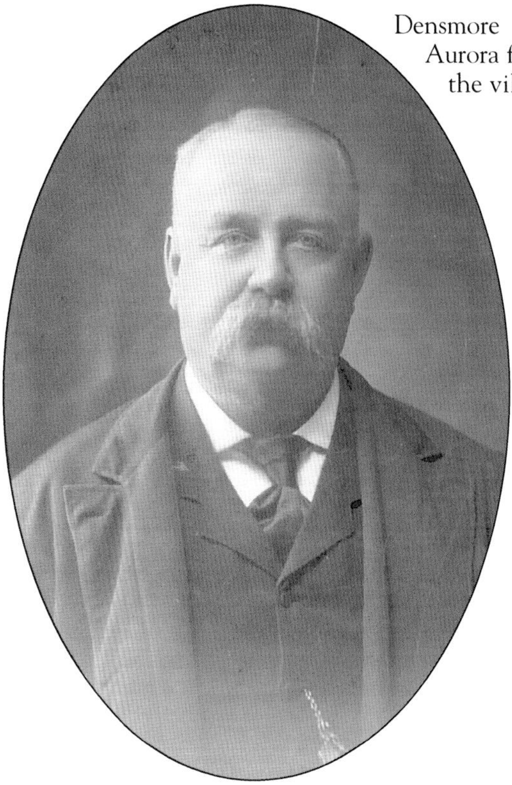

Densmore Pratt was president of the village of East Aurora from April 1901 to April 1907. In those days, the village had presidents instead of mayors.

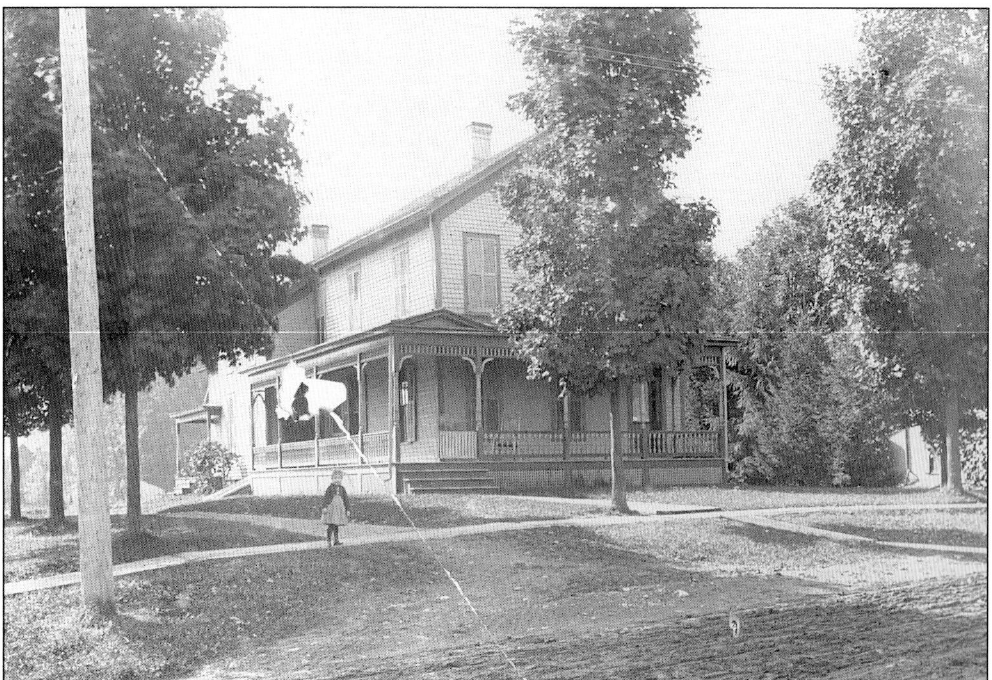

The Miles Williams house, which was on Oakwood Avenue, sits opposite the Immaculate Conception church. At one time, it was used as a home for the Sisters of St. Joseph.

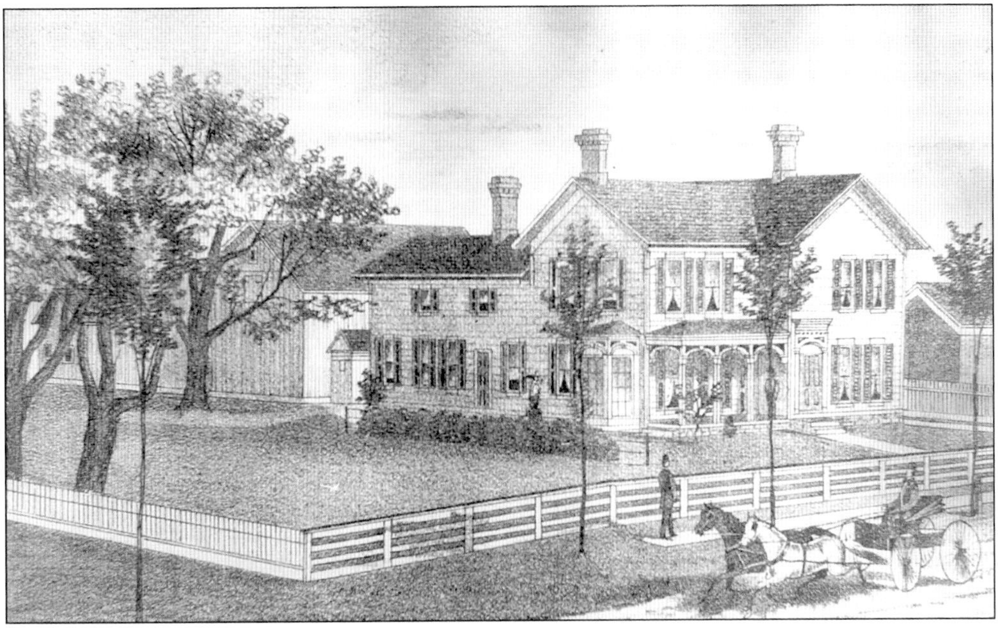

The residence of Rev. R.M. Sanford was on Pine Street in East Aurora. Reverend Sanford was pastor of the First Presbyterian Church from 1865 to 1887.

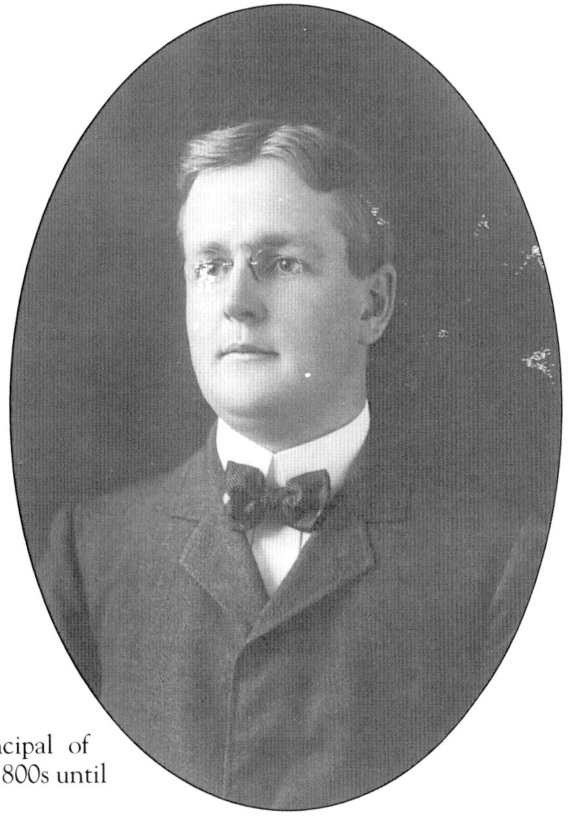

Charles Leighton McGavern was principal of East Aurora High School from the late 1800s until the beginning of the 1900s.

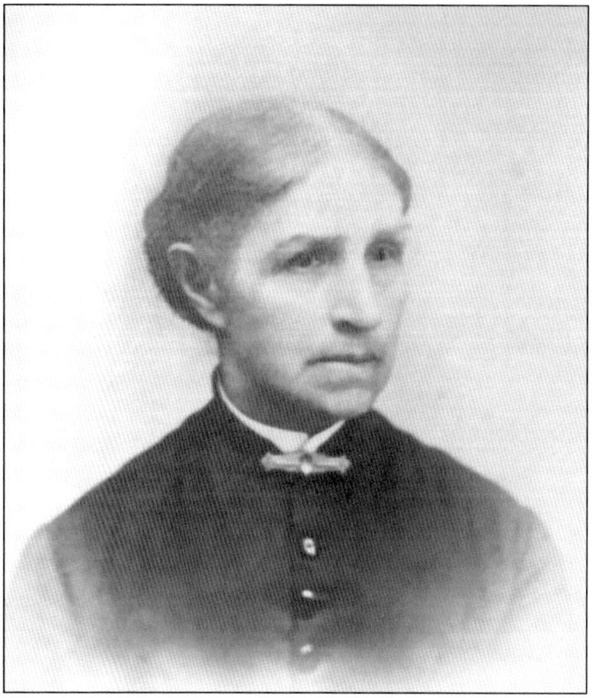

Elizabeth "Betsy" Gail Paine was born on September 25, 1820, in Ithaca, New York. She married Timothy Paine on February 14, 1839. They were the parents of Frank Paine.

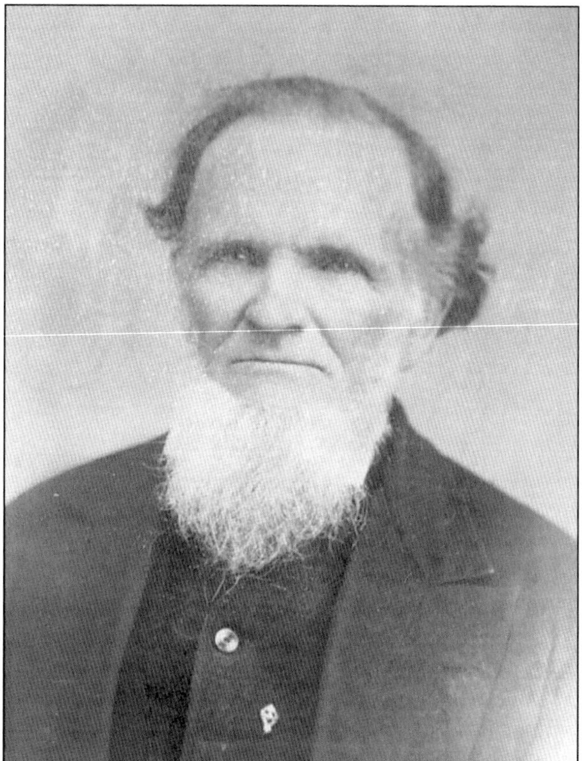

Timothy Paine was one of the earliest settlers to come to Aurora. From 1845 to 1890, he was a partner in the mercantile business with Henry Z. Persons.

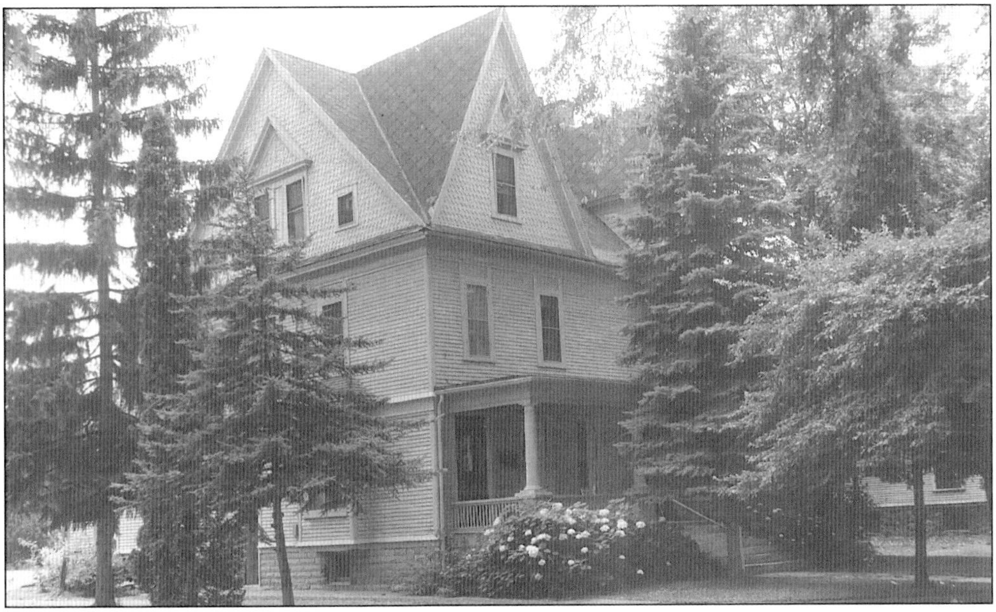

Depke's Big Tree Tourist Home is a "lost landmark" of the west end in East Aurora. Built in 1905 by Samuel Williams, it was known as Big Tree Tourist Home in the 1930s and possibly as late as 1960. The last owner, before the house was demolished in 1970, was Richard Depke.

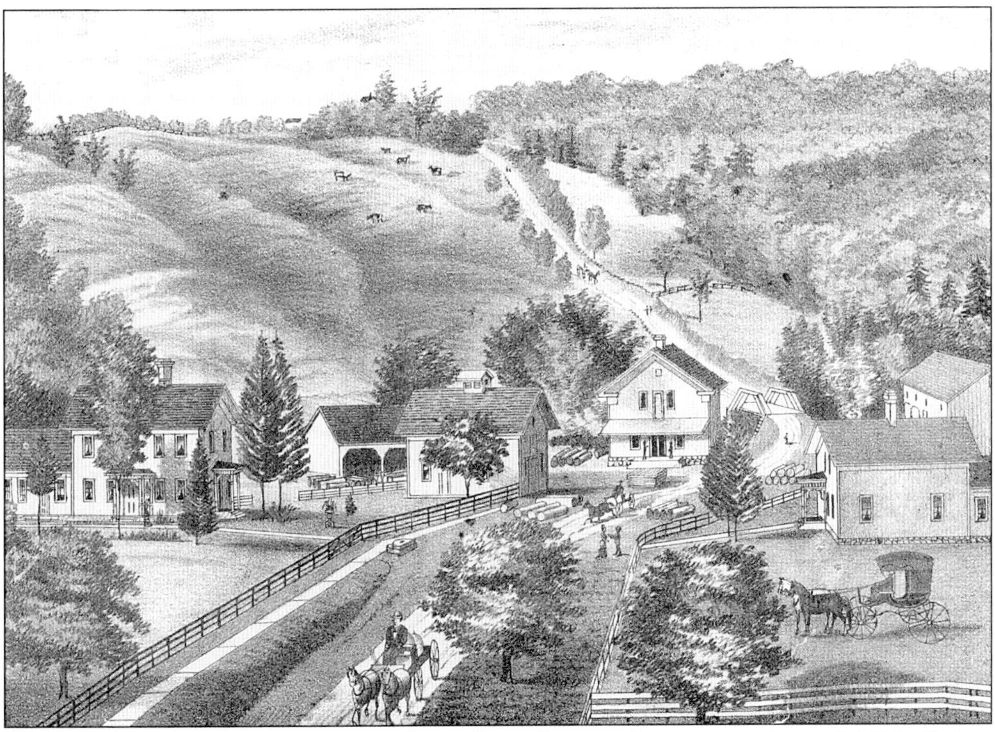

The residence and mills of L. Cornwall are shown here as they were in the mid-1800s. Before 1850 and for more than half a century, Lyman Cornwall operated a sawmill and gristmill on Emery Road in South Wales. This later became the site of Gow School. Cornwall was Aurora's town supervisor from 1876 to 1878.

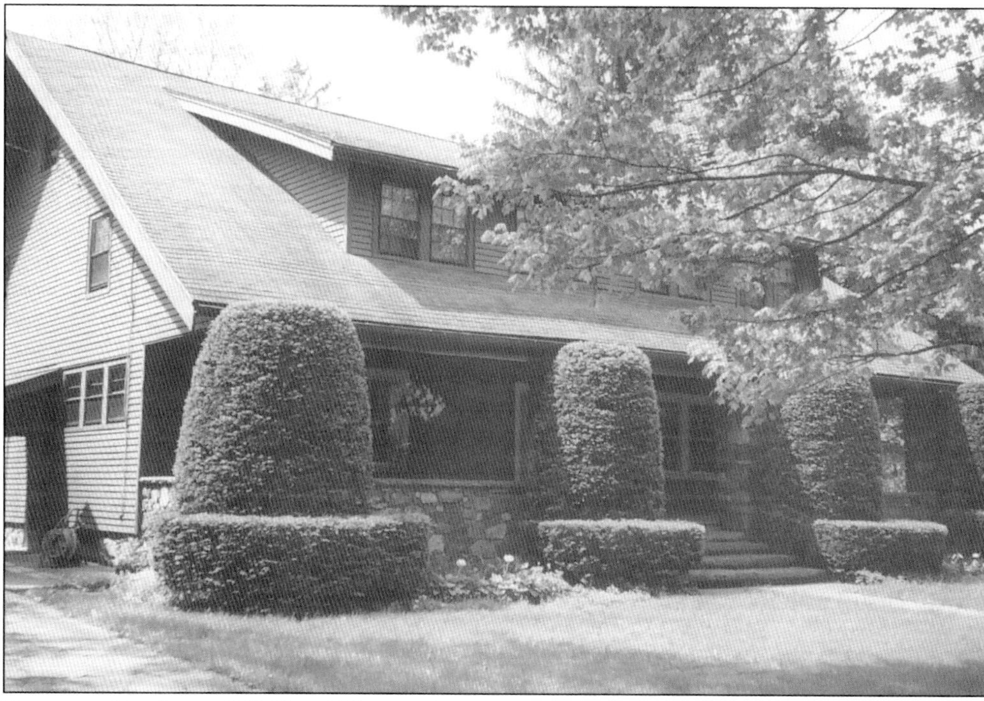

Harmony Castle, at 819 East Fillmore Avenue, was built in the early 1900s for Jean Kerr and Alice Charlesworth, who were workers at the Roycroft. They were famous for making Roycroft Maple Pecan Patties, which were sold through the Roycroft. The order form listed the following: "Carton of one dozen Patties each [$].90; quarts of pure 1916 first run Maple Syrup $1.25/quart." Pecan Patties boxes are now collectibles. See Charles Hamilton's *Roycroft Collectibles*. We have the recipe for those Pecan Patties, courtesy of A. Louis Zink

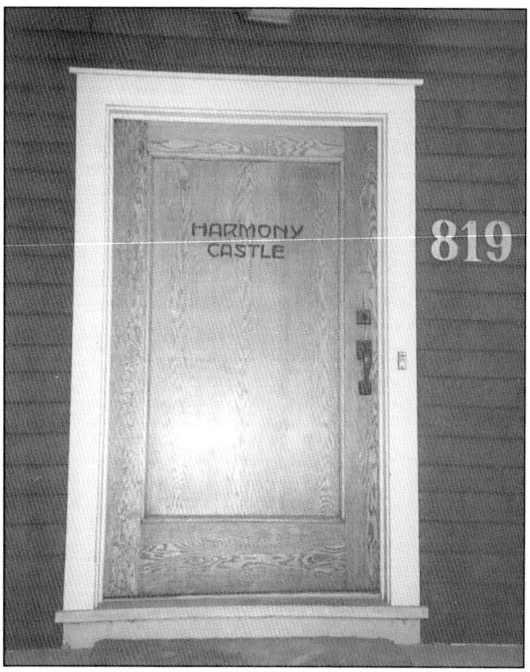

This large oak door with the name of the house on it (Harmony Castle) is true to the style and craftsmanship of the Roycrofters. At one time, Merle James, a Roycroft artist, was the owner of this house. While living there his daughter, "Betsy" James, married the well-known artist Andrew Wyeth. Ed Vidler remembers the day of that wedding because, as a 12-year-old boy, he taunted the groom with, "You'll be sorry." Check with Ed at his store on Main Street, and he will confirm this bit of little-known history. The house still stands on East Fillmore Avenue.

Martha Richardson Adams and Enos Adams were the parents of eight sons and four daughters. They were among the early settlers in Aurora, having come here in 1805. A great-great-granddaughter of Joel Adams, Mrs. William T. Forden Jr., was a former town and village historian of East Aurora. Her grandfather was the tenth child born to Enos and Martha Adams.

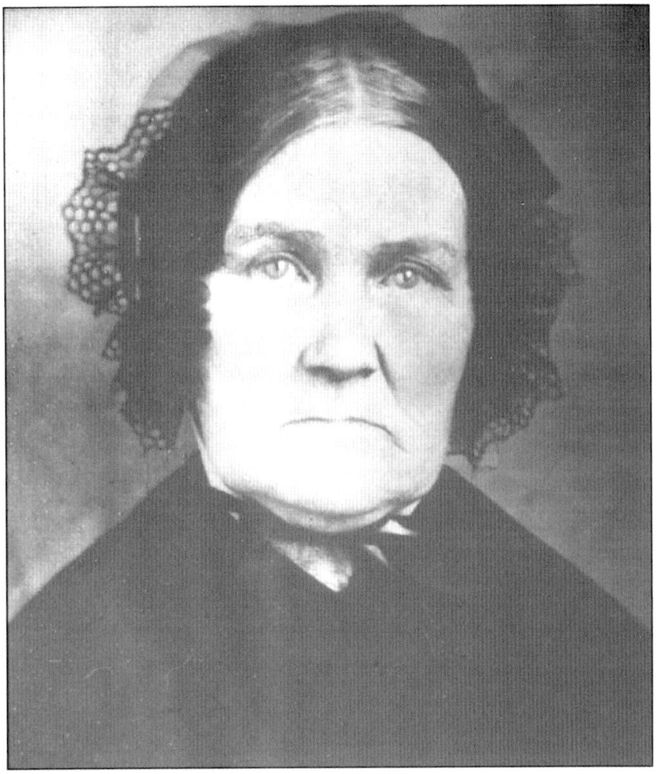

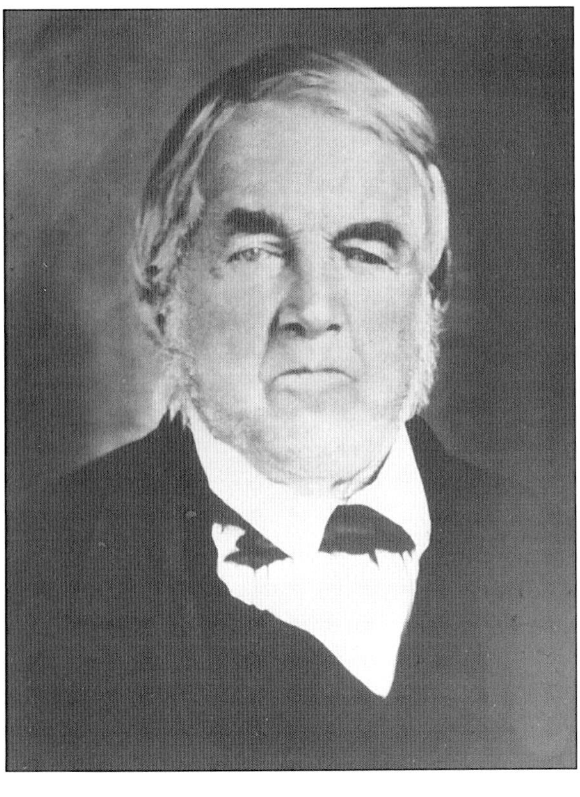

In 1805, Enos Adams came to Aurora from Braintree, Massachusetts, to live on land which his father, Joel, had bought in 1804. Enos traveled with the yoke of oxen while his wife, Martha Richardson Adams, rode horseback. She rode sidesaddle, carrying their infant daughter, Relief.

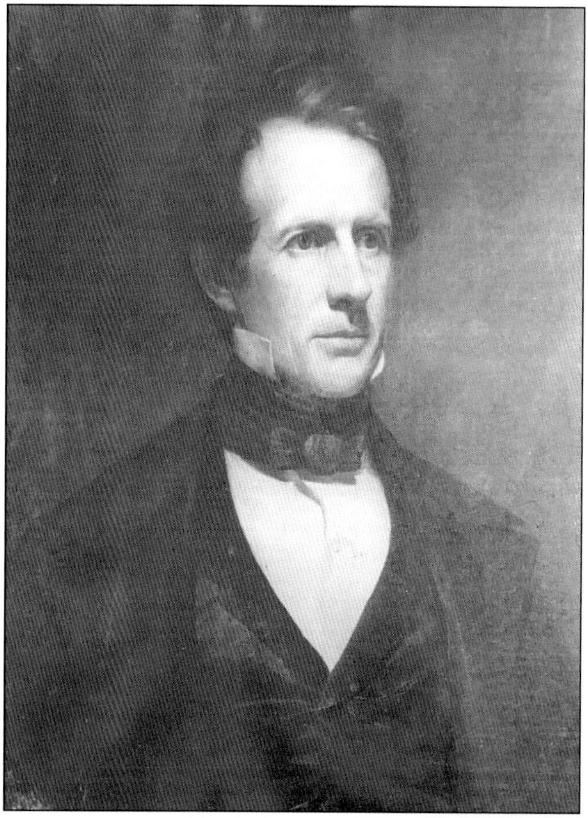

George Washington Johnson supervised the first select school in Aurora, a classical school. It was located at the east end of the village. He taught between 1828 and 1832 and was a graduate of the New England Institute. After leaving Aurora, he studied law with Millard Fillmore and Nathan Hall in Buffalo. For many years, he was clerk in the Holland land office in Batavia.

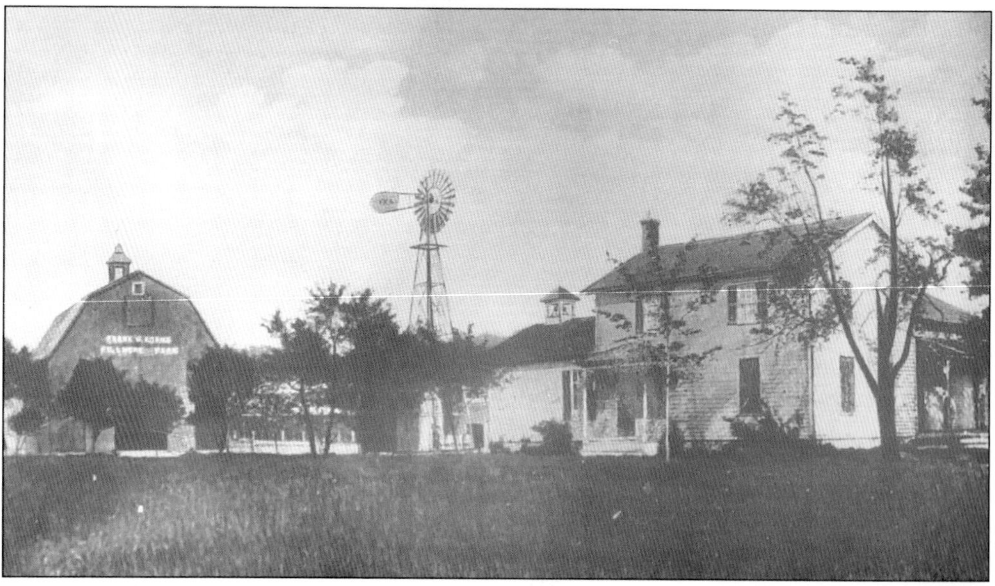

In 1819, Nathaniel Fillmore, father of Millard Fillmore, bought a farm on the southeast corner of Olean Street and Lapham Road. He built this house, which still stands in very good condition, and even today is known as the Fillmore Farm. At that time, Millard was an apprentice to a cloth-dresser; he later joined the family in East Aurora when he was about 21 years old. His parents lived on the farm until 1845, when they moved to 746 Main Street.

William E. Pierce was born in Colden, New York, on July 31, 1873. He was superintendent of rural schools from 1901 to 1929. As a member of the state commission to study the schools of New York State, he developed the first plans for central schools. His associates referred to him as "a just and kindly man, always looking for things to commend." He was the father of Dr. Edison E. Pierce.

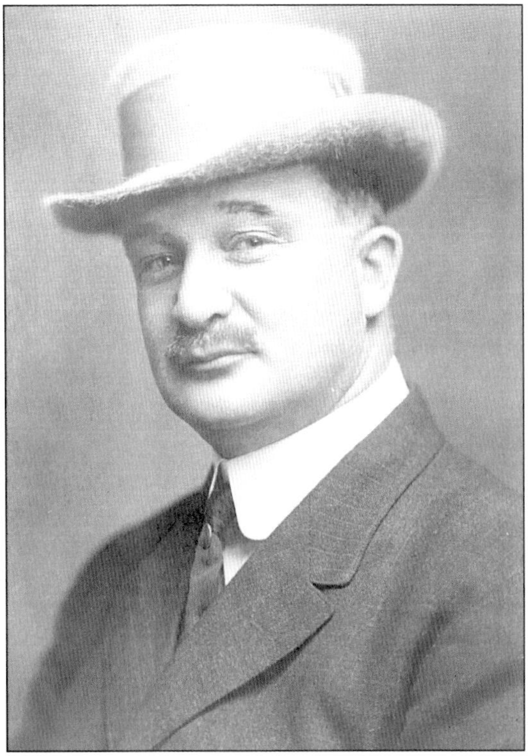

Clarence and Louise D. Bodiner Lamb were married in a public ceremony on September 15, 1887. The wedding took place at the East Aurora Fair. The fairgrounds were on South Street. It was held on a grandstand before 15,000 people. The event was one of Elbert Hubbard's ideas of showmanship and publicity. Lamb was an ardent supporter of light harness racing and was a great friend of Cicero J. Hamlin.

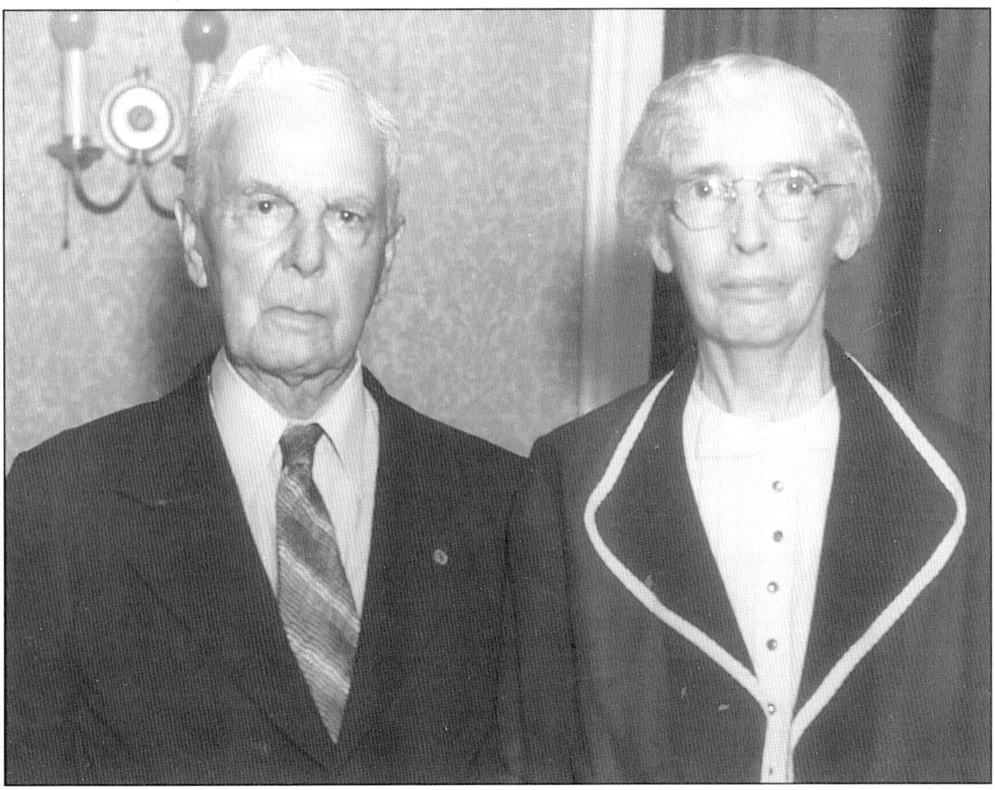

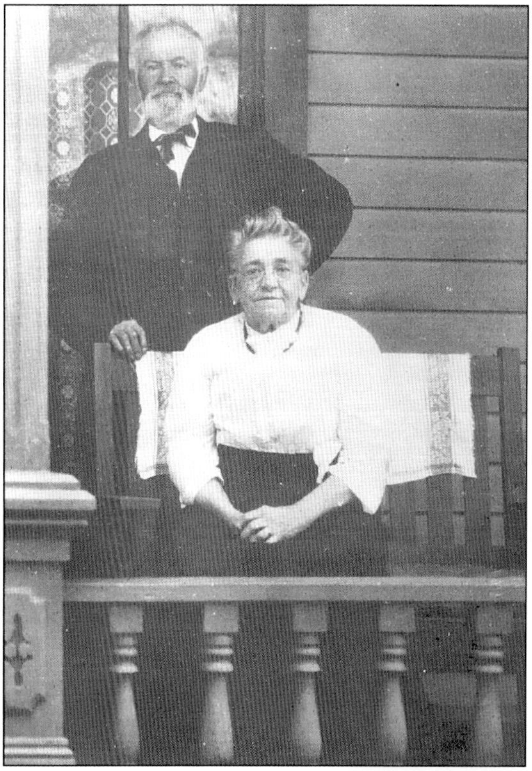

Anson Blackman, born in 1839 (shown with his wife, Abbie) was better known as "Ali Baba." To Elbert Hubbard, founder of the Roycroft movement, he was groom, handyman, traveling companion, and even babysitter for his children. Hubbard good-naturedly attributed some earthy mottoes to Ali Baba in his publications, *The Fra* and *Philistine*. His likeness appeared on Roycroft postcards. Years later, a bar was named for him at the Roycroft Inn. Ali Baba and his wife lived in a house on the corner of South Grove Street and Oakwood Avenue. They are buried at Evergreen Cemetery in Marilla.

Robert J. Donnor and Emma G. Lange Donnor were honored in February 1946 on their 57th wedding anniversary. They were married on February 26, 1889 by the Reverend Conrad Bodenbender of the First Baptist Church, Buffalo. Donnor was recognized for his oil paintings of seascapes and landscapes. Internationally known artists, including Alexis Fournier, praised his work. Mrs. Donnor was active in the First Spiritualist Church at Temple Place in East Aurora. The Donnors were best known for the development of Creekside, a pleasure resort along Cazenovia Creek at South and Center Streets. Donnor also built scores of canoes and a motorboat that seated 27 people.

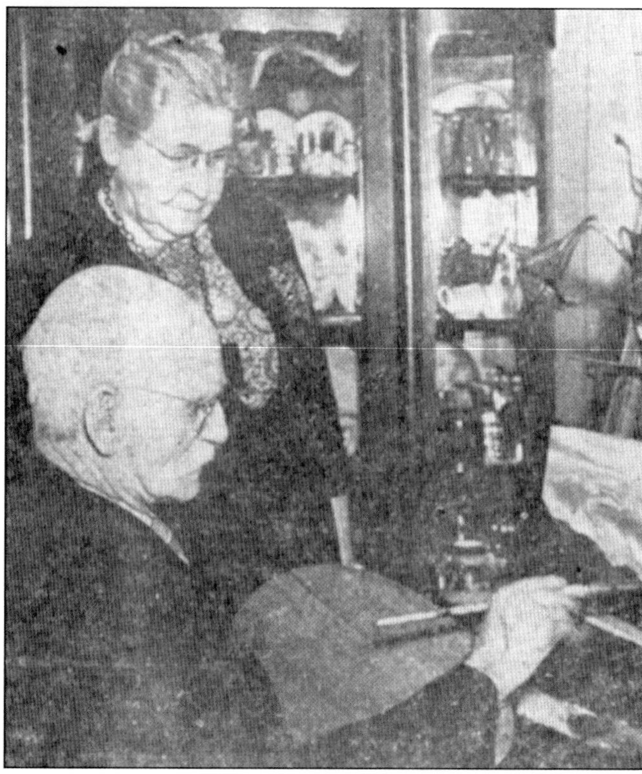

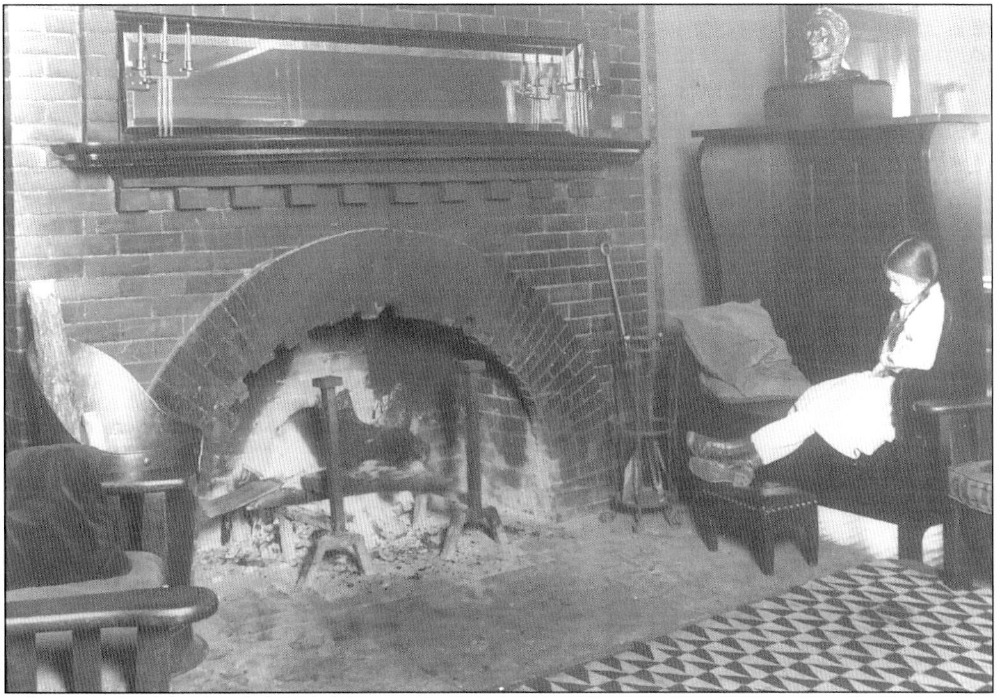

Elbert Hubbard's first grandchild, Lynette Hubbard Trefts, is seated in front of the lounge fireplace at the Roycroft Inn, *c.* 1914. (Courtesy of the Roycroft Inn.)

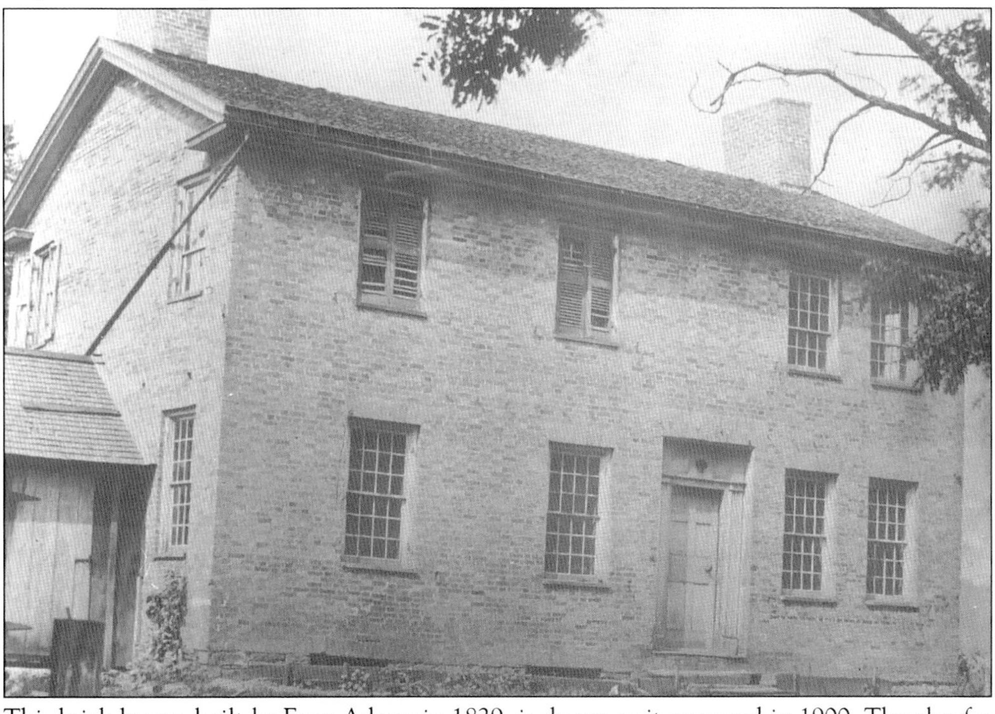

This brick house, built by Enos Adams in 1829, is shown as it appeared in 1900. The clay for the bricks was obtained from the Adams's farm near Cazenovia Creek. The two-story dwelling is on the west side of Olean Street, 4.5 miles south of East Aurora's Main Street.

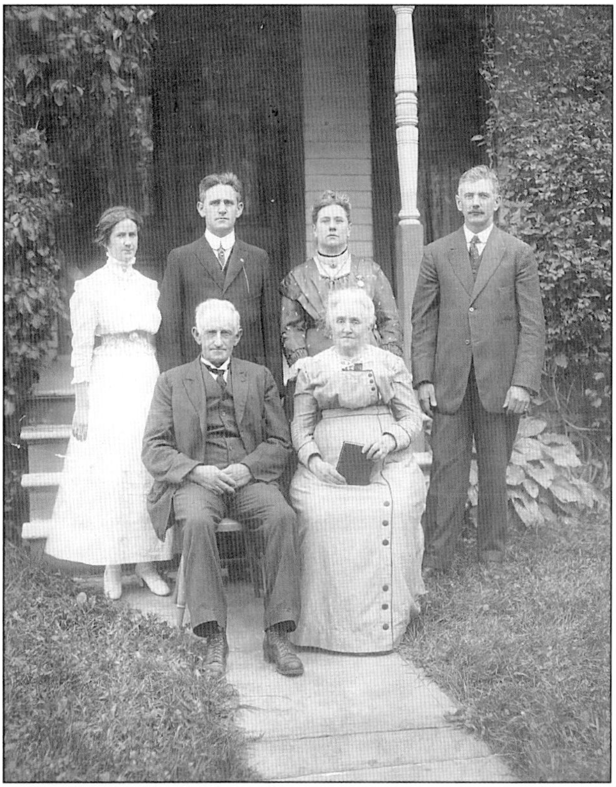

This Ball family group photograph was taken at their Porterville Road farm. They are, from left to right, as follows: (seated) Mr. Ball Sr. and Mrs. Ball; (standing) Ruby Adams, Harris Adams, Mrs. Leander Griffin, and Fay Ball.

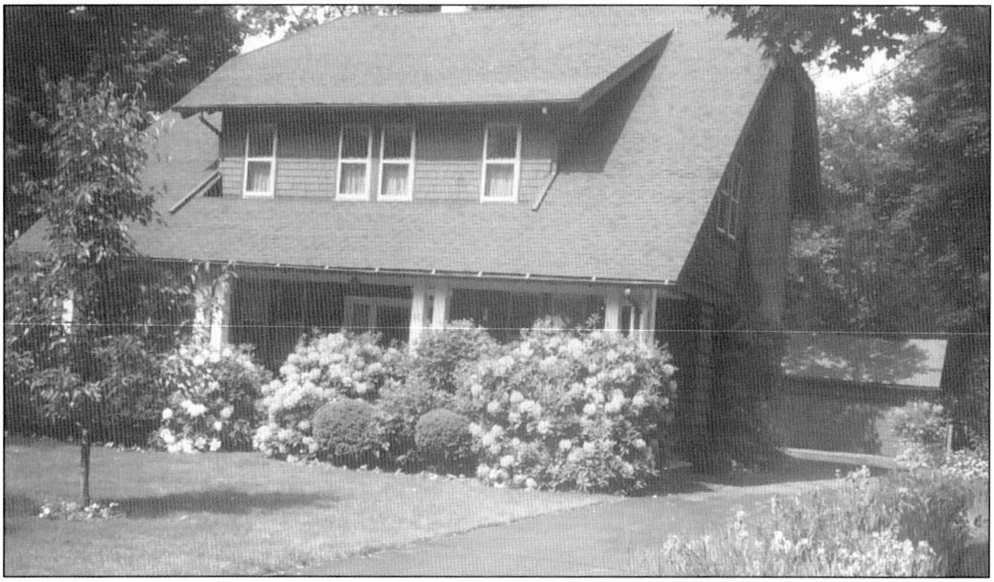

The most common Arts and Crafts–style home in the Aurora area is the bungalow. It is characterized by low sweeping roofs, prominent front porches, exposed interior beams, central fireplaces, and an open first-story plan. In the East Aurora area, bungalows are made primarily of wood or stone. The house in this photograph, 107 Center Street, was built in 1910 for Frederick Krantz. He was a Roycrofter and head of the Leather Bindery. (Courtesy of Neal and Evelyn Jacobus, owners since 1957.)

Two

Main Street

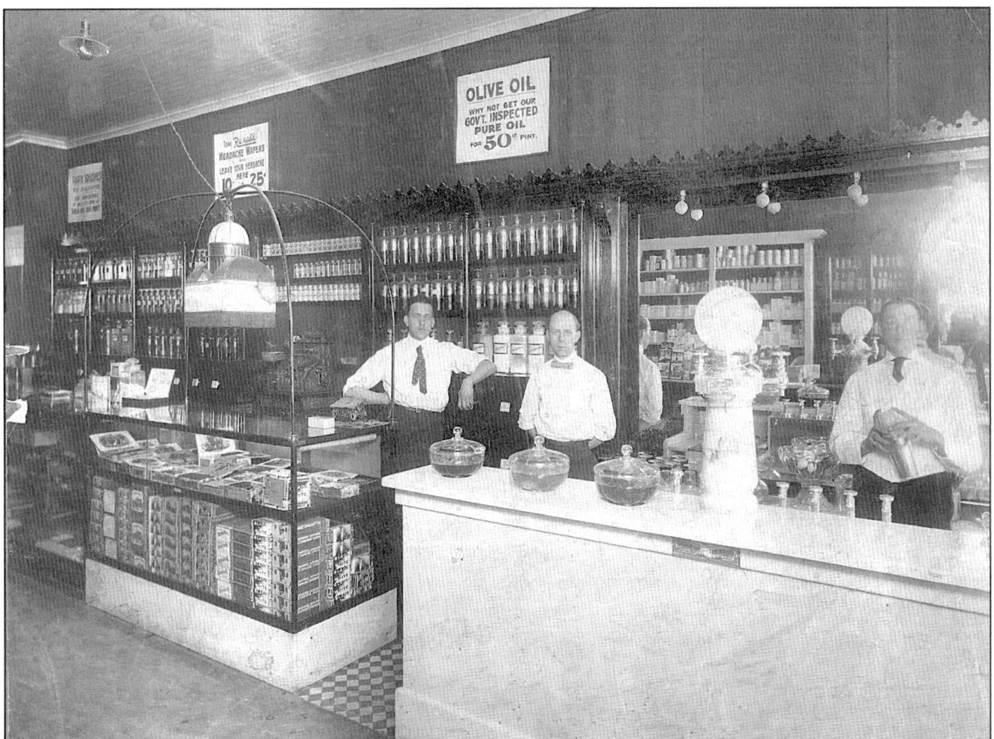

This view shows the interior of Cummings Drug Store in 1908. It was next-door to the bank on Main and Church Streets.

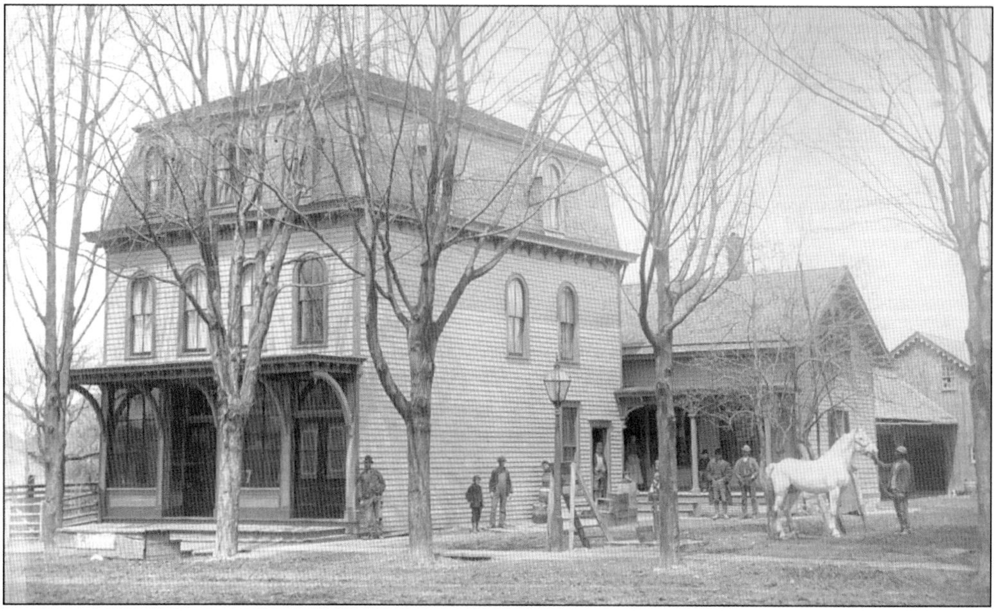

Wallenwein Hotel (also known as Maple Leaf Hotel) is shown as it looked *c.* 1890–1900. It stood on Main Street across from the village hall. The hotel was demolished to make way for a parking lot east of the Independent Order of Odd Fellows building. Holding the horse is Fred Bender.

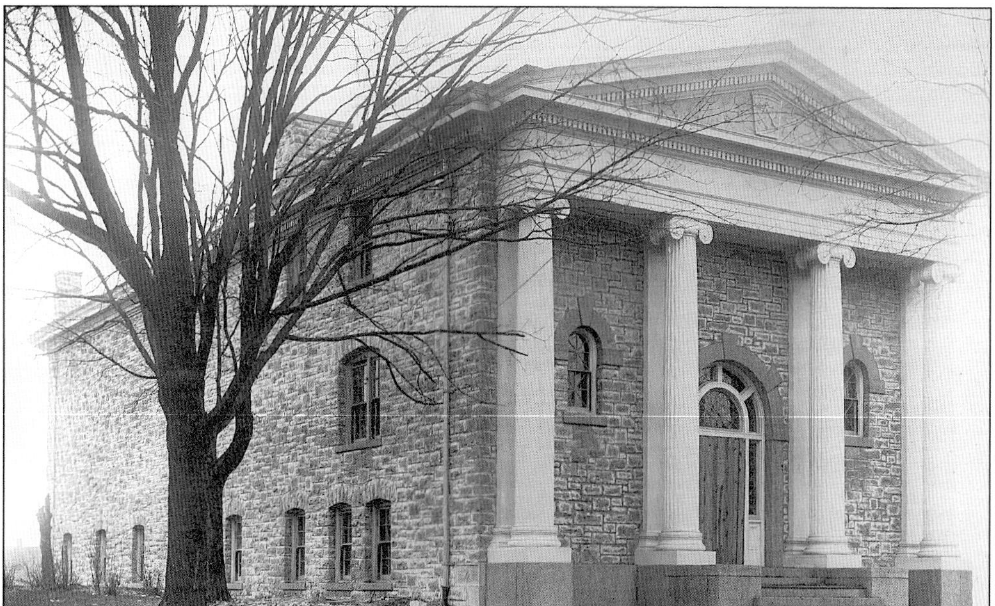

The Masonic Temple was built near the corner of Main and Elm Streets. The Masons occupied the fourth story of the Persons building on Main Street sometime before 1906, when the Persons building was destroyed by fire. The cornerstone of this structure was laid on July 25, 1906. Smith's Silver Coronet Band met the train, which brought the Grand Lodge officers and the delegation of Masons from Buffalo to East Aurora and led the delegation to the ceremony. The charter for Blazing Star Lodge was issued in 1869, but the history goes back to 1817, when it was known as Blazing Star Lodge of Willink.

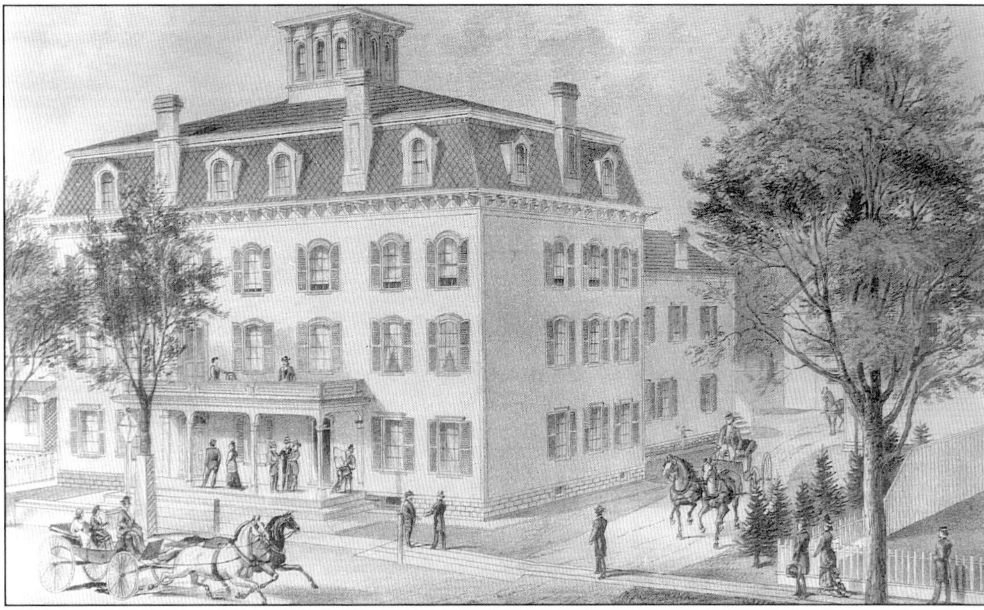

Byron D. Persons built this structure in 1872. This fine three-story hotel occupied the present site of the Aurora Theater. A fourth floor was added later and rented to the Masons. This facility was operated at times under different names: Yoeman House, Warren House, Hotel Eulalia, and Aldrich House. It was destroyed by fire *c.* 1905.

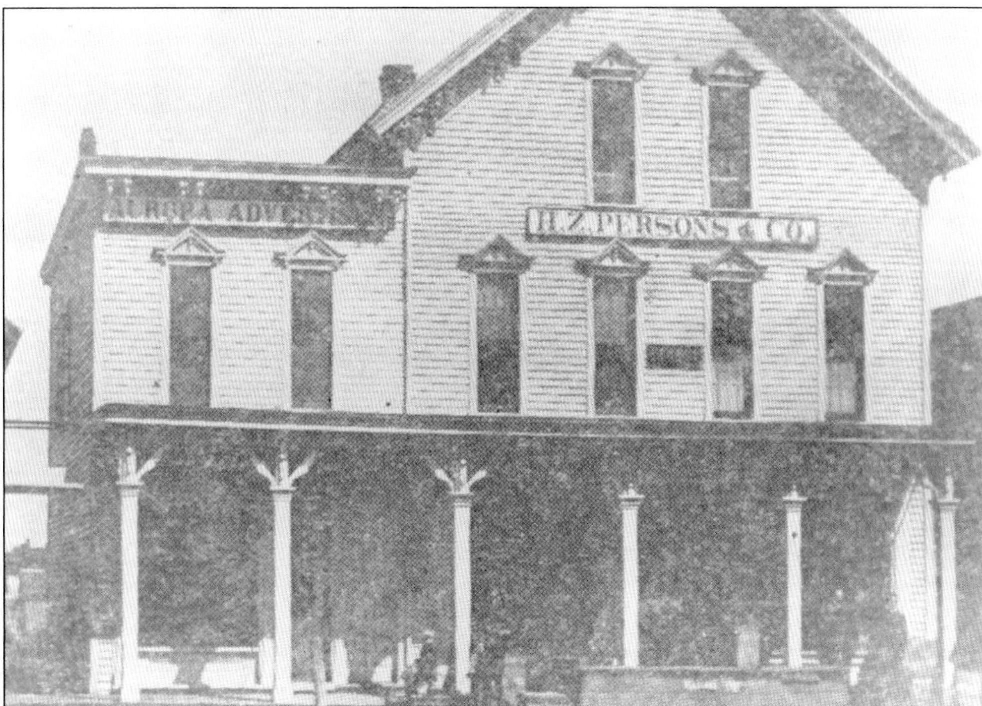

Henry Z. Persons and his son, Henry H. Persons, founded the first bank in Aurora in 1882. It was known as the Bank of East Aurora. The smaller building to the left is the office of the Aurora Advertiser.

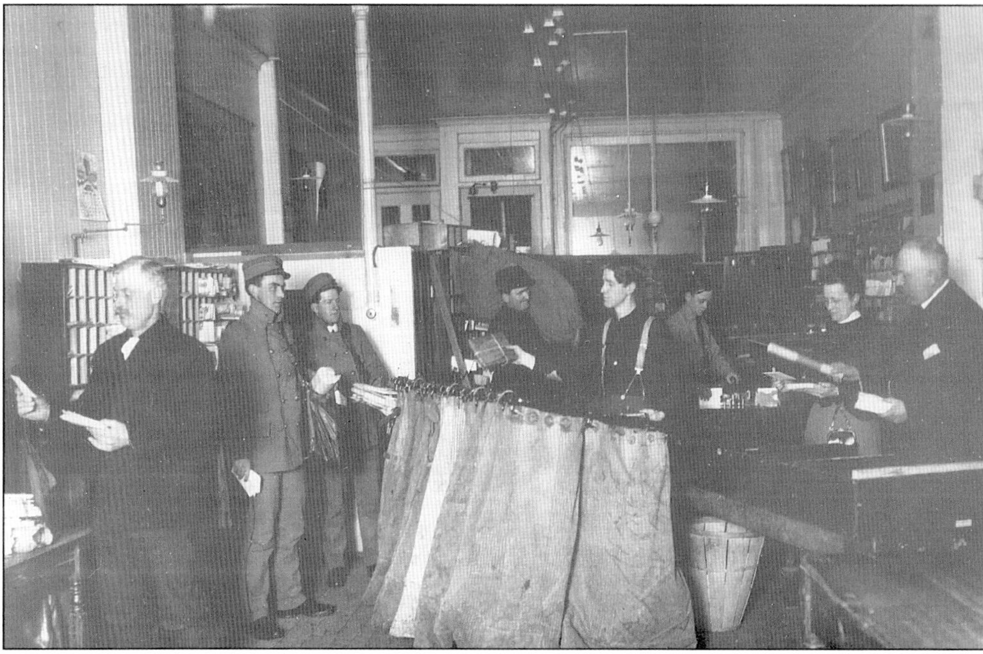

Posing are the East Aurora Post Office employees on February 15, 1905. From left to right, they are John J. Marshall, RD carrier; Henry A Pierce, city carrier; Charles H. Norton, city carrier; Robert Galvin, carrier from depot; Guy H. Rogers, mailing clerk; Herbert Tackbary, clerk; Katherine P. Mead, assistant postmaster; and A.H. Lapham, postmaster.

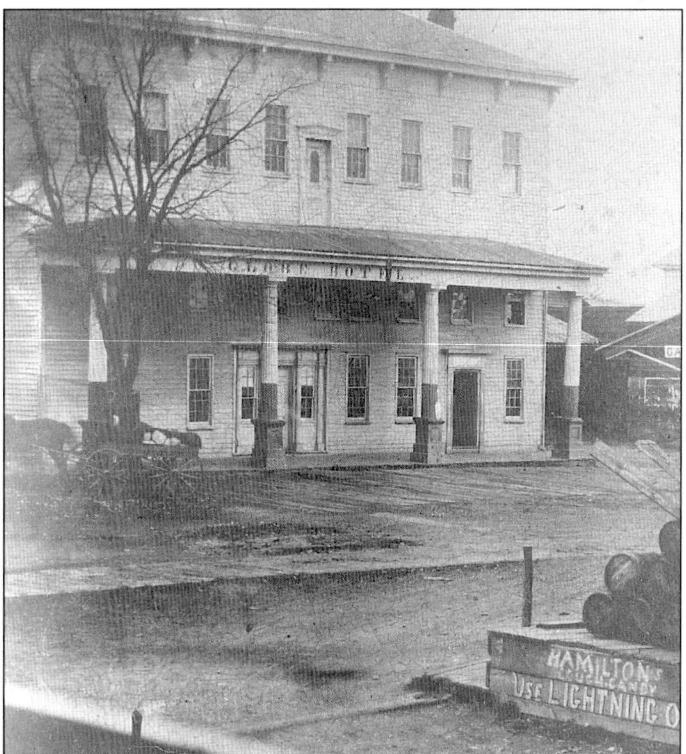

The Globe is the oldest hotel in existence in East Aurora. Built in 1824 by Charles Persons, it was a stopping place for the stage line that ran between Buffalo and Olean. The Balthasar family became owners c. 1906. For many years, the third floor was used as a meeting place and a dance floor. This photograph was copied from a tintype and was probably taken c. 1865–1870.

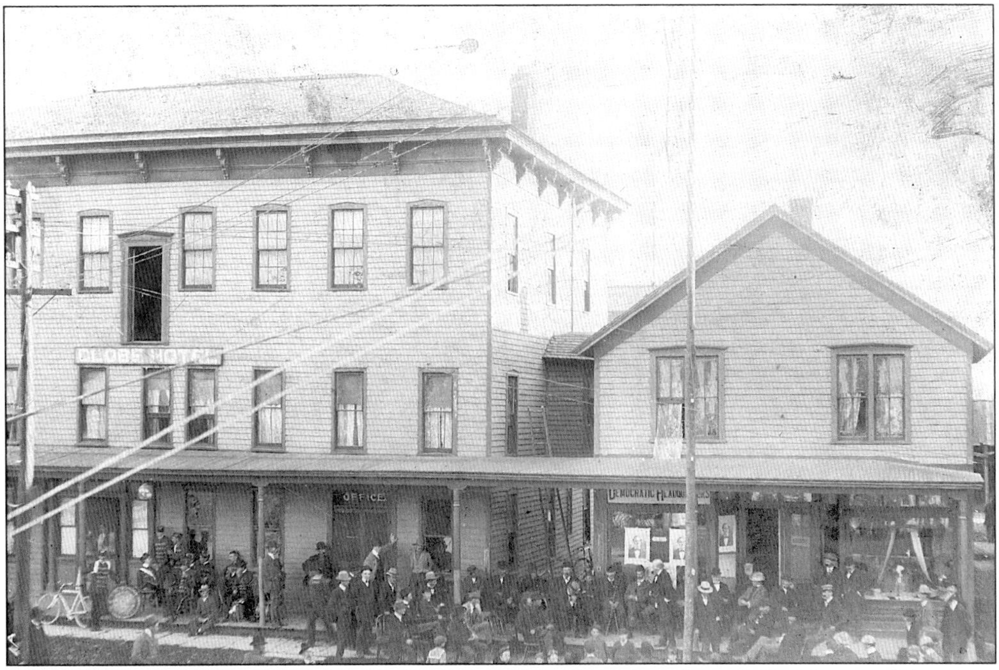

This photograph shows a political gathering at the Globe Hotel, *c.* 1900. The small building on the right was later the Offhaus Meat Market. The speaker standing near the "Democratic Headquarters" sign could be William Jennings Bryan. His uncle is standing and leaning against the post by the band.

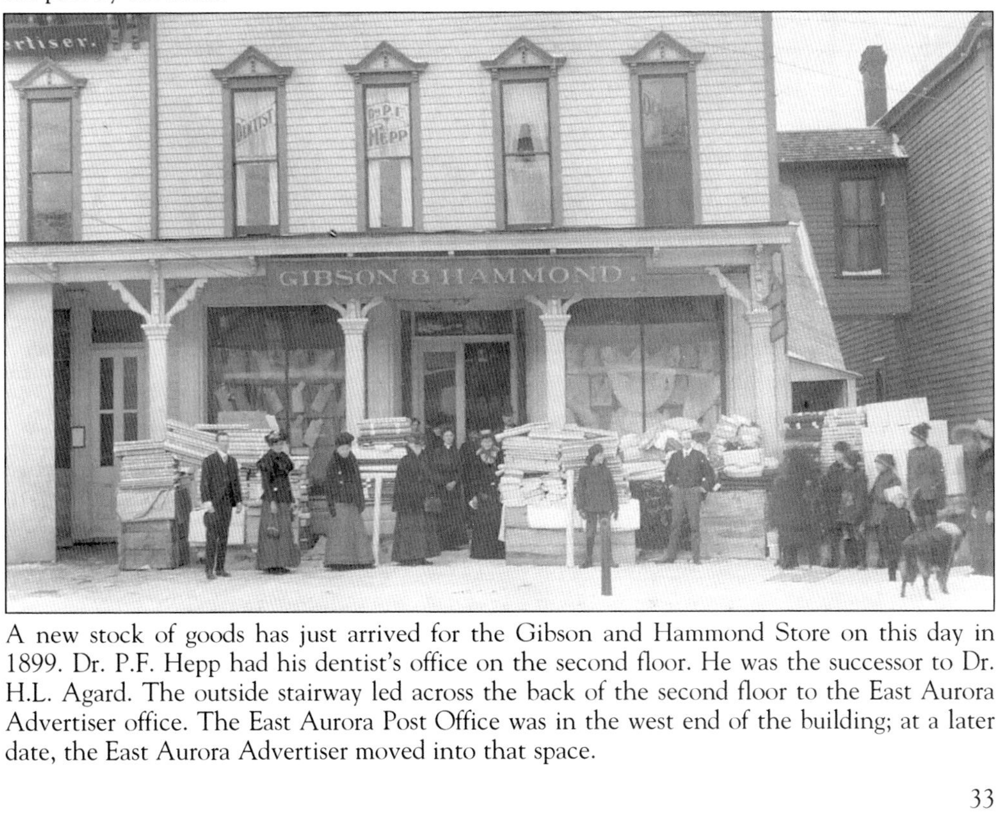

A new stock of goods has just arrived for the Gibson and Hammond Store on this day in 1899. Dr. P.F. Hepp had his dentist's office on the second floor. He was the successor to Dr. H.L. Agard. The outside stairway led across the back of the second floor to the East Aurora Advertiser office. The East Aurora Post Office was in the west end of the building; at a later date, the East Aurora Advertiser moved into that space.

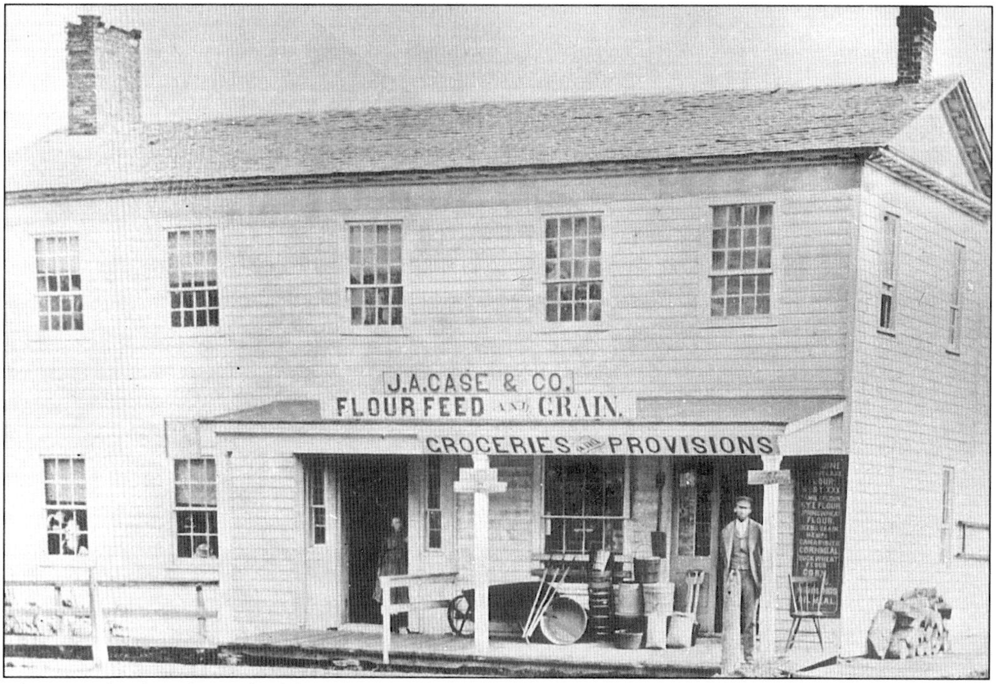

This was the first frame building in Upper Town Aurora. It was a tavern when William Warren built it in 1816. Warren sold it to Calvin Fillmore in 1820, and it remained on Main Street until 1884. At the time of this photograph, it was occupied by J.A. Case and Company. The man on the porch is unidentified.

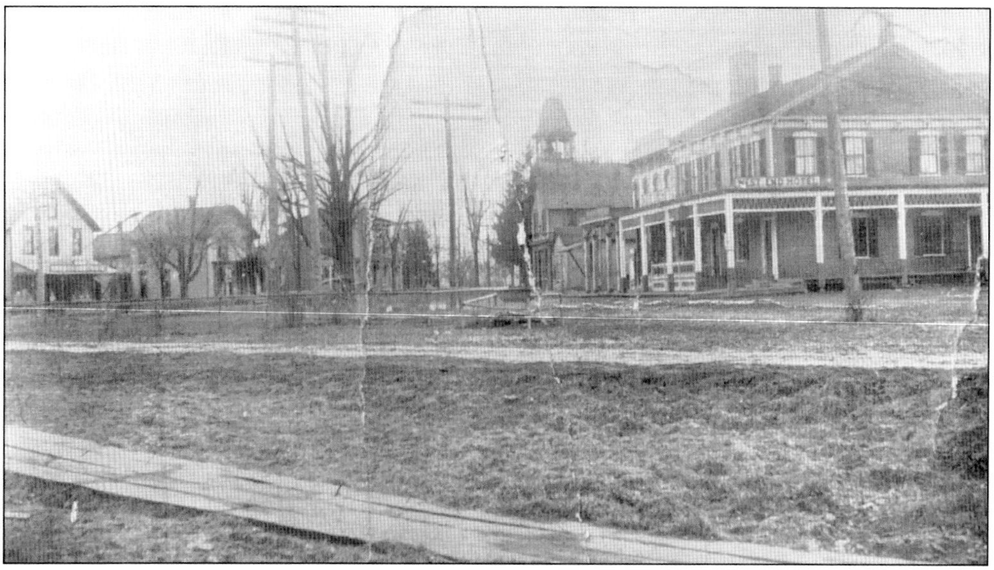

This site dates back to 1812, when the Eagle Tavern, a log building, occupied the spot. After a series of fires and a number of different owners, Harry Benedict bought it in 1909. He named it the West End Hotel. It continued under that name until the 1940s, when a fire caused damage in the amount of $75,000. It was rebuilt as Shore's Circle Inn. To the left is the bell tower of the West End Firehouse, which was built in 1880 when the Cazenovia and Pioneer Hook and Ladder Companies combined resources to build a common fire hall.

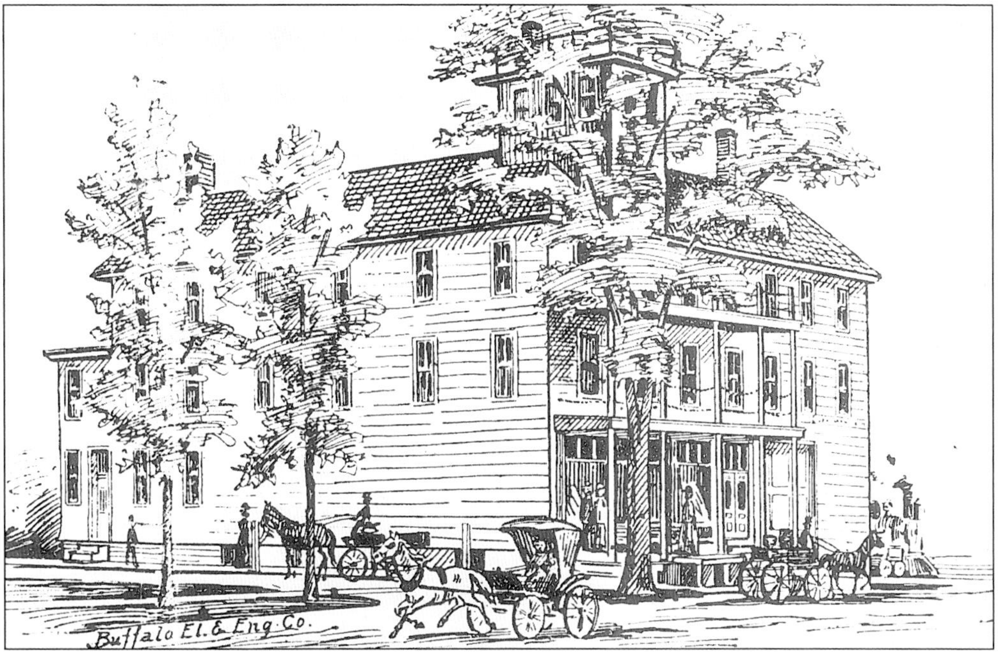

The Pfifferling Block was built in 1893 and was destroyed by fire in 1915. It contained three stores on the first floor, two apartments on the second, and a dance hall on the third. In 1899, Hooles Hardware specialized in the making of milk cans and pails. In 1904, Will Bragg opened a barbershop in the west side, Frank Hammond had a poolroom, and Billy Letson (a shoemaker from Germany) occupied the middle store. The first basketball games were played there. Elbert G. Hubbard managed wrestling matches there, and kindergarten classes were also held in this building. An item in the *Advertiser* on January 30, 1894, stated that Peter Caseman, cigar maker, was the first tenant. The article also stated that George Pfifferling "had completed a sightly clock tower" on Main Street at the railroad crossing. The clock had three dials, a 500-pound bell, and cost $650.

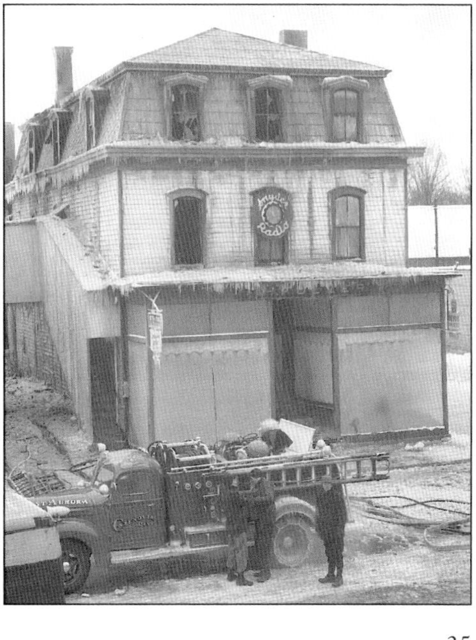

Fuller's Store, which was built in 1870, was burned and badly damaged on a subzero night in December 1948. Cazenovia firemen are shown after responding to the fire.

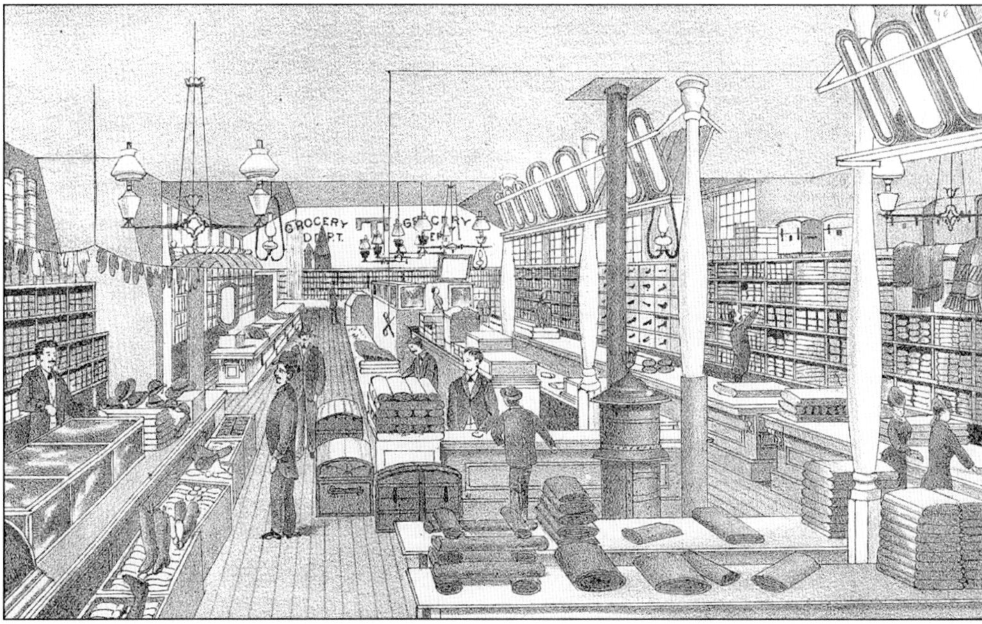

S.B. Thomson's General Store was in the Regulator Block. The interior of this store measured 134 feet by 32 feet.

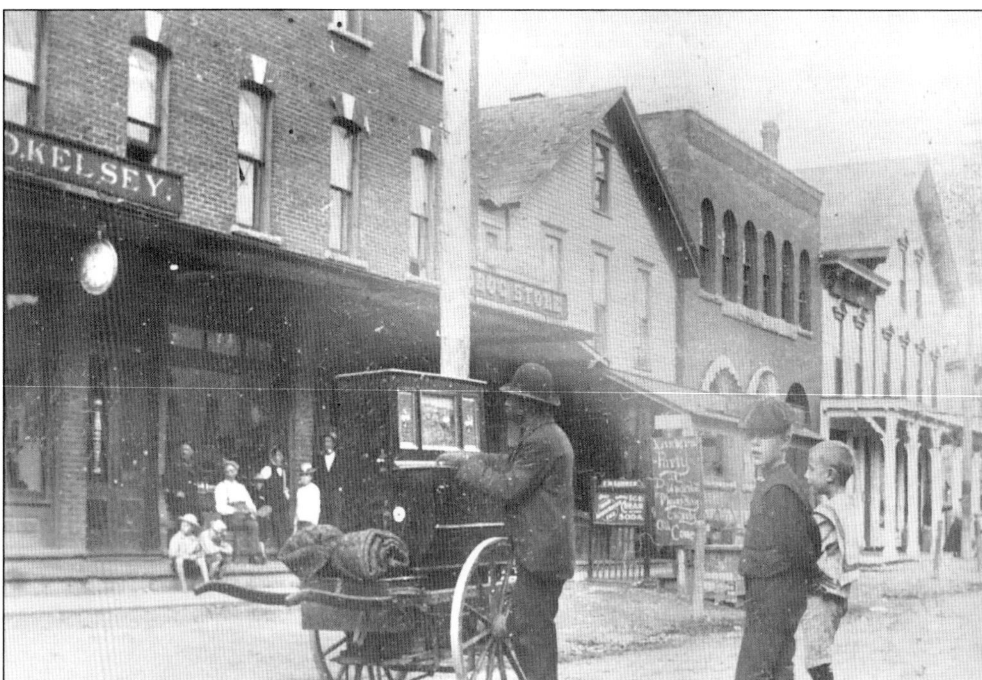

The buildings shown in this photograph were in the F.N. Spooner Block. From left to right are Kelsey Jeweler, Moore's Barbershop, Gardner's Drug Store, Heineman's Grocery, Bank of East Aurora, the post office, and Gibson Hammond. The organ grinder is unidentified.

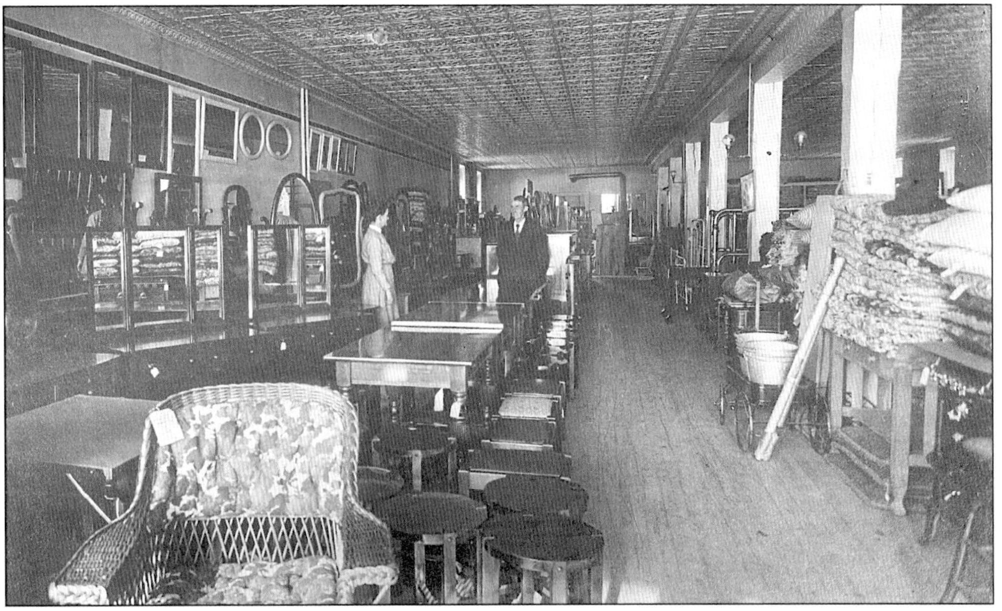

Shown is the interior of the Tackbary Furniture Store in 1915, with owners Kate and William Tackbary. The business was opened in 1895 in the Regulator Building. Shortly after that, they moved the store into a new three-story building next to the opera house. The original lumber for that building came from some of the Pan American buildings. When the exposition ended, Tackbary drove his team of horses to Buffalo to bring the lumber to East Aurora. In 1908, a fire destroyed both the store and the opera house. The store was rebuilt. Four generations of Tackbarys were involved in the business.

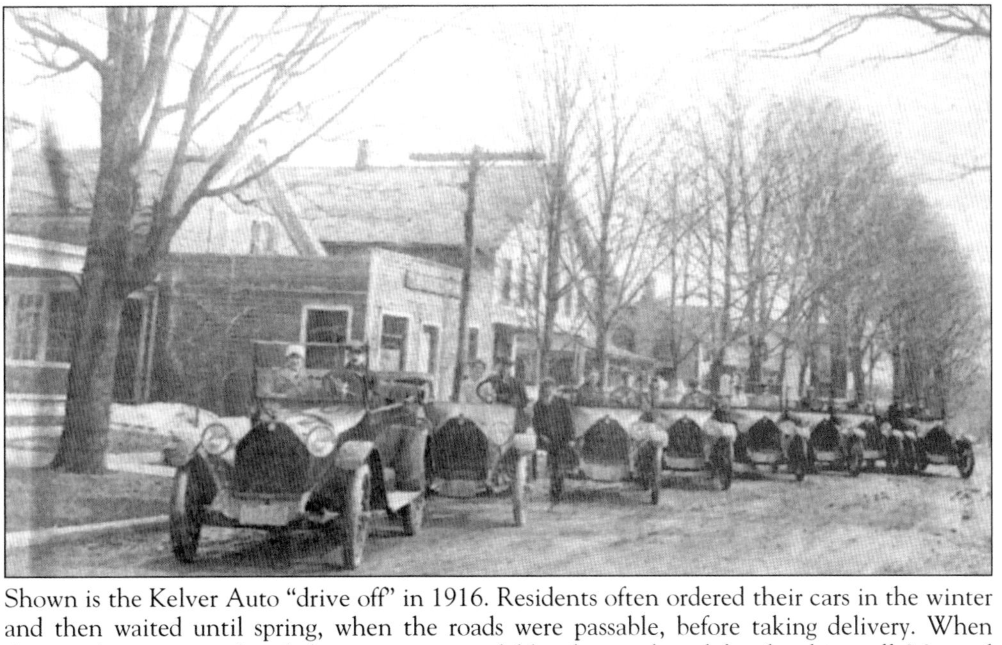

Shown is the Kelver Auto "drive off" in 1916. Residents often ordered their cars in the winter and then waited until spring, when the roads were passable, before taking delivery. When the weather permitted and the cars were available, they gathered for the drive off. Mr. and Mrs. W.A. Kelver led the way. The Flanders automobiles are shown here. Later, the Flanders Company was sold and the name was changed to Studebaker.

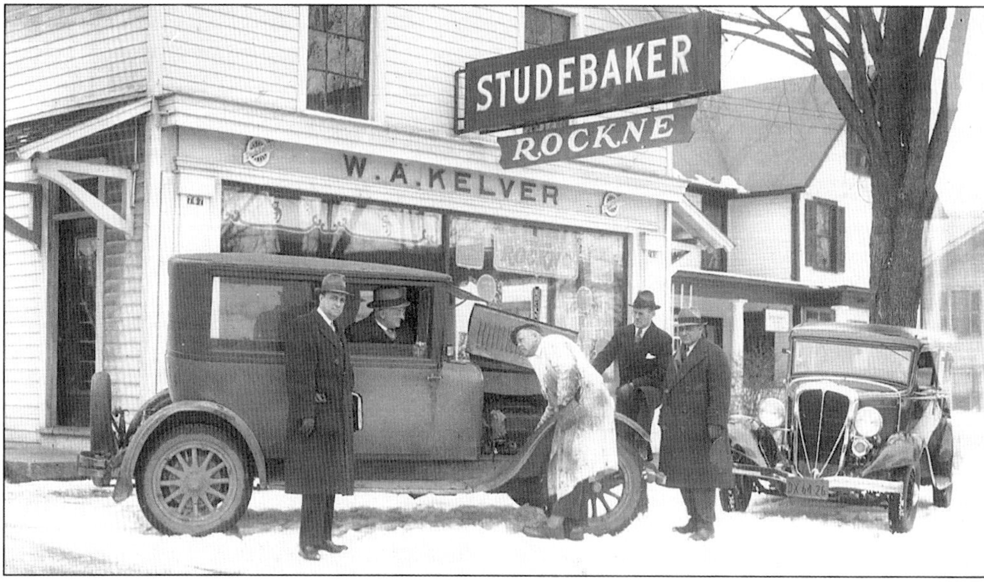

Bill Kelver began his auto business c. 1911 at Wales Center. In the 1920s, he moved the business to East Aurora, where more paved roads made sales prospects brighter. The building purchased for the showroom on East Main Street had been the Roger's Carriage Company, which had gone out of business. Over the years, Kelver Auto grew from a one-man operation to a corporation with 14 employees.

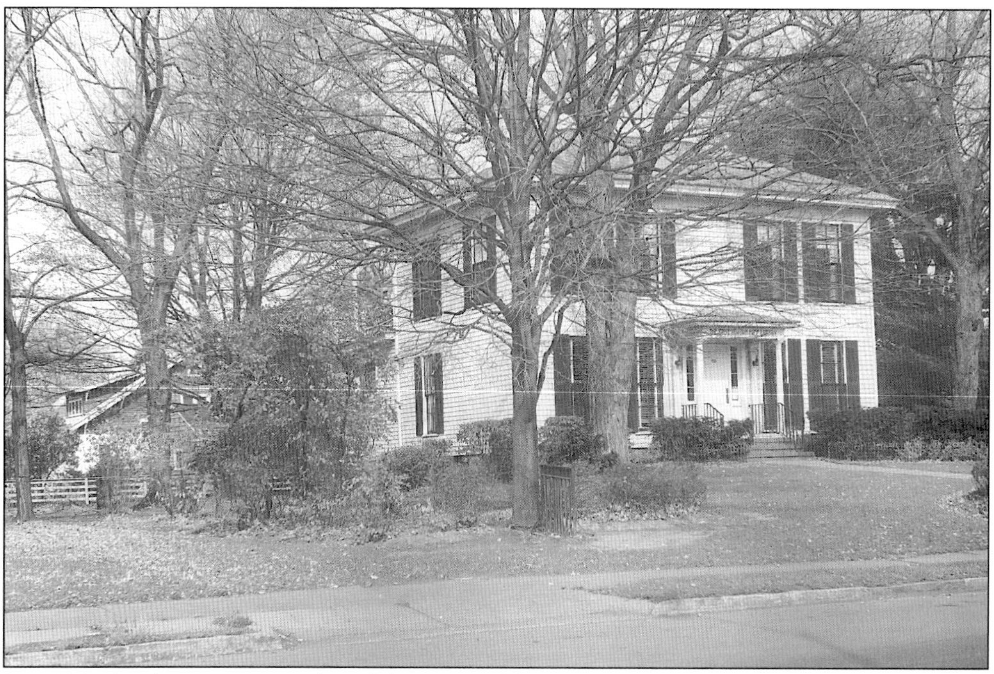

In 1922, this house was purchased by Mrs. Abbott S. Griggs and presented to the library association. A community fair was held to raise money to convert the home for library use. For the next 42 years, it was used by the East Aurora Free Library. Levi Pratt built the house in 1835 on the corner of Main Street and Whaley Avenue. It was demolished to make room for the new library building.

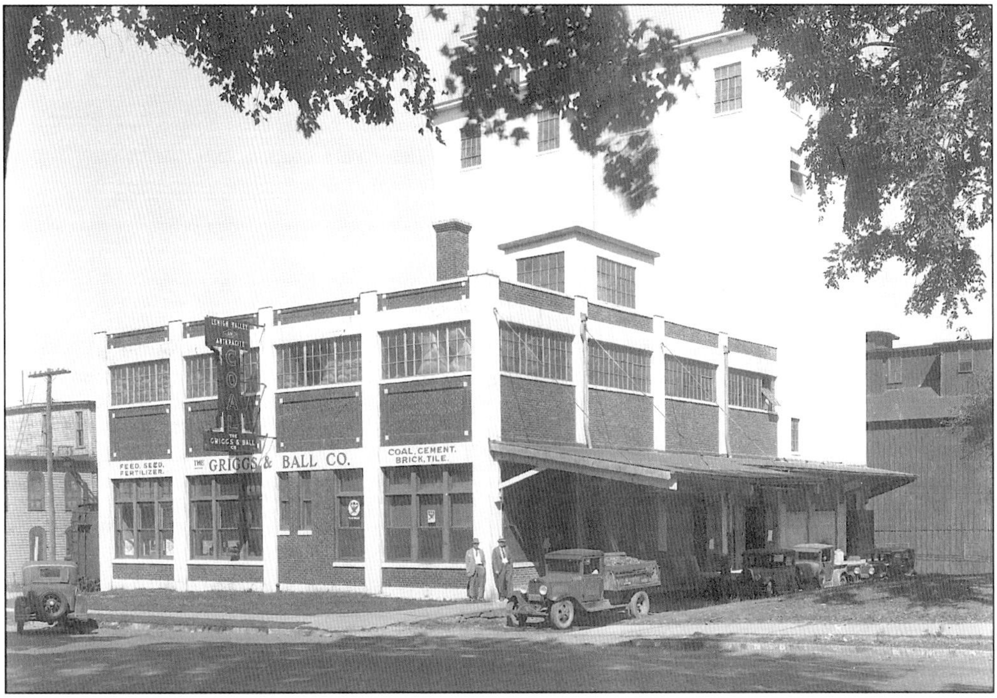

Sylvester Griggs opened a flour and feed business on Main Street in 1882. In 1893, F.H. Ball became a partner. After a fire in 1917, a new mill was built and became known as Griggs and Ball Company. They added mason's supplies and fertilizer to their inventory. Officers of the company have included Fay H. Ball, Haines R. Merritt Sr., Stan Hitchings, and H. Reuben Morse.

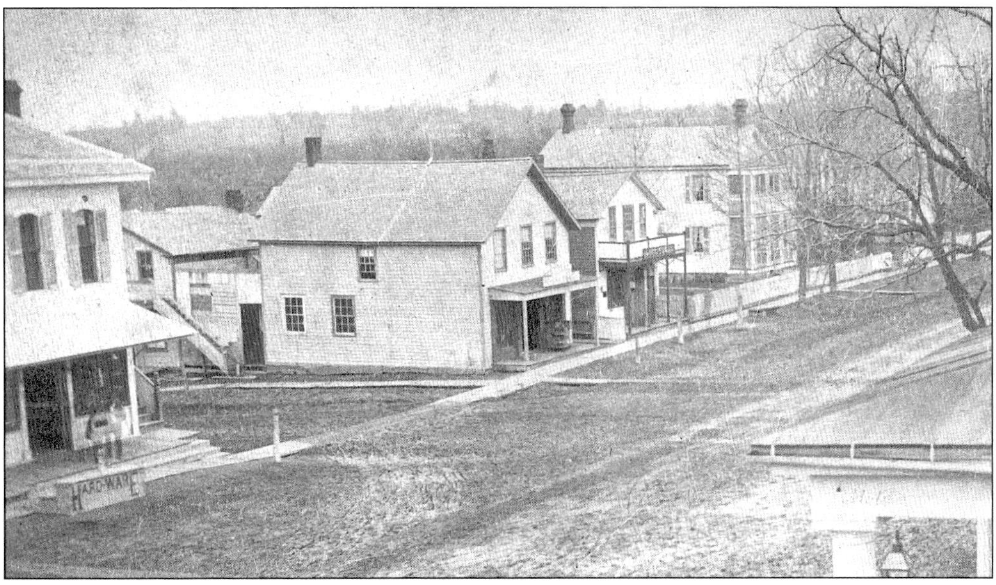

Looking east from the corner of Pine and Main Streets, the second building is East Aurora's first drugstore, which was opened c. 1834. Dr. Jabez Allen operated the business for 46 years. His motto was, "No cure, no pay." On the list of items sold were a complete line of wines and liquors, Hatch's Universal Cough Syrup, and Davis Home Relief for Pains. The little drugstore was a waiting place for the Buffalo stagecoach patrons.

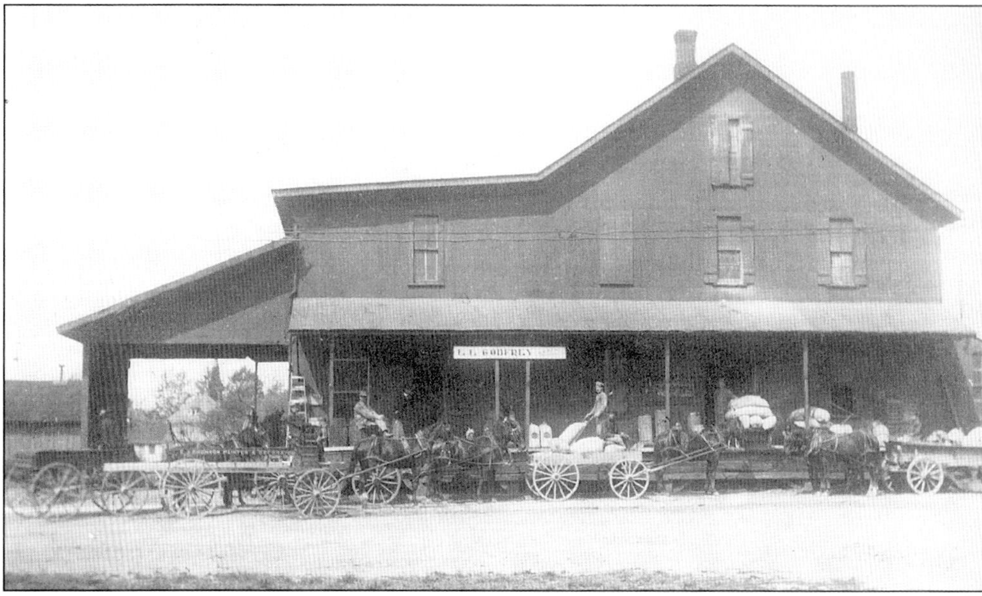

E.E. Godfrey's first mill, which was on Elm Street, burned in 1914. It was a prosperous feed business, which Godfrey entered into in 1887, when he came to East Aurora. He joined the general milling business with his father-in-law, Erasmus R. Adams. At the death of Adams, Godfrey rented the mill for several years. On February 6, 1911, he purchased the mill and the property.

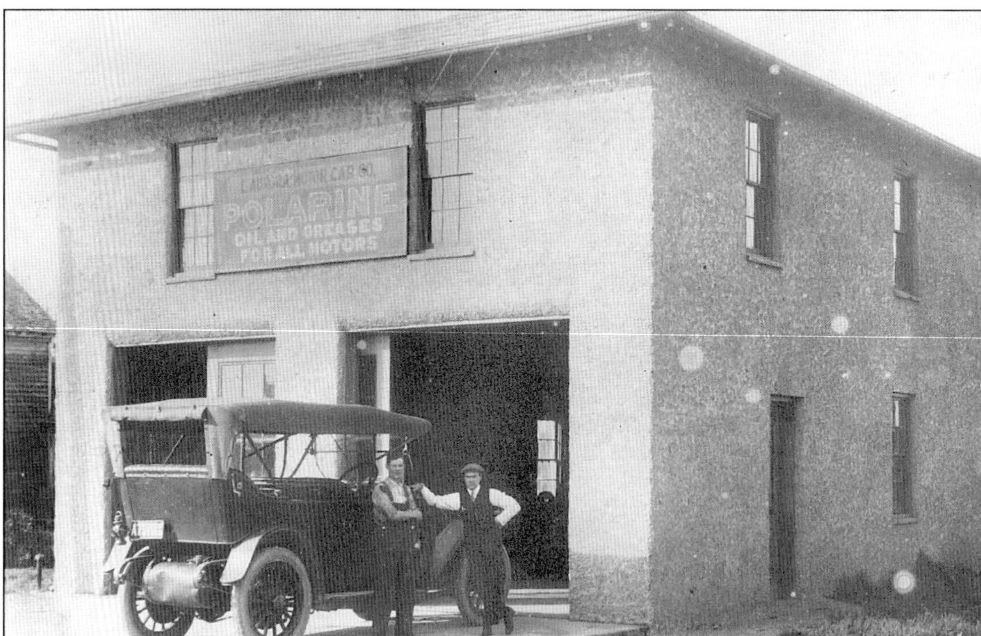

In 1914, the location of the East Aurora Motor Car Company was 16 Buffalo Road at the circle. Later, the front of this building was converted to a laundromat, and Aurora Glass occupied the rear. The man wearing the cap is Arthur L. Pierce.

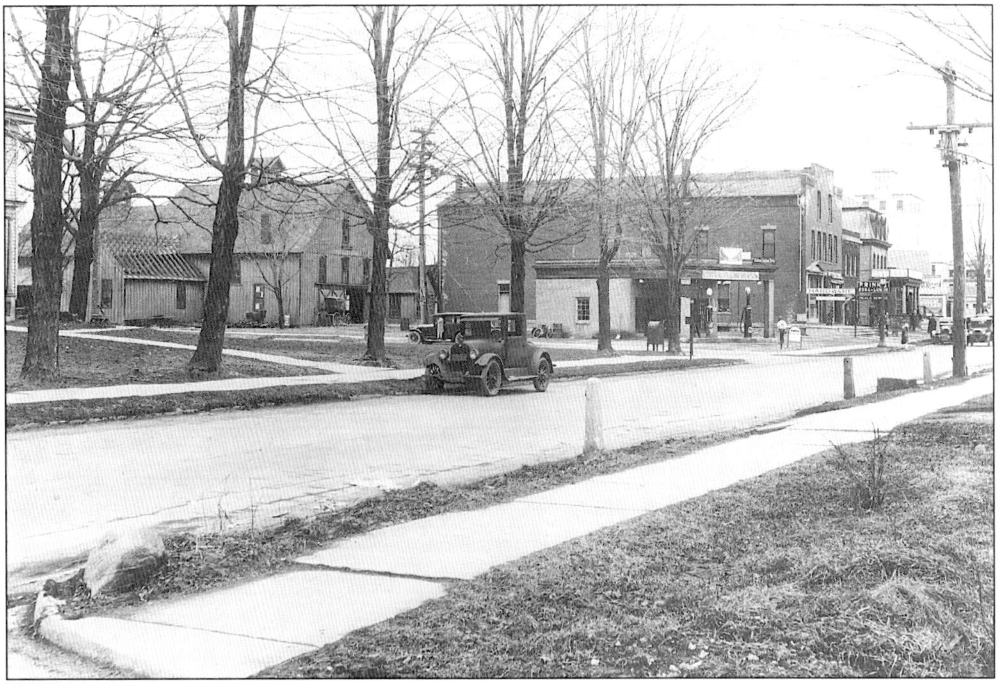

This scene features Main Street from the corner of Whaley Avenue, *c.* 1928. The large building in the upper right corner is the property owned by the Independent Order of Odd Fellows. At the time of this photograph, a hardware store was on the first floor, and Frink's Soda Bar and Restaurant was next-door. At the corner is Frink's Filling Station, which later became the Ernst Oil Corporation. Goodrich Livery Stable, built in 1885, is in the background.

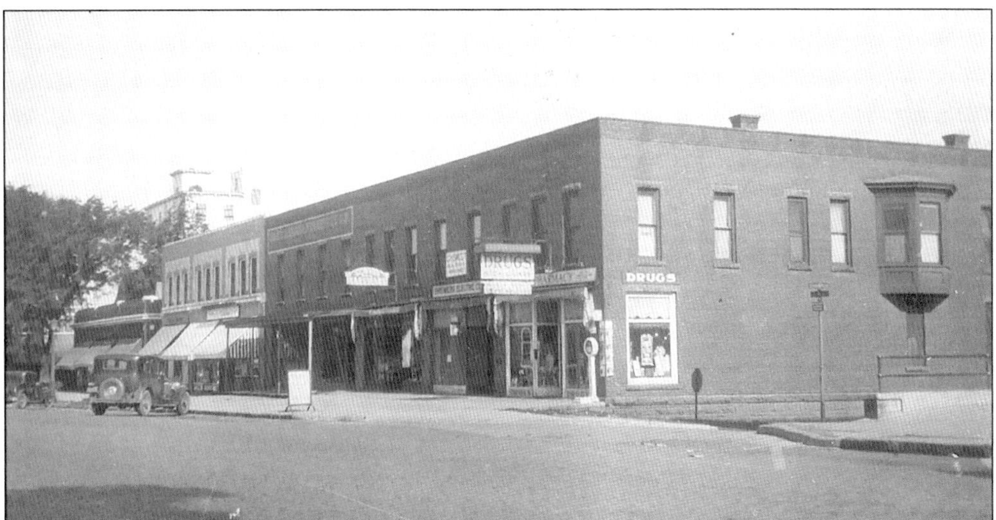

Shown is Main Street in the 1920s at the northwest corner of Church Street. On the opposite corner is Washburn's Drug Store. Griggs and Ball is the tall building in the left corner. To the far left, the lower building is Seaman, Hood, and Morey.

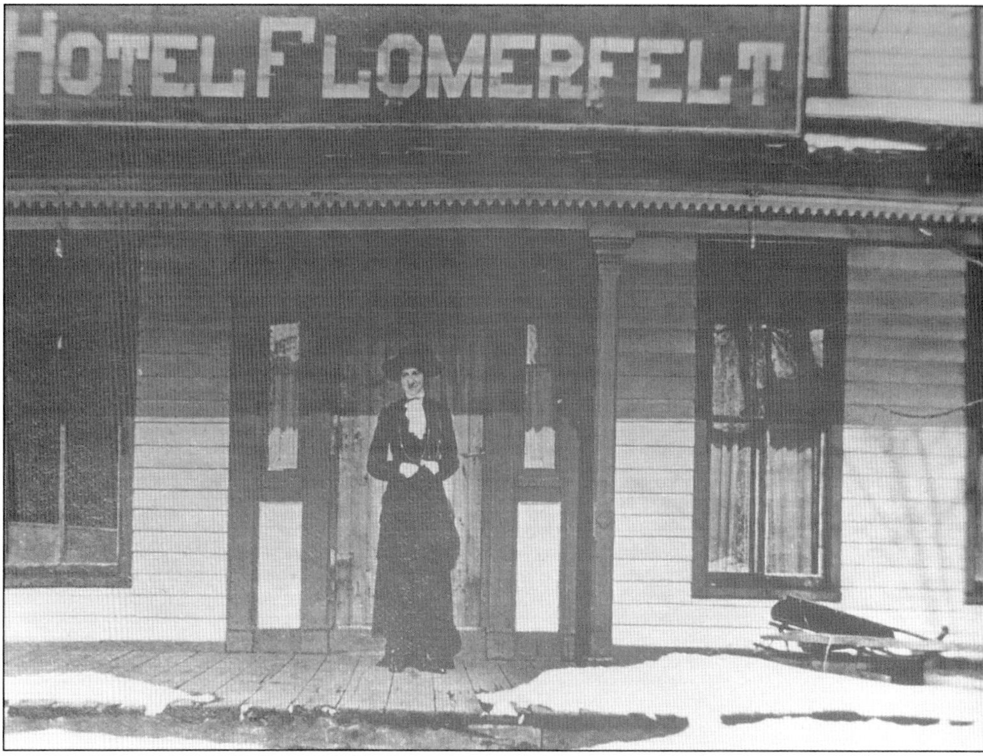

Hotel Flomerfelt, shown here in the late 1890s, later became the Curtis Hotel.

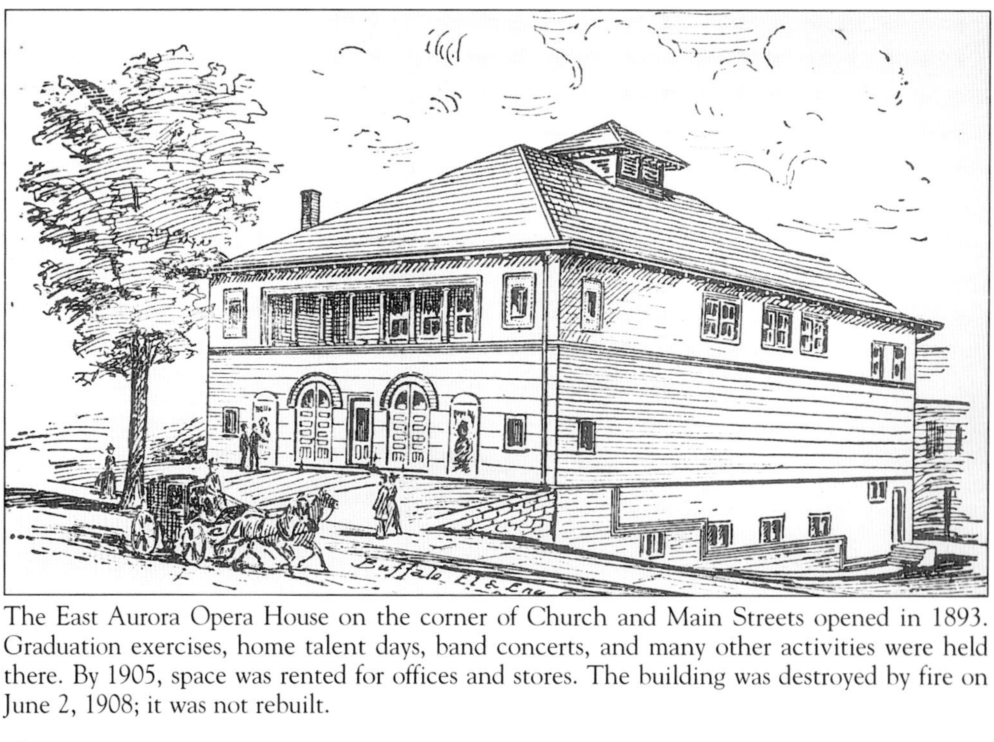

The East Aurora Opera House on the corner of Church and Main Streets opened in 1893. Graduation exercises, home talent days, band concerts, and many other activities were held there. By 1905, space was rented for offices and stores. The building was destroyed by fire on June 2, 1908; it was not rebuilt.

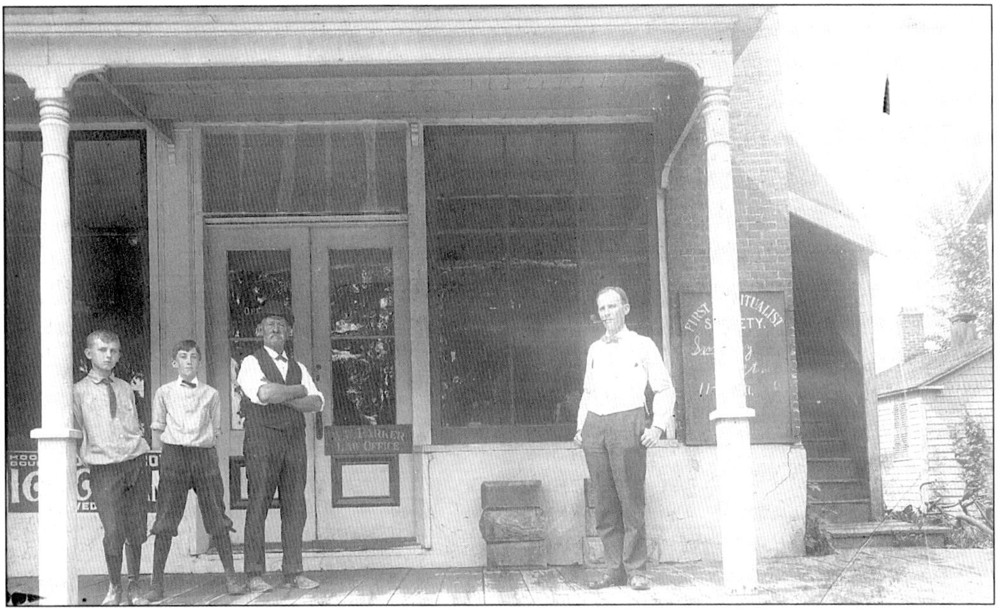

Standing in front of the Parker law office are, from left to right, George M. Houliston, Paul Whipple, Theodore Baetzhold, and Wells W. Parker. The First Spiritualist Society held meetings in the upstairs rooms. The Regulator Block later became Seaman, Hood, and Morey, and then a drugstore, a copy shop, and the toy museum.

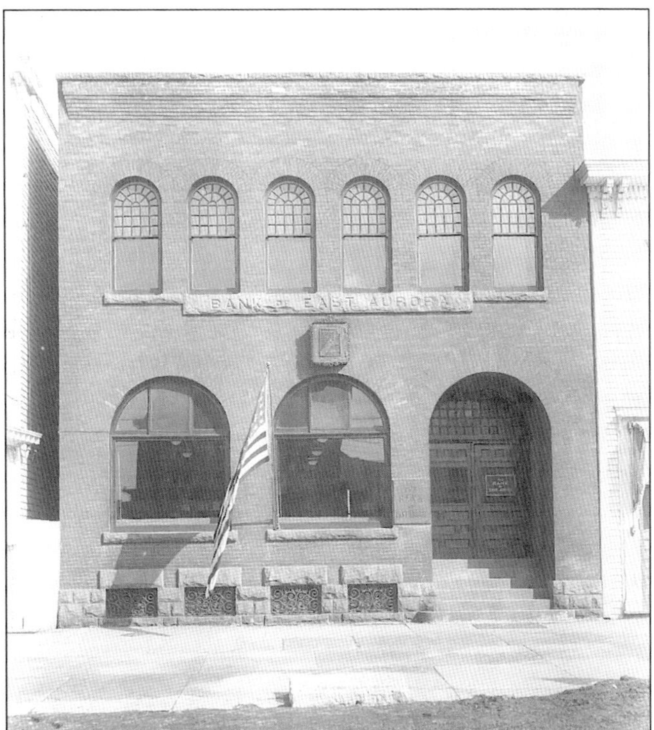

This is the second location of the first bank in the town of Aurora in 1882, known as the Bank of East Aurora. Henry Z. Persons and his son, Henry H. Persons, founded it. In the 1930s, this bank merged with the Marine Trust Company. The second floor of this building, at 706 Main Street, was occupied by the New York Telephone Exchange.

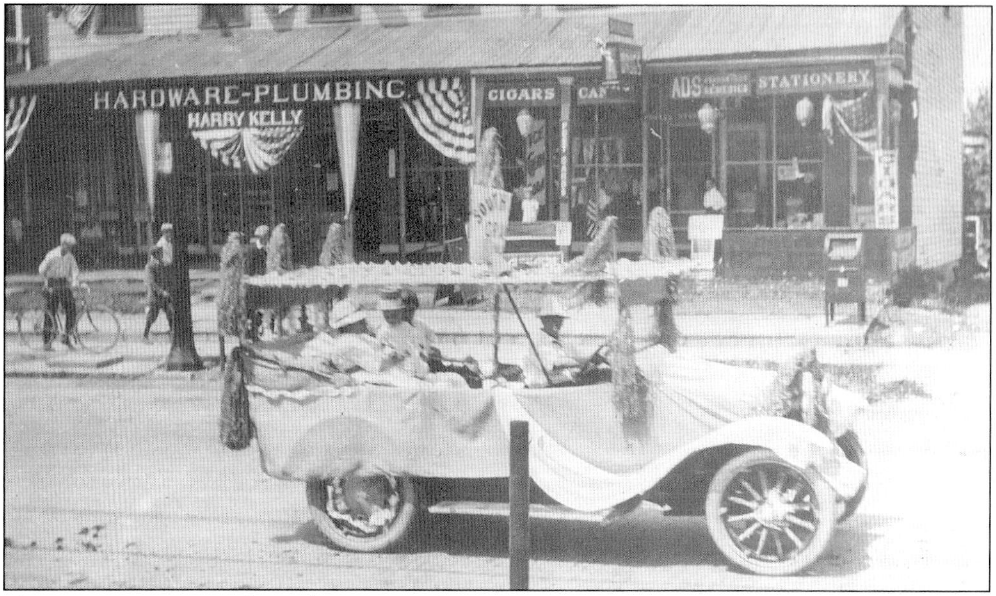

Shown is a 1920s parade at the corner of Main Street and Hamlin Avenue. Harry Kelly had bought out Sommers' Hardware. Darrin Drug Store is on the corner.

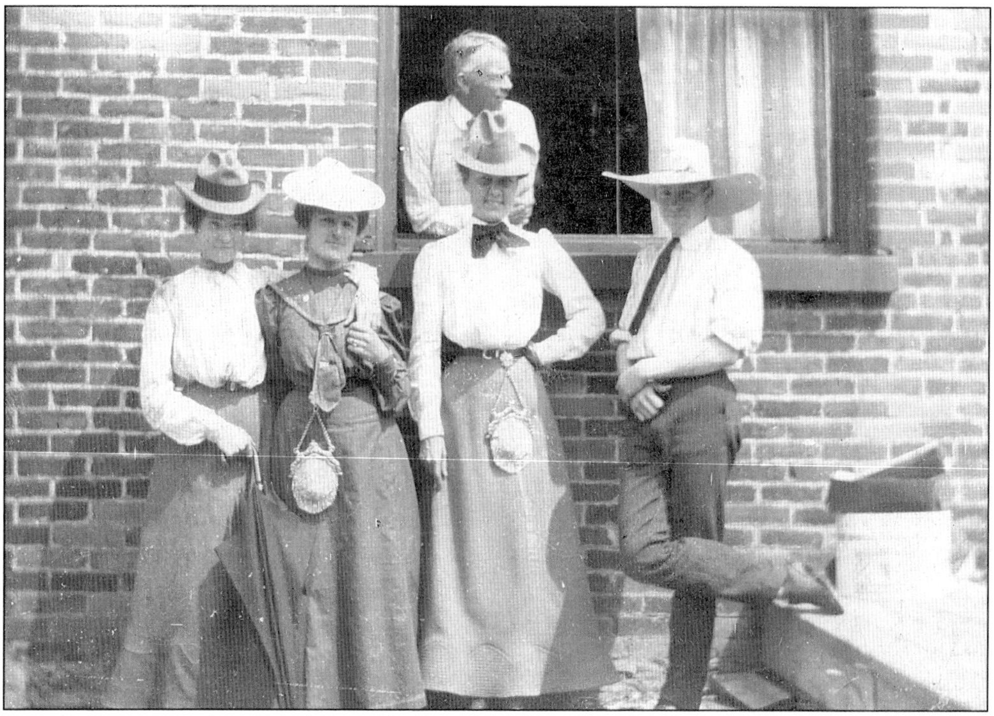
F.H. Fuller is standing in the window. Four of his employees are, from left to right, an unidentified woman, Alma (Nellie?) Paine, Ella Nye, and an unidentified man. The store was west of the Globe Hotel and later became the site of Sweet Memories. This general store was started in 1872 by Turner Fuller. His son, F. Henry Fuller, bought out his father's business in 1882 and continued there for 48 years. A son-in-law of F. Henry Fuller, Harrison Hall, joined the firm in 1923, continuing there until the building was badly damaged by fire in 1948.

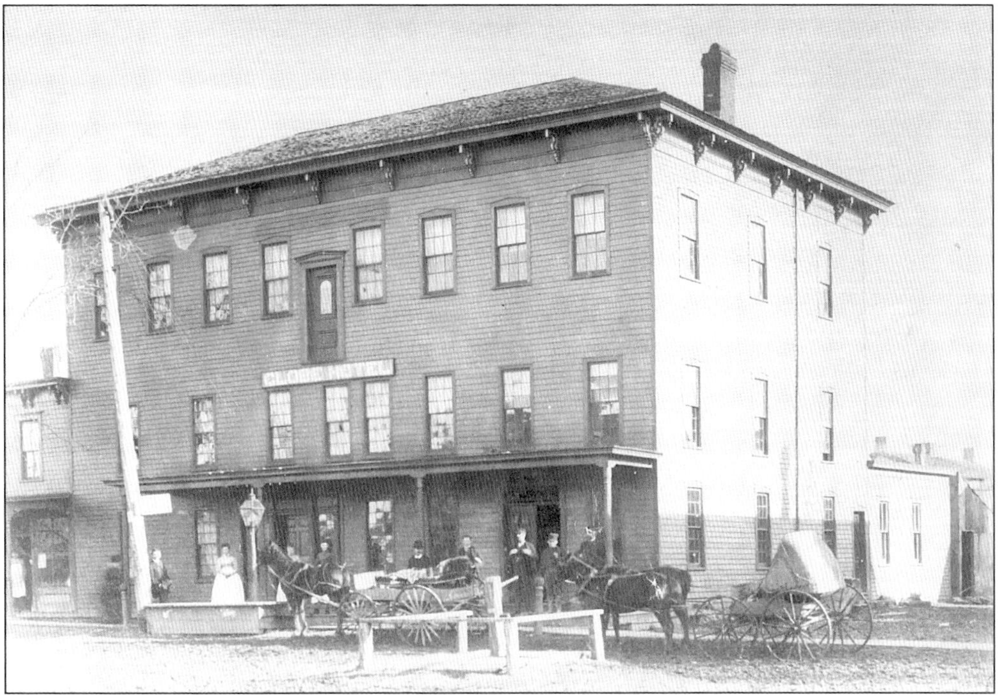

Horse-drawn carriages and the Globe Hotel are shown in 1885. Pattengill market is to the left of the hotel.

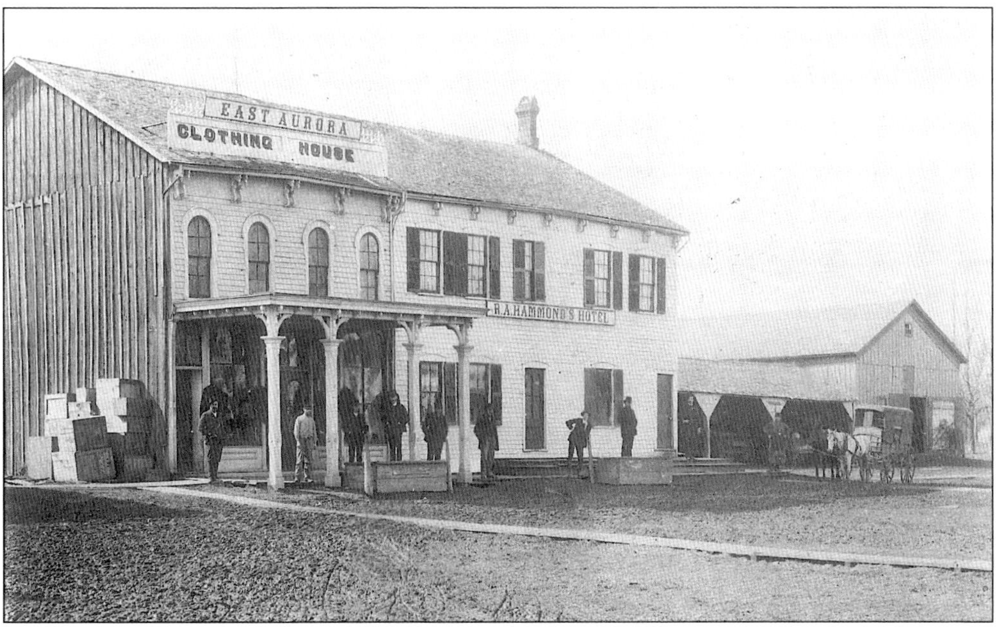

The East Aurora Clothing House and the Hammond Hotel at the circle are shown *c.* 1885. The history of the Hammond Hotel begins with the Eagle Tavern, which was built in 1812. A frame building replaced the original log structure that burned in 1869 and again in 1897. Robert A. Hammond rebuilt it. The people on the porch are, from left to right, Joe Wiser, unidentified, unidentified, and Byron D. Gibson. The wagon belongs to Frey's Bakery of Ebenezer.

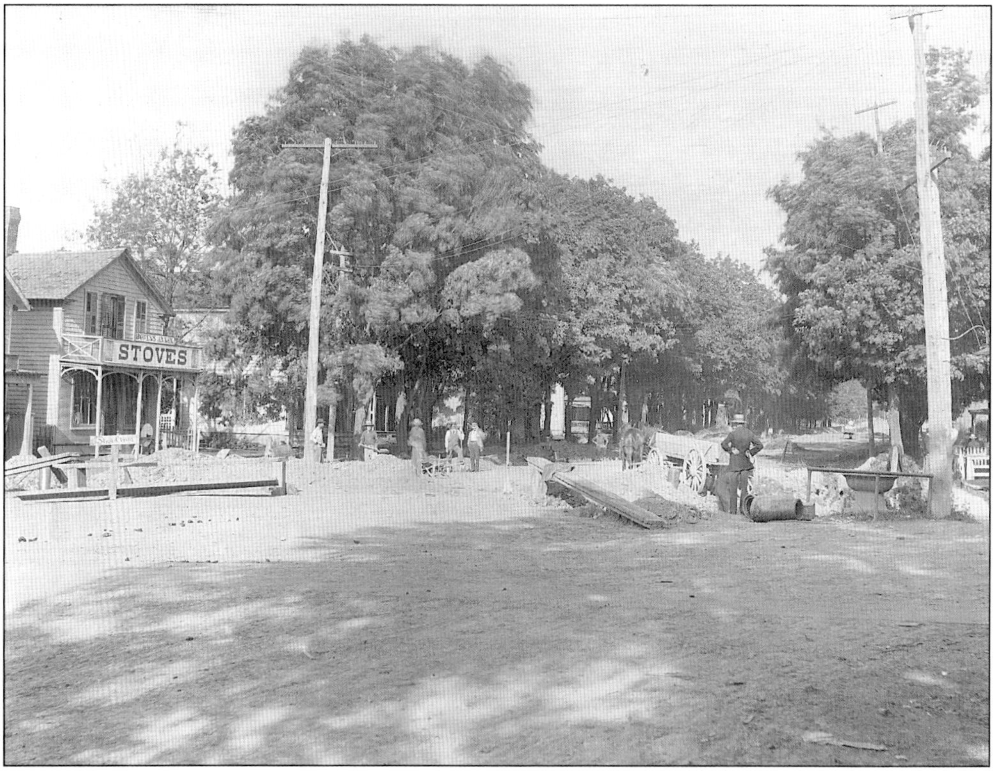

Workers put in water mains at the corner of Main and Pine Streets, *c*. 1890. Bowen's Store and the Allen home are on the right side of the photograph.

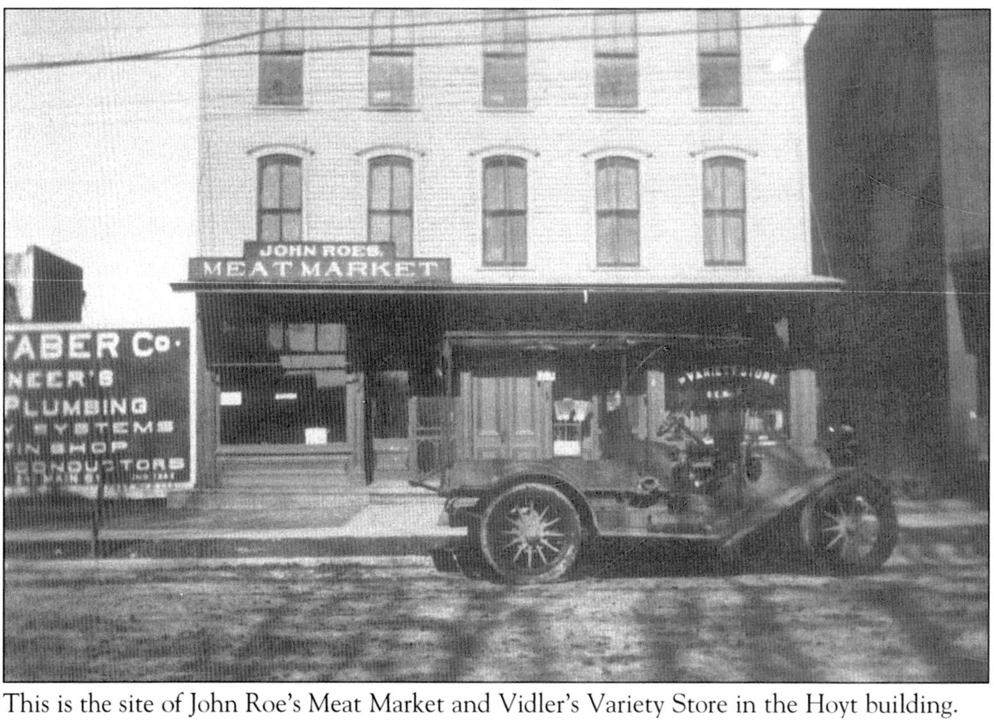

This is the site of John Roe's Meat Market and Vidler's Variety Store in the Hoyt building.

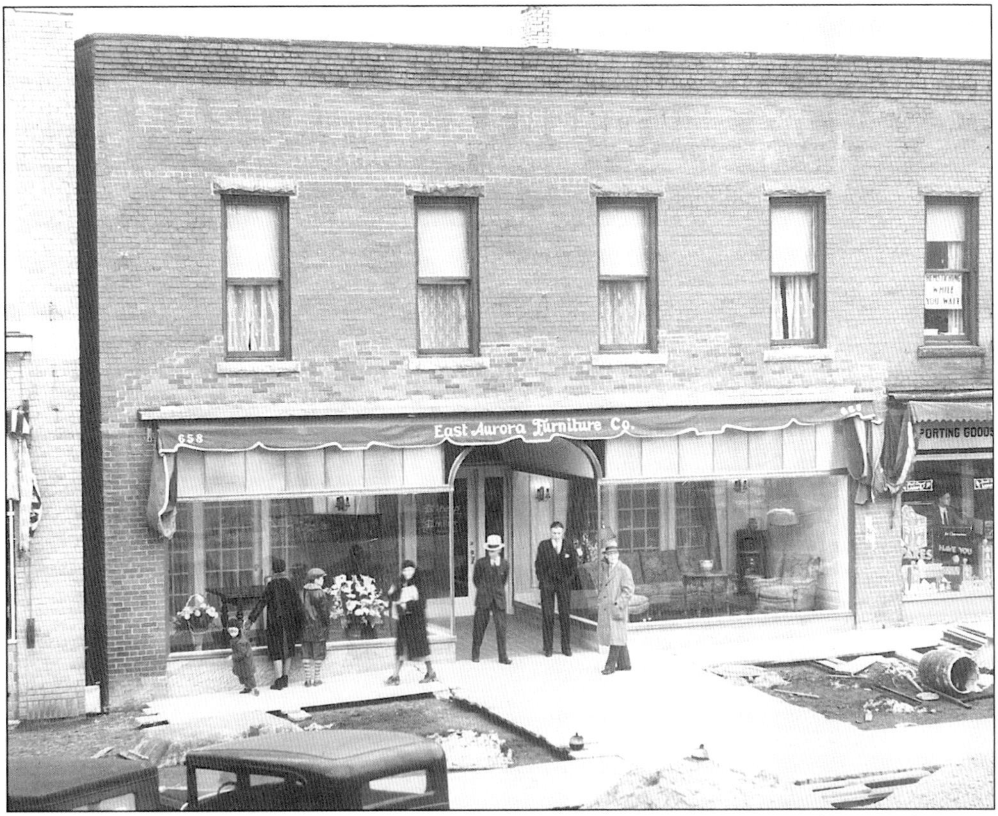

In his spare time, William Tackbary made and sold furniture. In 1895, he opened his own business in the Regulator Building and purchased an interest in the East Aurora Furniture Company.

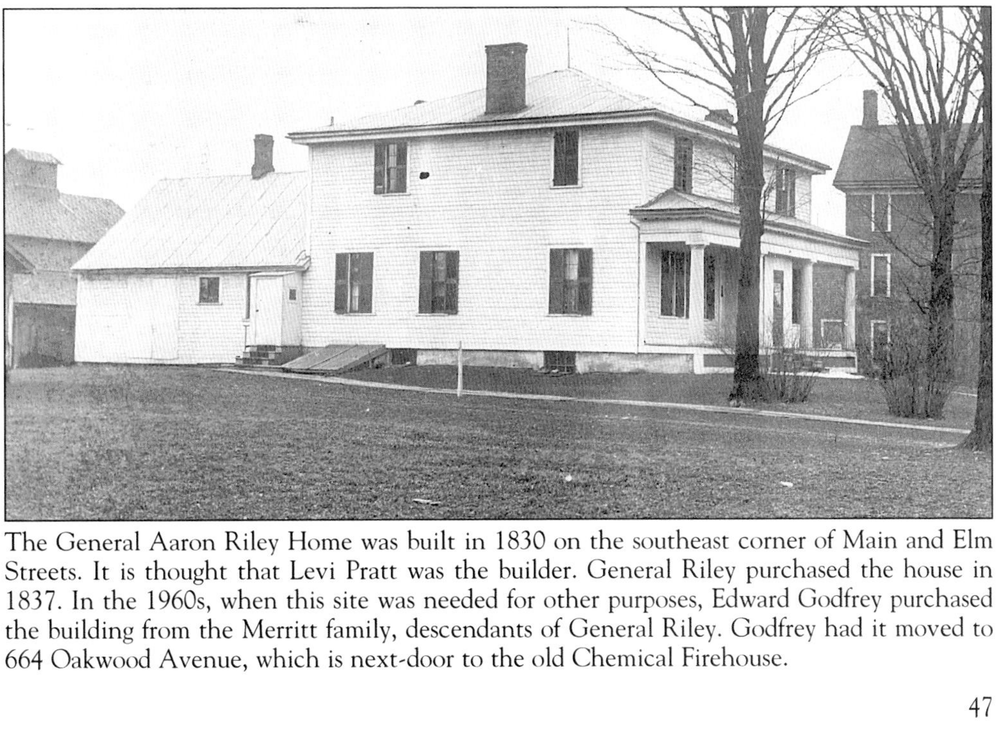

The General Aaron Riley Home was built in 1830 on the southeast corner of Main and Elm Streets. It is thought that Levi Pratt was the builder. General Riley purchased the house in 1837. In the 1960s, when this site was needed for other purposes, Edward Godfrey purchased the building from the Merritt family, descendants of General Riley. Godfrey had it moved to 664 Oakwood Avenue, which is next-door to the old Chemical Firehouse.

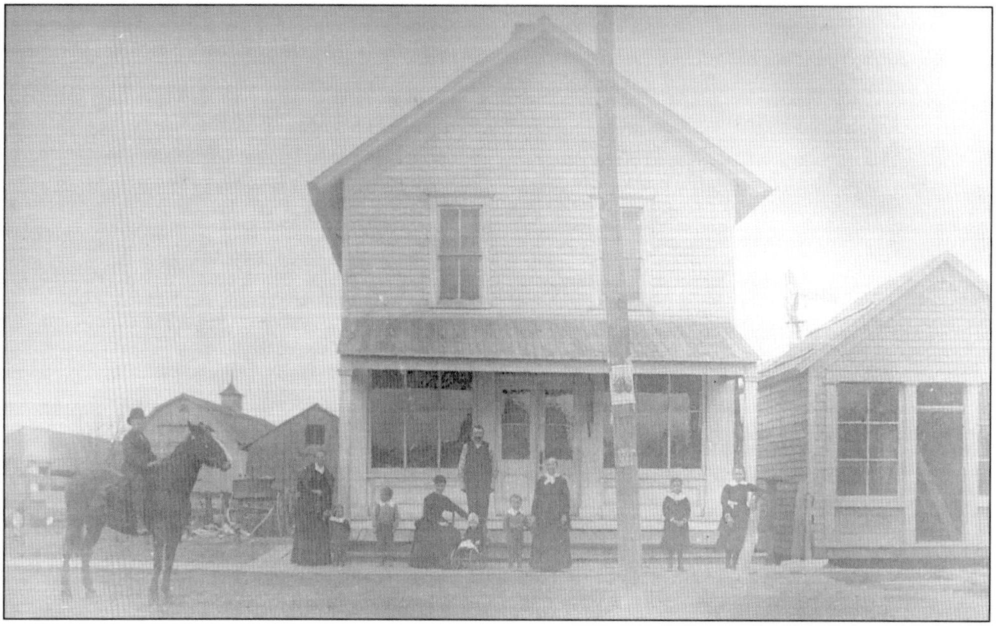

Around 1900 or 1910, Tasker's Store was on the north side of Main Street. In the 1920s, this business was Tasker's Confectionery. Later this site was Dusel Brothers, then Bell's Supermarket, and then Tops Supermarket. On the left, behind the horse and rider, are the Hamlin Farm buildings.

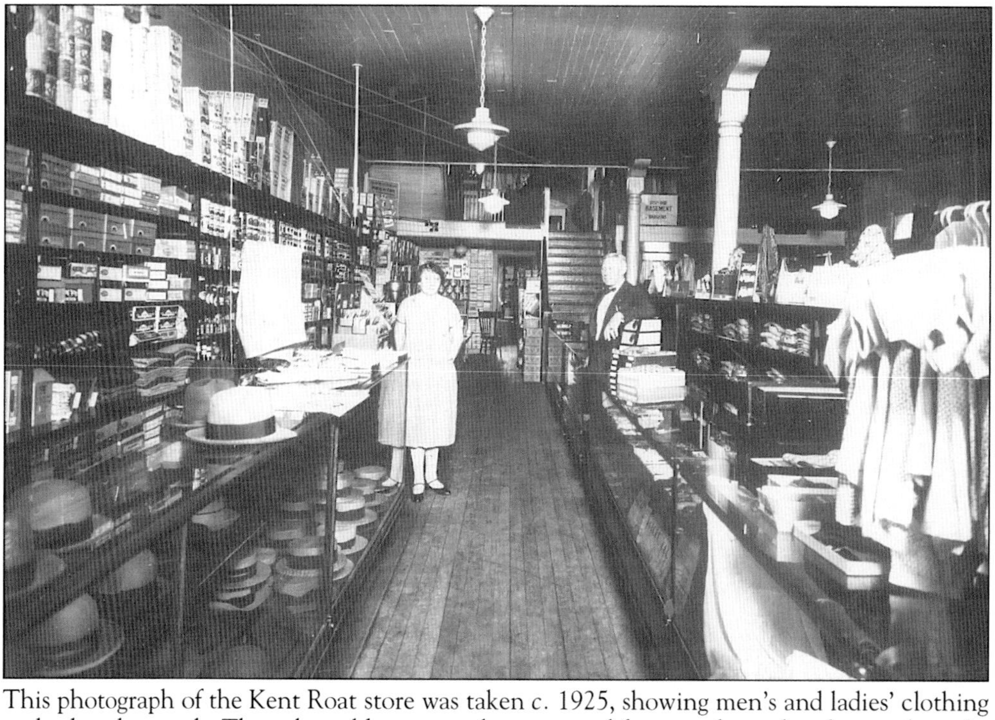

This photograph of the Kent Roat store was taken *c.* 1925, showing men's and ladies' clothing and other dry goods. They also sold eggs, maple syrup, and farm products that farmers brought in exchange for their family's needs. The balcony visible in the back was added for a better display of goods.

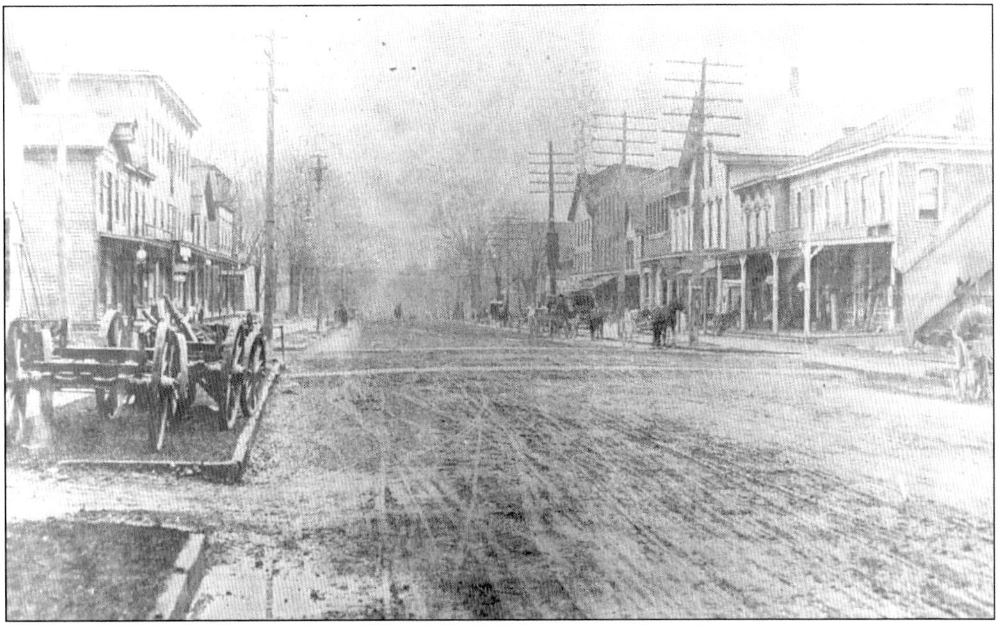

This early street scene in East Aurora shows the corner of Main and Olean Streets, looking west. The photograph was taken after 1891 and before 1904.

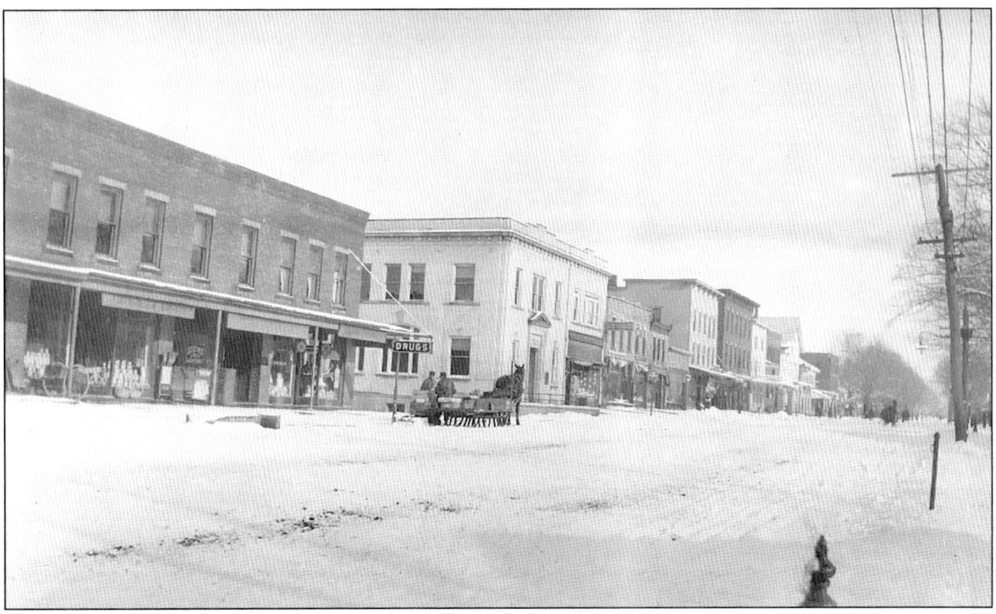

This view looking east shows the Tackbary and A.S. Griggs Block on the north side of Main Street in 1916. From left to right are George Persons Grocery, Adams Express Office, Mason Brown's Pharmacy, Church Street, the bank, and Cummings Drug Store.

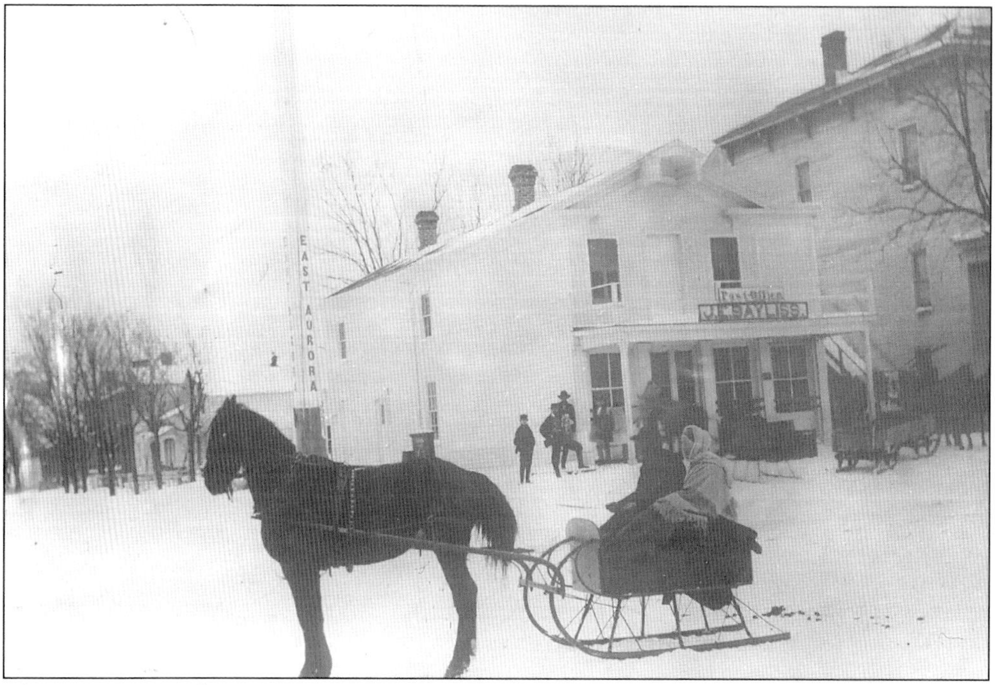

The street sign reading, "East Aurora" is on the corner of Olean and Main Streets. James Bayliss and his wife are riding in the sleigh. Bayliss was postmaster in East Aurora from 1867 to 1872. The post office was in his store. A part of the Globe Hotel can be seen at the right corner of this photograph, which was copied from a tintype.

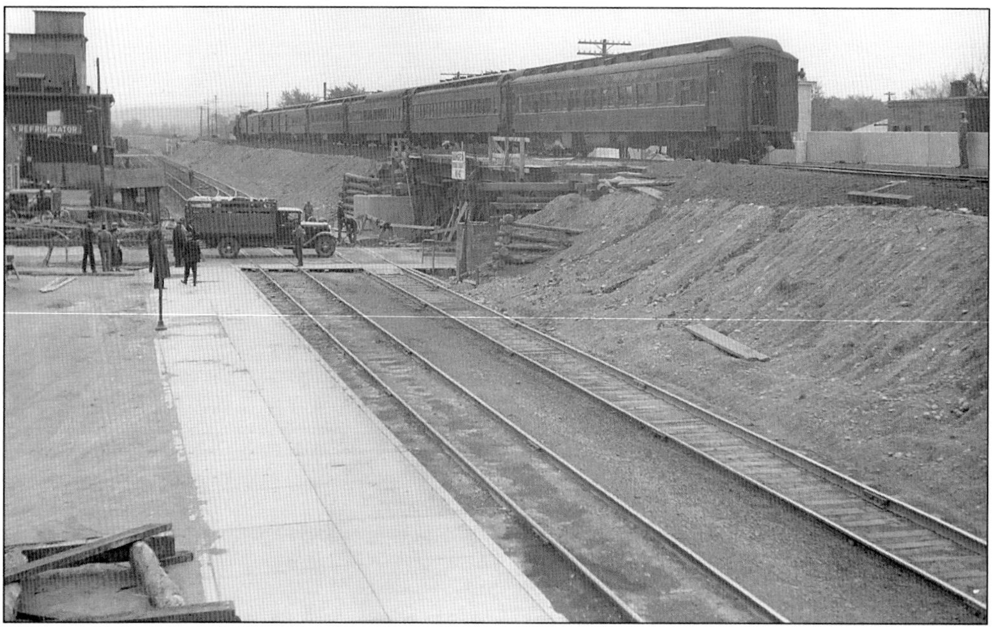

The Pennsylvania Railroad tracks were raised in 1934. The Main Street grade crossing was eliminated by the elevation of the tracks. Upon completion, the tracks were 13 feet above grade and the street was depressed about 7 feet. Ferguson and Edmondson Company of Pittsburgh, Pennsylvania did construction. The first train went over the elevated tracks on October 15, 1934.

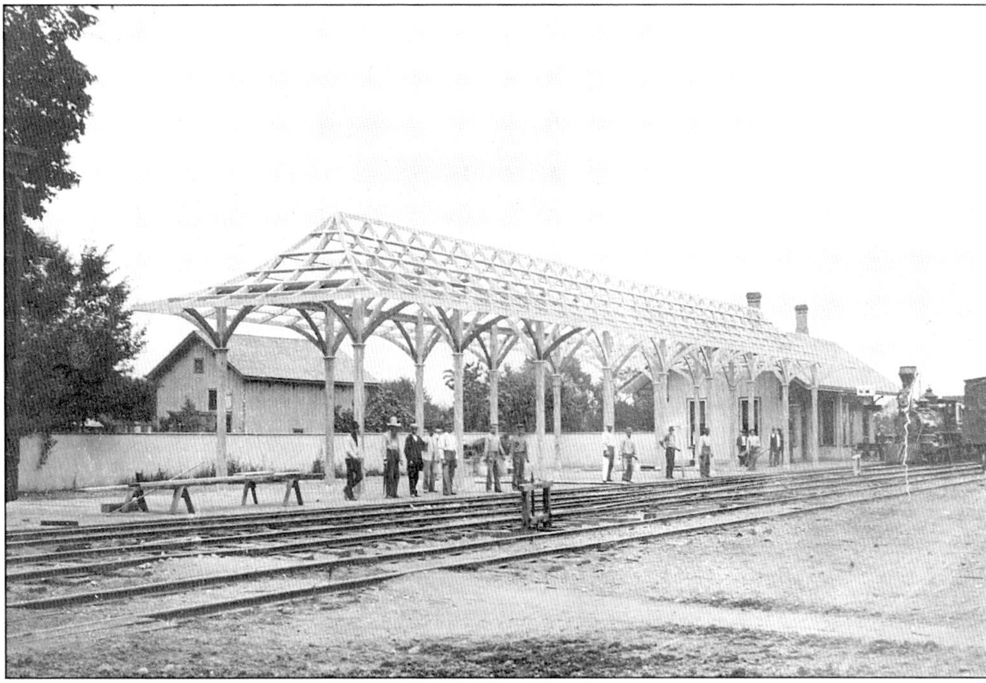

In this photograph, the shelter for the Western New York and Pennsylvania Railroad is under construction in East Aurora.

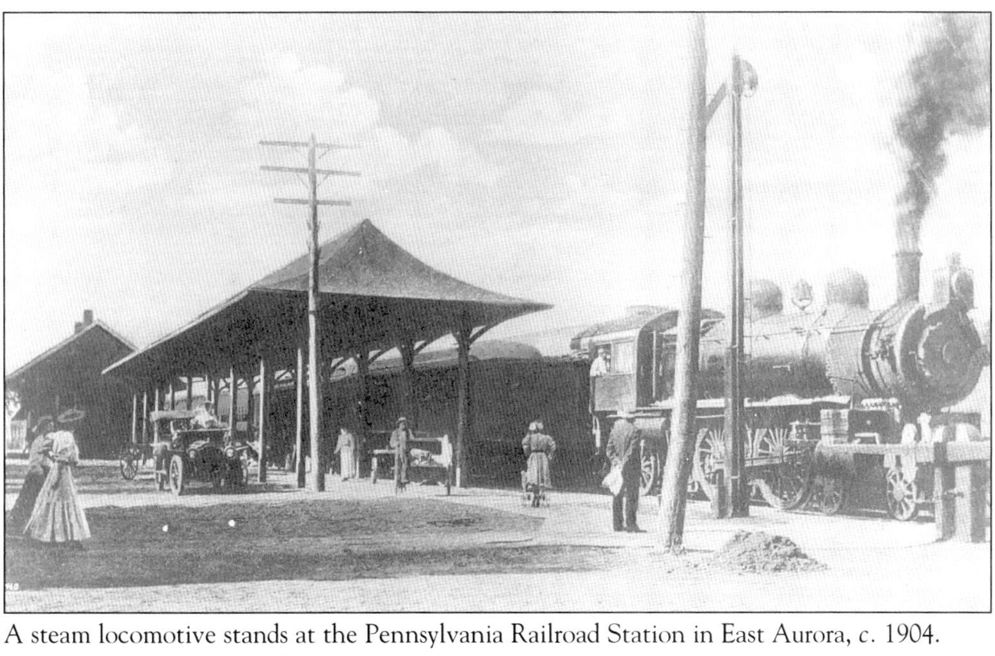

A steam locomotive stands at the Pennsylvania Railroad Station in East Aurora, c. 1904.

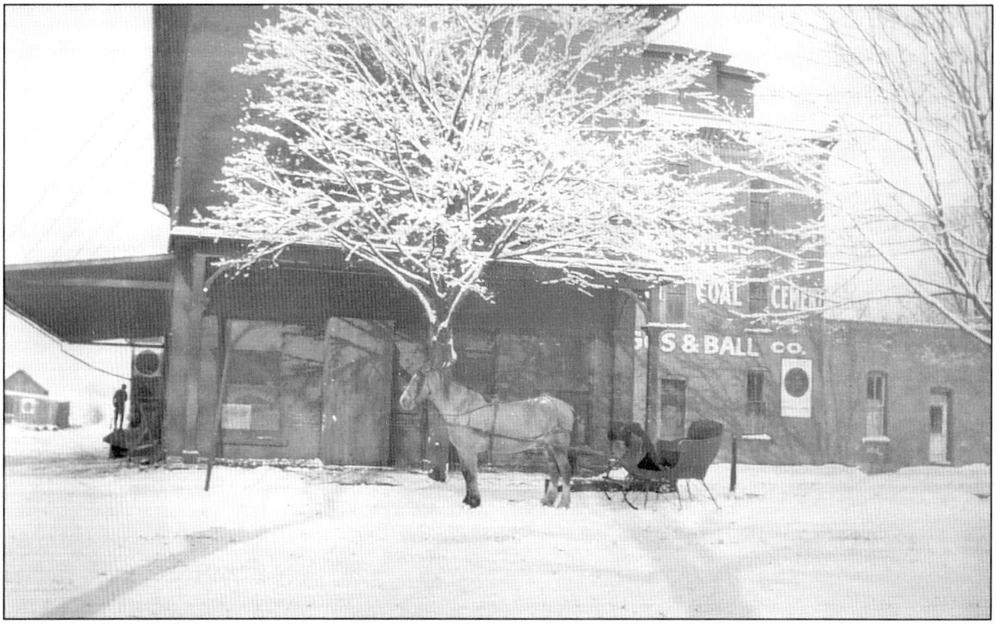

This winter scene with a horse and sleigh at Griggs and Ball Company shows the mill from the east side. The old mill burned in the early 1900s.

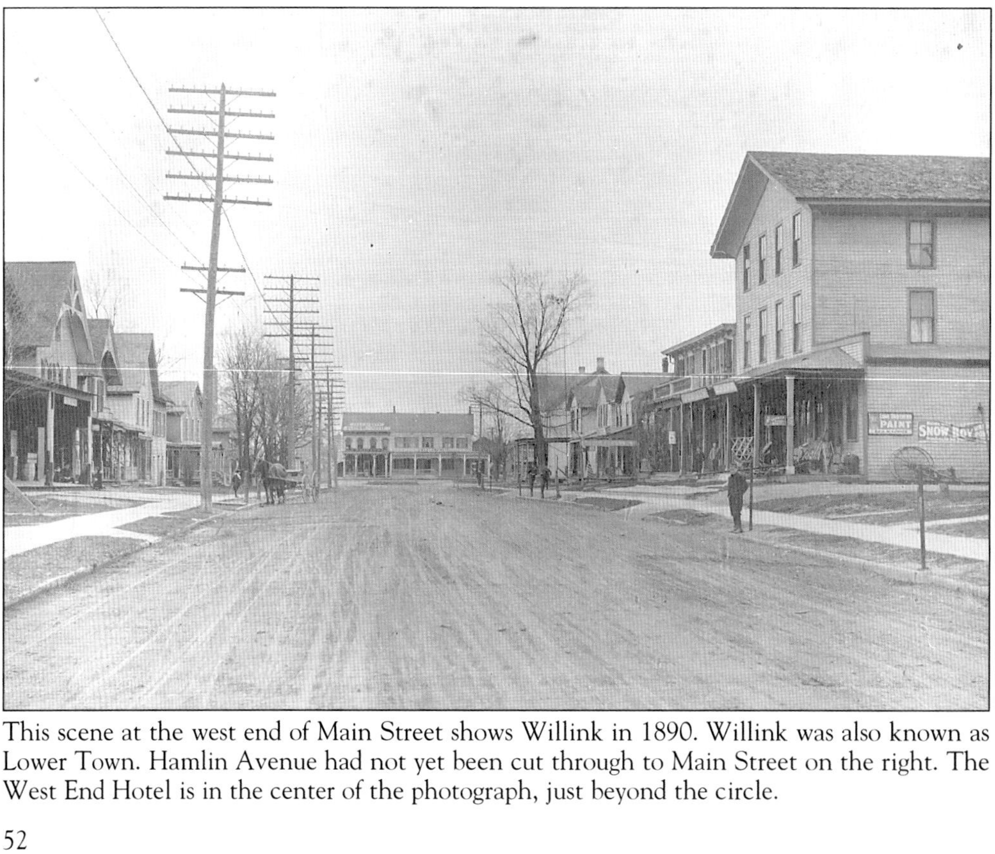

This scene at the west end of Main Street shows Willink in 1890. Willink was also known as Lower Town. Hamlin Avenue had not yet been cut through to Main Street on the right. The West End Hotel is in the center of the photograph, just beyond the circle.

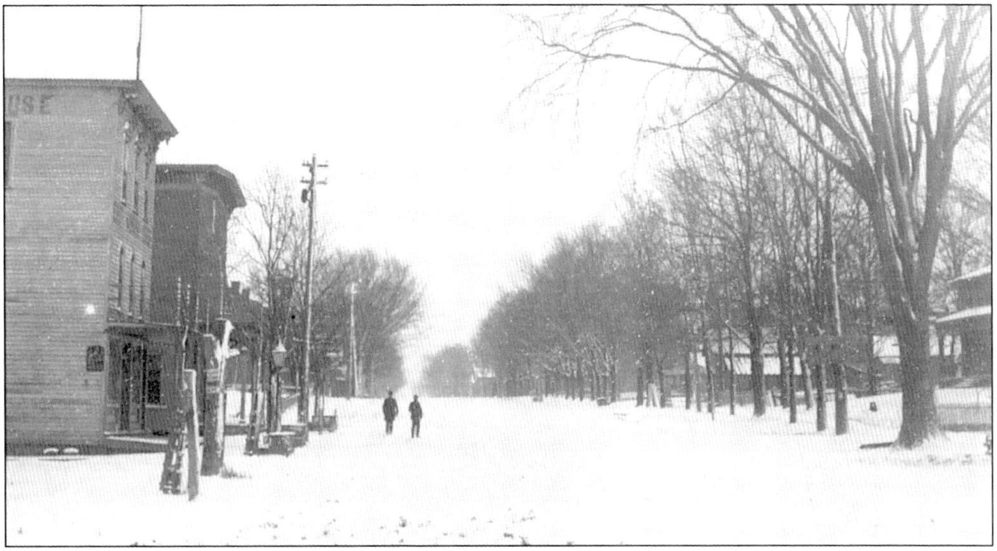

This view of Main Street looks east from the railroad in the early 1880s. The house of Aaron Riley is on the right, and the monument works of Harding Kyser, Pfiffering House, is on the left.

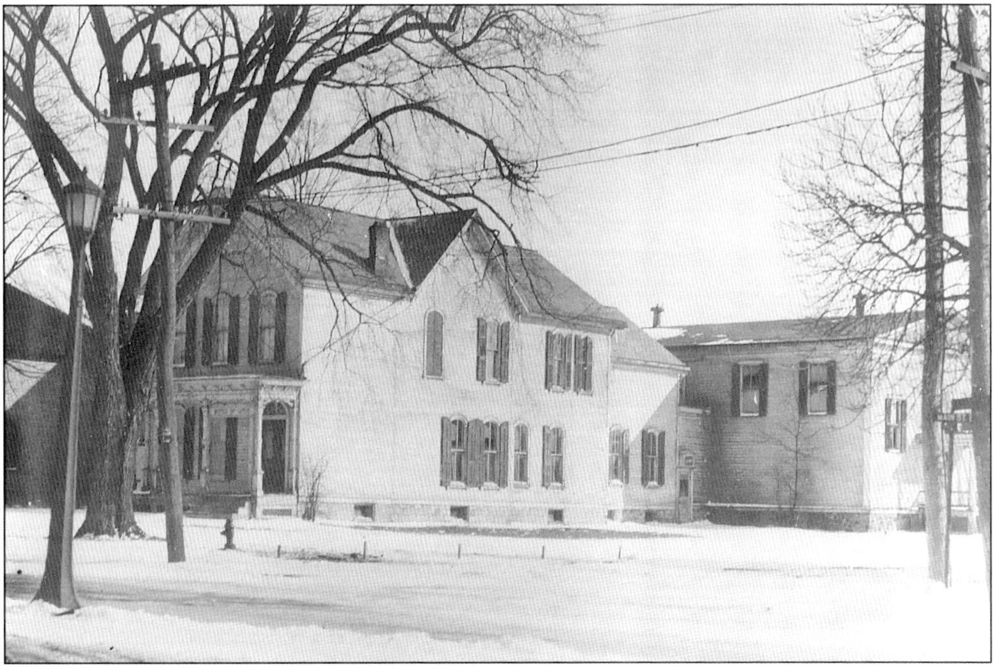

The large building on the corner of Main and Paine Streets has been known as the McCrea House, Clement Hall, and the Boys' Club. In October 1907, the East Aurora Guild rented this property for their guild house. The guild was formed on April 20, 1900. Their object was to "relieve the sick and needy of this community, both monetarily as well as materially." They paid grocery, doctor, and electric light bills and furnished shoes, clothing, bedding, and even coal for those in need. In November 1908, Stephen Clement made a gift of $2,000 to be used for a new gymnasium, which became known as Clement Hall. It was eventually owned by the village and used for the Boys' Club.

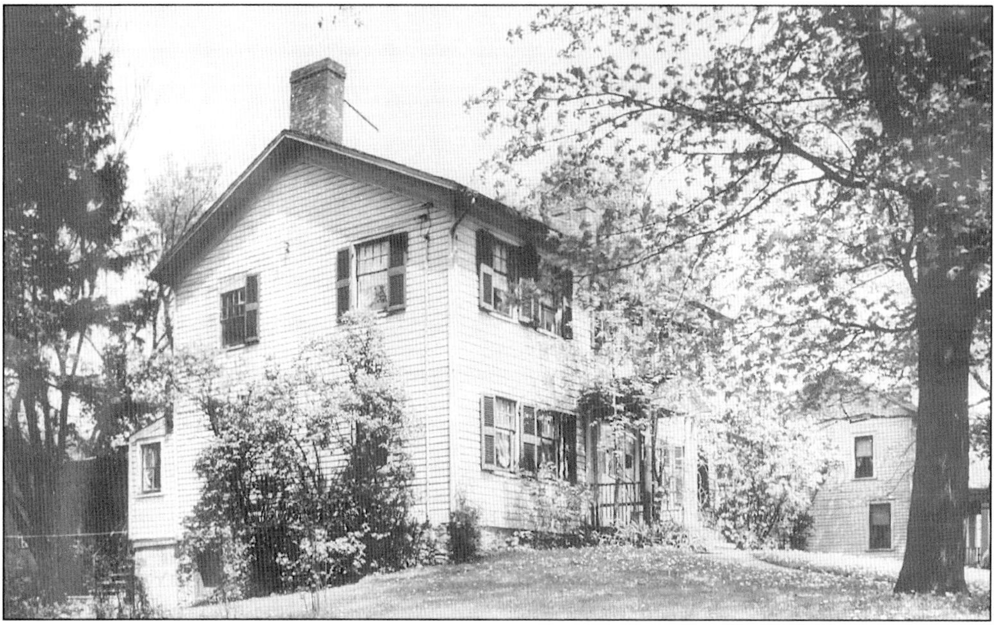

The Shearer Home was built in 1828 by Daniel D. Stiles and was purchased by Noah and Betsy Shearer in 1838 or 1839. Their son, Joseph H. Shearer, lived there until the time of his death in 1915 at the age of 91. Joseph was one of Willink's foremost citizens. He was a teacher, a lawyer, and later operated a grocery store west of the high school on Main Street. He was an enthusiastic member of the Academy Lyceum, a debating and dramatic society. Millard Fillmore visited this home frequently because of the great respect he had for Joseph and the intellectual stimulation those visits fostered. The house is on Main Street across from Baker Memorial Church.

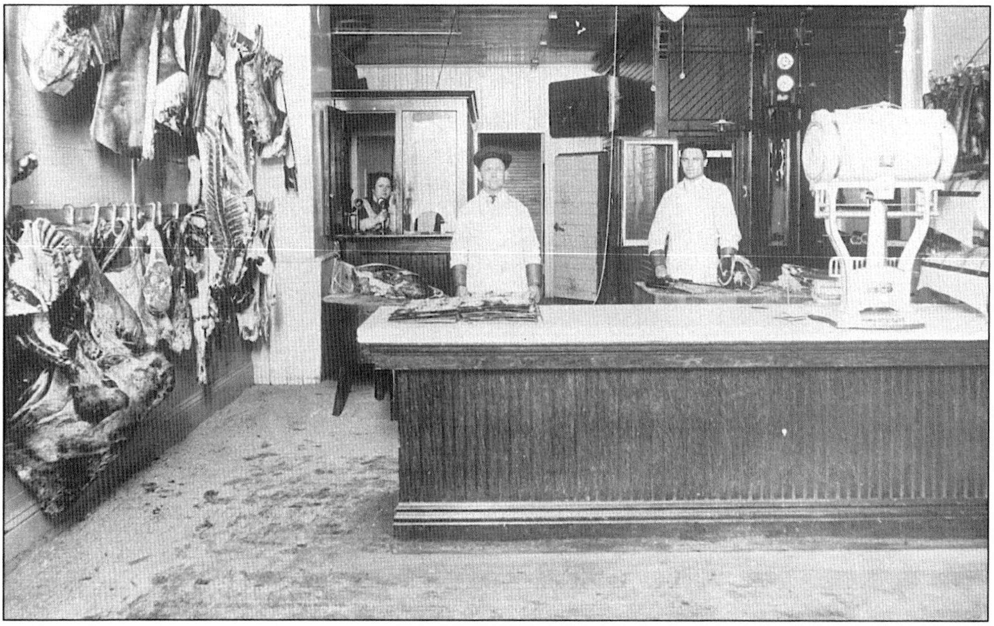

This is the interior of Roe's Meat Market in 1918. In the office is Christian (Dena) Roes. Standing are John Roes (left) and Frank Suttel, the great uncle of Norman Suttel.

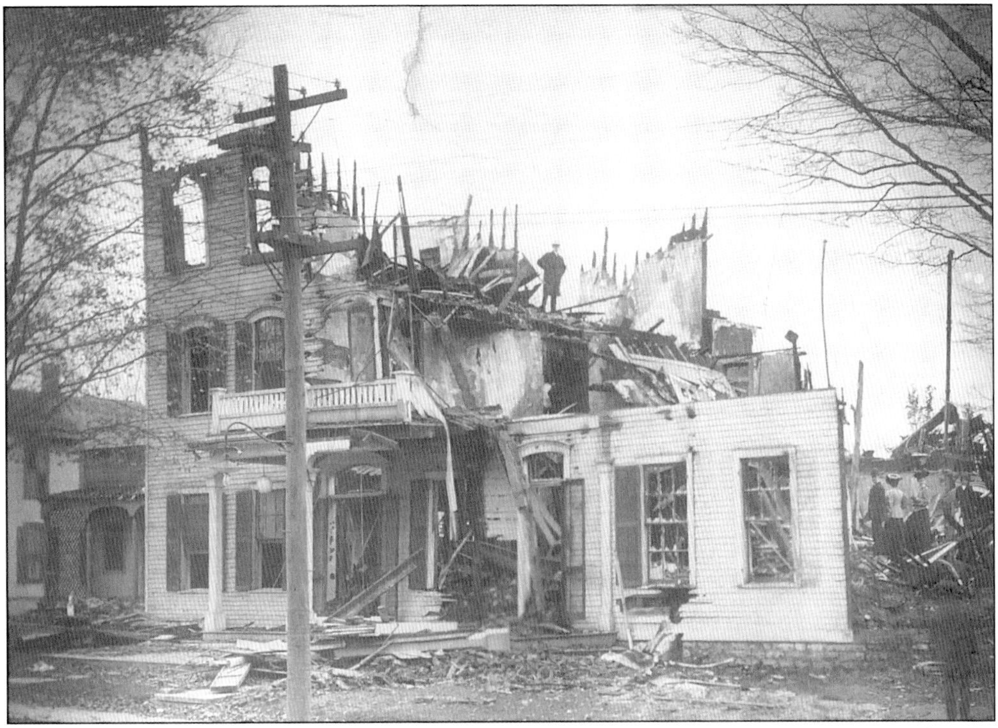

The Persons House was destroyed by fire on October 22, 1905. The building was operated under different names over time: Aldrich House, Hotel Eulalia, Yoeman Hotel, and Warren House.

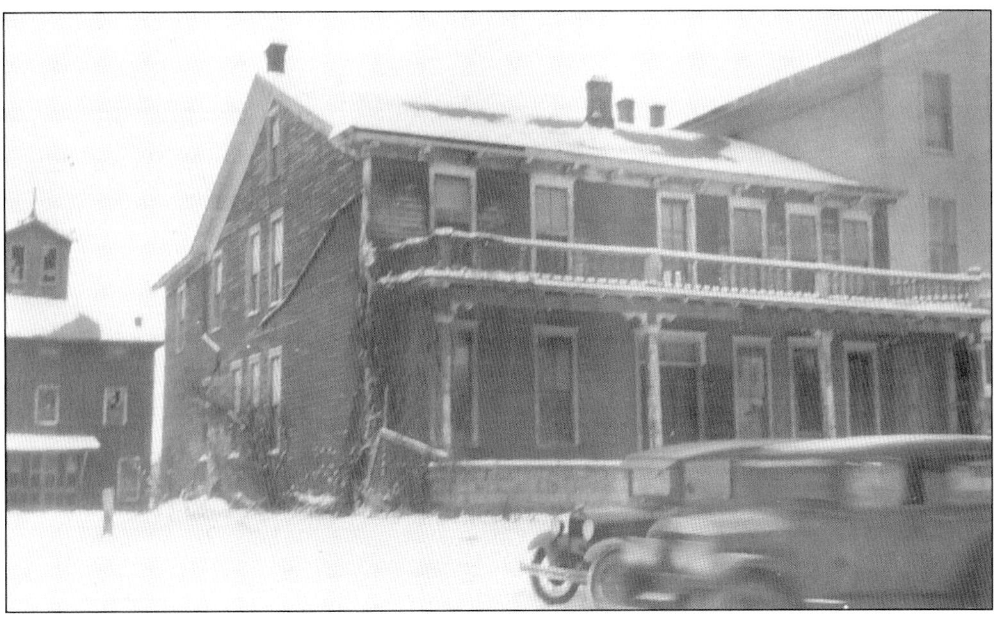

The H. Damon Hotel occupied this site, which later became Tops Supermarket. The hotel was extensively remodeled in the early 1930s and became Lange's Village Inn. It was destroyed by fire in 1933. The livery stable can be seen on the left and back of the hotel.

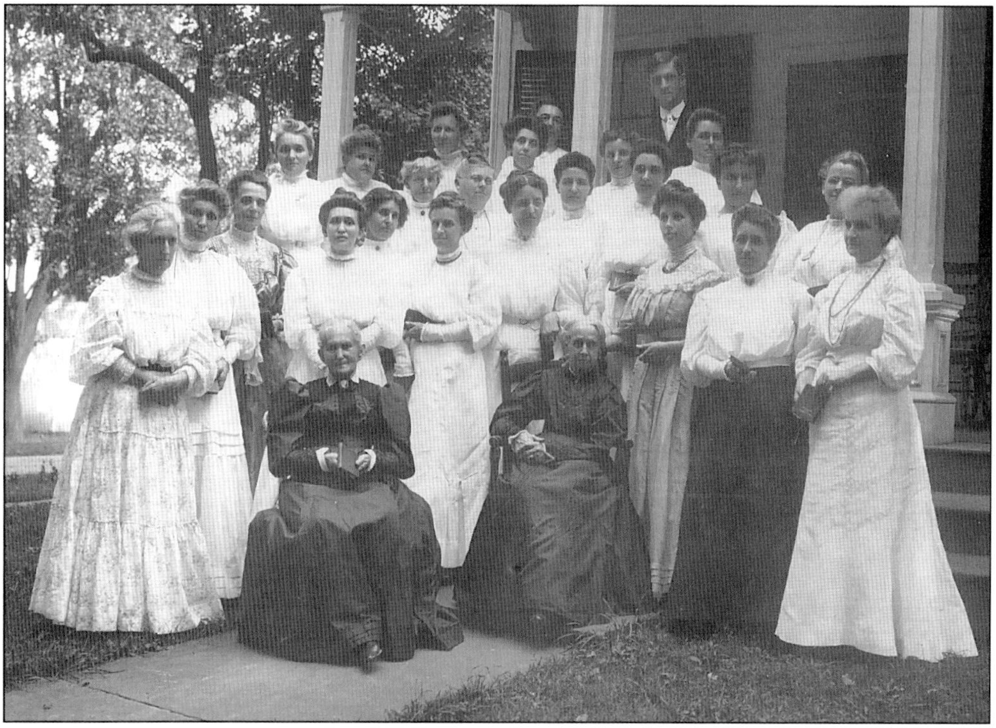

This photograph was taken on Main Street at the home of Mrs. H.Z. Persons c. 1903–1906. Seated are Mrs. Chase (left) and Mrs. H.Z. Persons. The others, from left to right, are as follows: (front row) Ellen Perkins (H.H.), Mrs. Elliot Hambleton, unidentified, Catherine Chase, unidentified, Mrs. McMillan, Mrs. Waters, Mrs. Higgins, Mrs. Wright, and Mrs. Torrence; (middle row) unidentified, Mrs. Frank Whaley, Mrs. Dwight Spooner, unidentified, unidentified, Mrs. Frank Higgins, Mrs. Robert Nye, Mrs. Russell, and Quincy Whaley; (back row) Mrs. Wallace Perry, Mrs. Burgette, Odell Rodney, and ? Tackbary. Standing in the back is the Reverend Henry S. Brown.

Three

Groups and Organizations

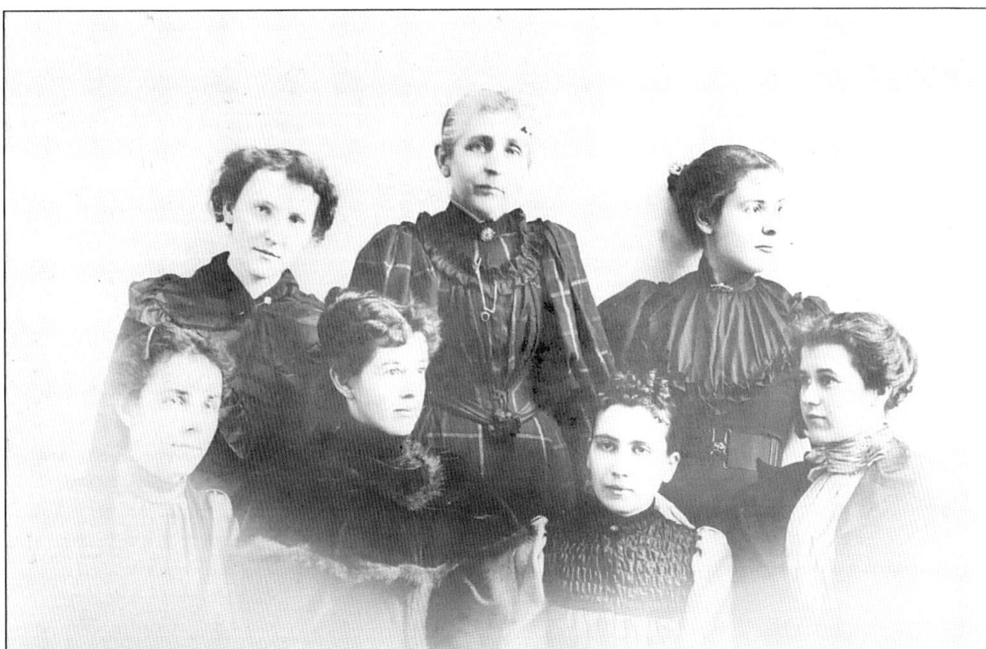

Members of the Historical Society of Willink pose here between 1890 and 1895. Pictured, from left to right, are the following: (front row) Louella Heaton, Mary Wilson, Cora Mae Wolcott, and Fanny Trantor; (back row) Minnie Boise, Miss Hamilton, and Nellie Cutter. They were photographed by another member, Mae Hitchcox.

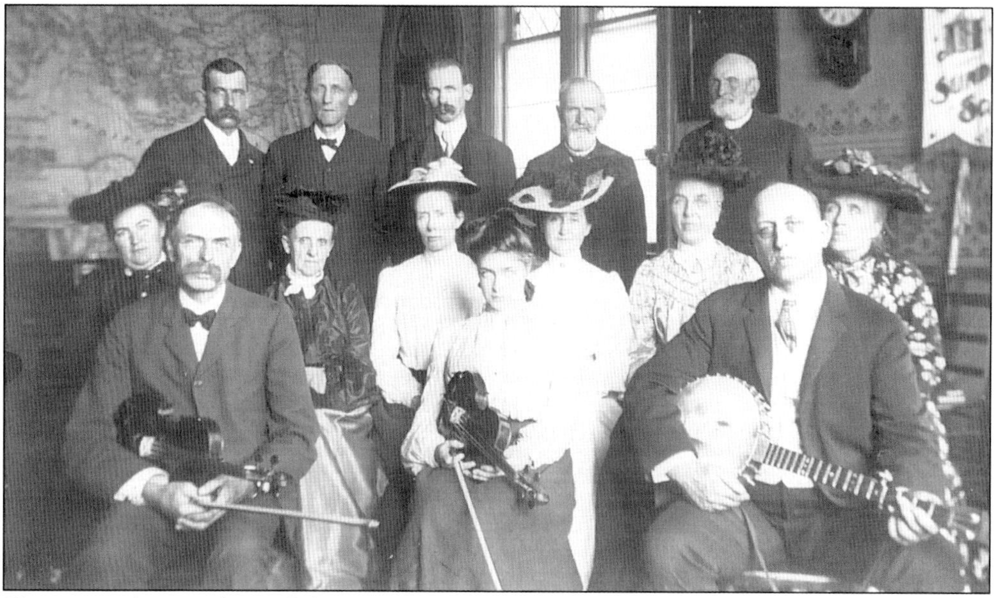

Shown are the members of the Aurora-Wales Sunday School Association of the Methodist Episcopal Church 1910–1915. They are, from left to right, as follows: (front row) Louis Bowen, his daughter Ethel, and Watson Moore; (middle row) Nettie Letson Newell, Mrs. Ruel Paul, Clara Shearer Persons (Mrs. Lester), Mrs. Watson Moore, Mrs. Seth Fermer, and Mrs. Louis Bowen; (back row) Clarence Howard Newell, Lester F. Persons, Charles Rosen, Ruel Paul, and Seth Fenne.

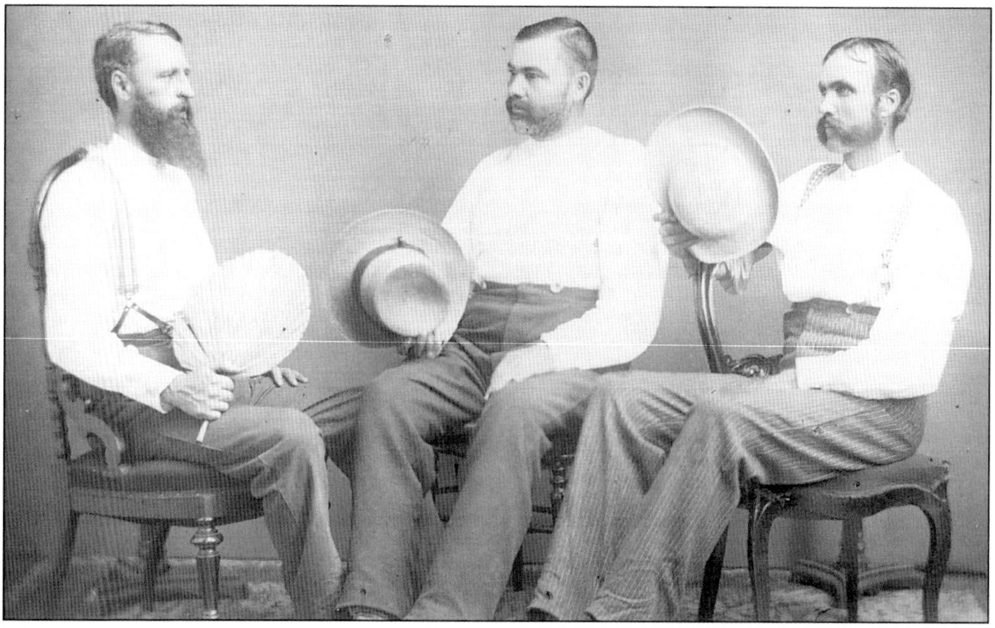

This photograph was taken on August 29, 1881, when it it may have been 94 degrees in the shade! Posing, from left to right, are Dr. Gail, Adin Perry, and Josiah B. Wolcott. Adin Perry was a teacher and scholar. He married Mandane Kent of Vermont Hill, town of Holland. Her family settled there in 1811. There were two daughters, Mrs. Robert Nye, and Mrs. Eva Rodney. Dr. William Gail was in active medical practice in East Aurora in the late 1890s.

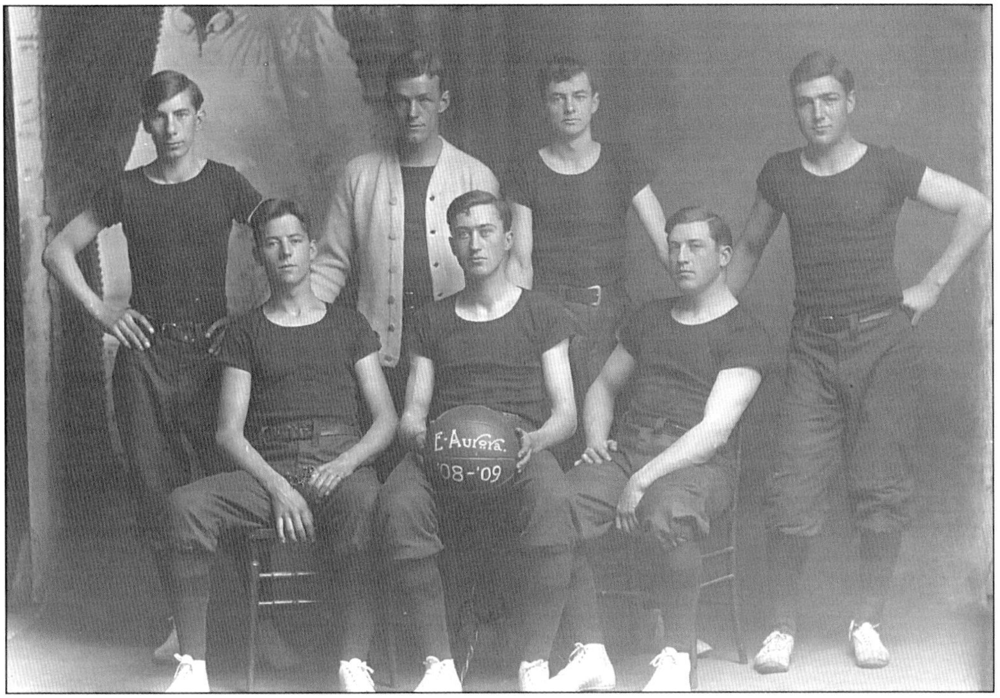

Members of the East Aurora Basketball team pose *c.* 1908–1909. Pictured, from left to right, are the following: (front row) William Bagley, unidentified, Harlan Abbott; (back row) ? Perry, ? Miller, ? White, and Joe Ehrenburg.

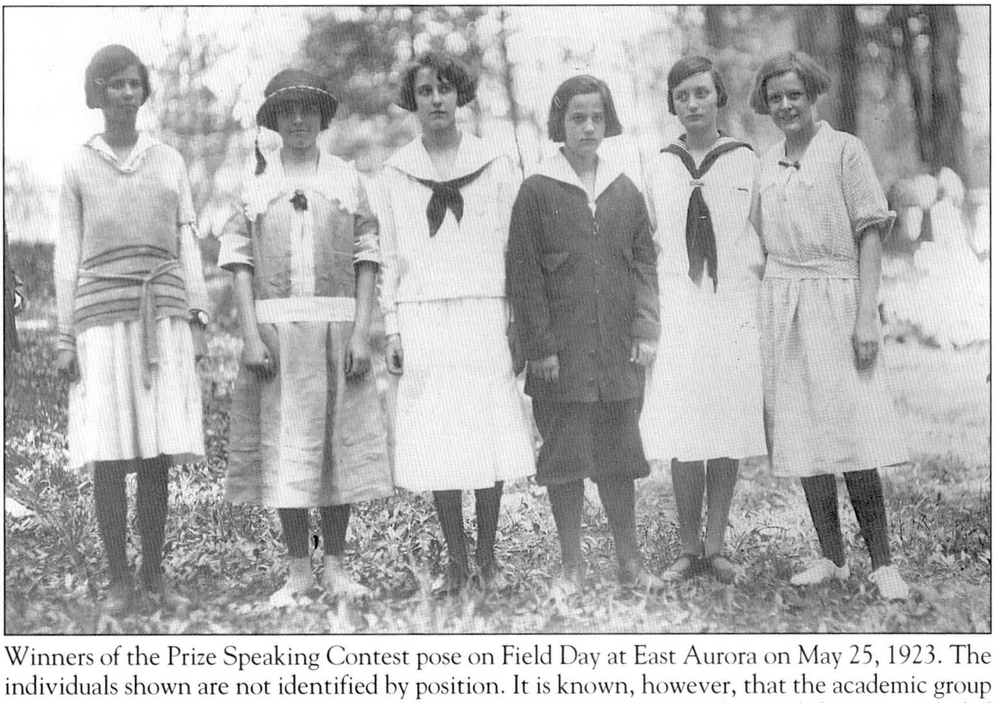

Winners of the Prize Speaking Contest pose on Field Day at East Aurora on May 25, 1923. The individuals shown are not identified by position. It is known, however, that the academic group included Catherine Mead, Margaret Crain, and Bessie Summers. The rural division included Aurelia Hesse, Helen Moran, and Margery G.

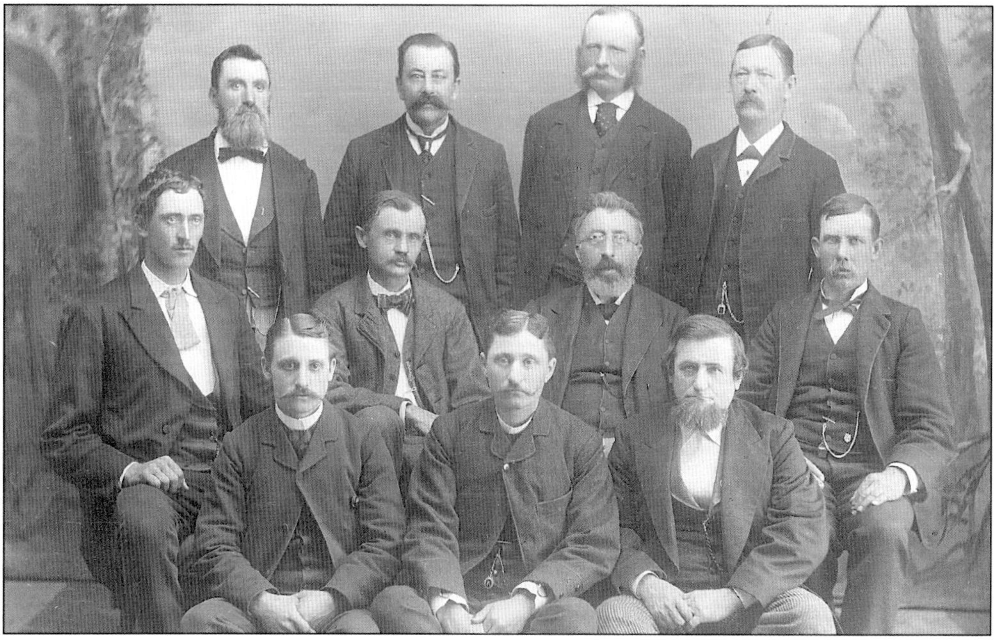

This is the German Singing Society of the Immanuel Lutheran Church *c.* 1883. Shown, from left to right, are the following: (front row) William Letson, Fred Kissinger, and Adam Wallenwein; (middle row) John Weinheimer, C. Kuhn, the Reverend Juergens, and Phillip Wagner; (back row) William Quade, E. Keller, J. Kreiger, and Theodore Baetzold. Absent is Henry Killian.

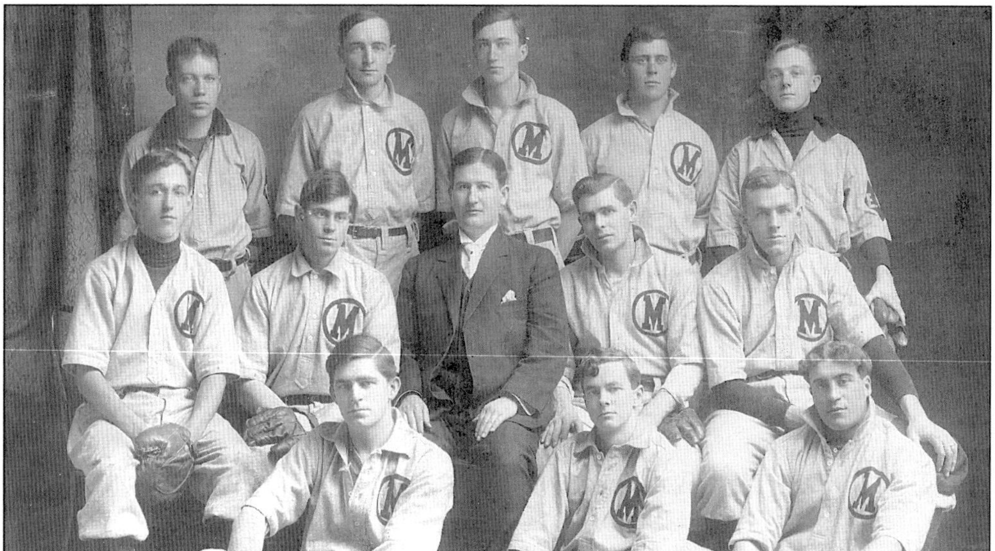

The members of the Mercury baseball team (1908–1910) are, from left to right, as follows: (front row) Frances Bowen, Joe White, and Bob Schang (AA baseball in Midwest who became manager); (middle row) John Whiting, Lynn Brown (in Yankee farm system), Mr. Burns, Herbert Bowen, and Albert Miller; (back row) Clarence White, Roy Wheeler, Elmer Bagley, Wally Schang (Baseball Hall of Fame inductee who played with Philadelphia Athletics, Boston Red Sox, and New York Yankees), and Bob Helern. Team meetings were held over the Offhaus Meat Market, and games were played in Hamlin Park.

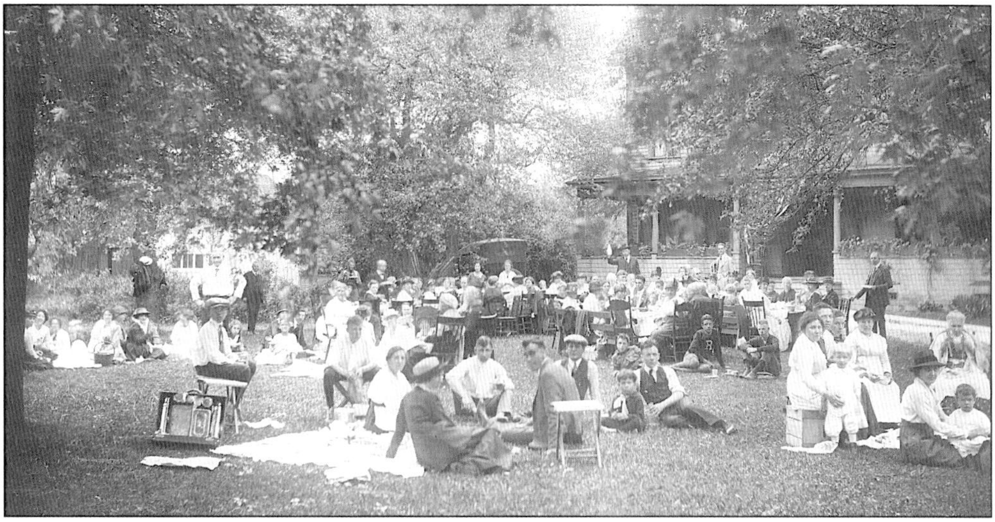

Ursula Havens's dream to provide a home for elderly citizens was finally realized just before 1890. She was able to purchase a small tract of land on the corner of Prospect and Center Streets. A large frame building was erected with rooms for about 35 people. Many village churches and organizations contributed to the support of the Home for Aged People. By 1923, the residents were moved to a similar institution in Florida. The building still stands at the corner of Center and Prospect Streets. This photograph was taken *c.* 1910.

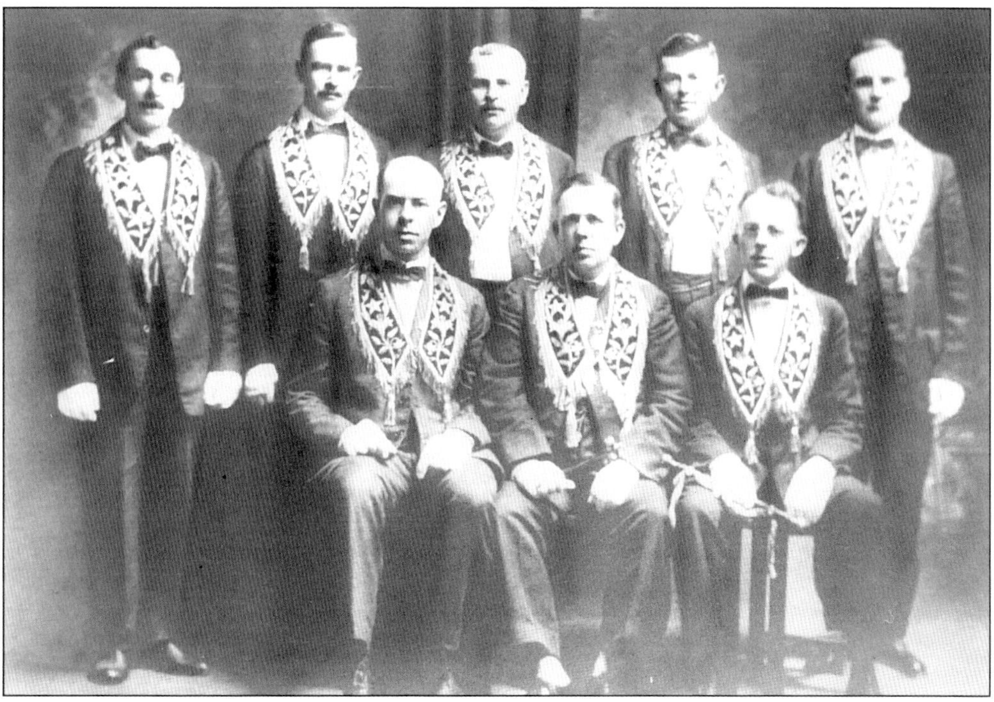

Shown are members of the Independent Order of Odd Fellows, Erie District No. 4 in 1918. Pictured, from left to right, are the following: (front row) Christian Schopper (DDGW), Frank O. Persons (DDGM), and Everett C. Stratton (DDGM); (back row) John H. Claringbold (DDGH), Merritt H. Jackson (DDGC), George J. Heim (DDGG), Andrew Marks (DDGT), and Martin J. Schaug (DDGS).

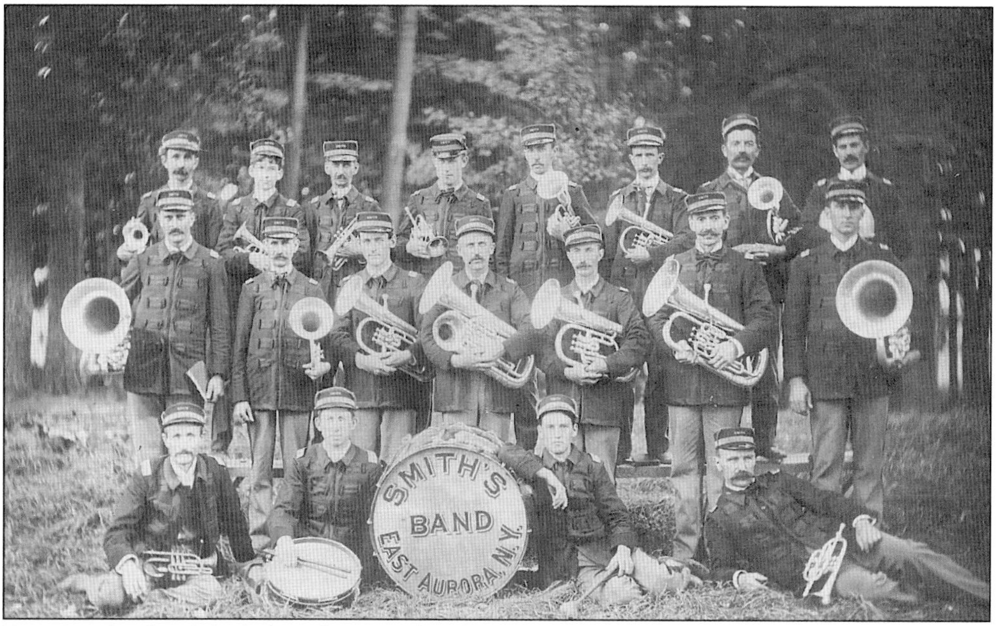

Ezra Smith's band had this photograph taken in 1893. Shown, from left to right, are the following: (front row) Frank Kelsey, Dick Hubbard, Harry Buffum, and Frank Spooner; (middle row) Henry Heller, Frank Brown, George Stackman, Seth Cole, Frank Durstein, Gene Gross, and Will Connell; (back row) Frank Higgins, Merritt Kyser, Orlando Winch, Theodore Bean, Louis Heim, George Durstine, Frank Hatch, and Herbert Buffum.

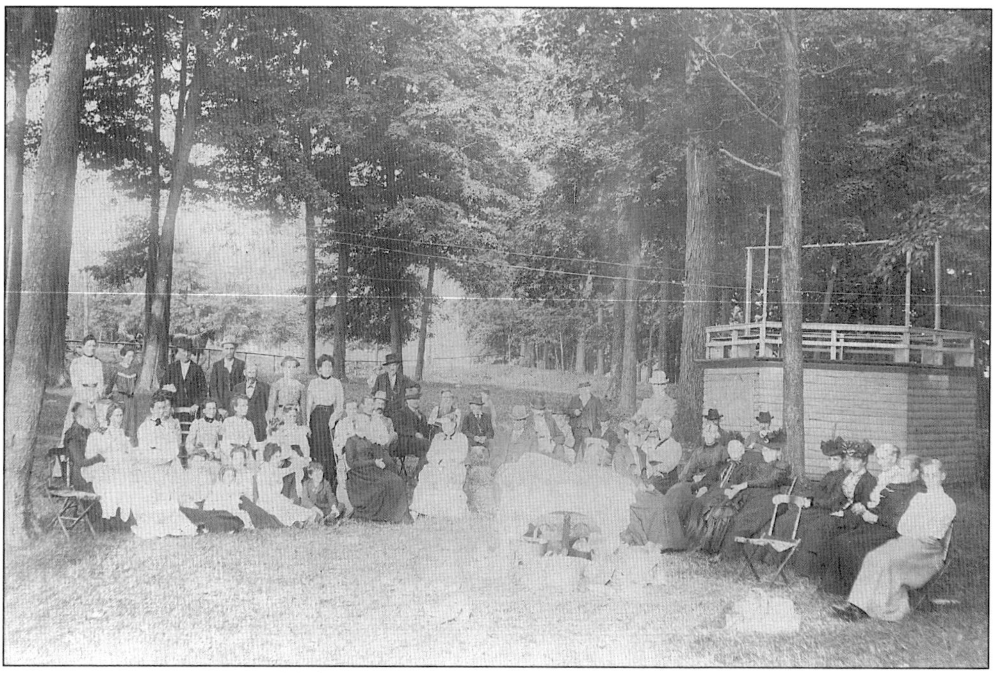

Everyone is enjoying an old-fashioned picnic at Hamlin Park in East Aurora, c. 1900. The bandstand can be seen in the background.

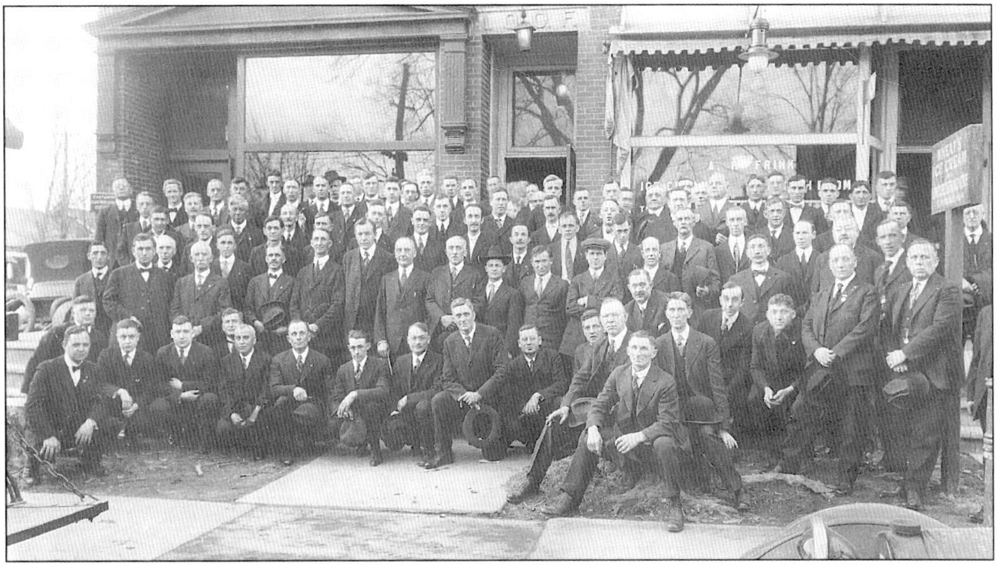

Shown are the members of Erie District No. 4 Independent Order of Odd Fellows. The hall is on Main Street in East Aurora, across from the village hall.

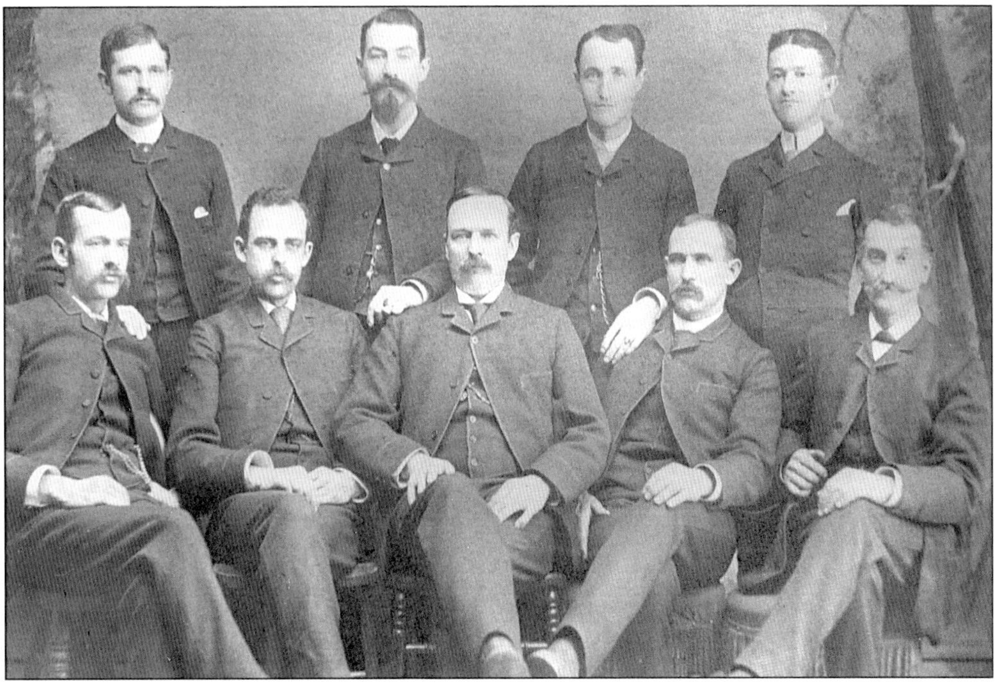

This 1886 photograph of East Aurora businessmen, includes, from left to right, the following: (front row) Willis Mead, Edward K. Emery, Charles Peek, Frank R. Whaley, and George Hall; (back row) Fred Fink, Charles H. Addington, Frank Kelsey, and Albert Hoyt. Emery, Addington, and Whaley were lawyers. Frank Kelsey was a prominent jeweler. Charles Peek owned and operated a livery, and George Hall operated a carriage shop. Fred Fink was in the collection business. Albert Hoyt, one of the few Democrats in town, owned Tammany Hall, now the Vidler building. Willis Mead lived in the homestead on East Main Street that later became the Gaylord Mead home.

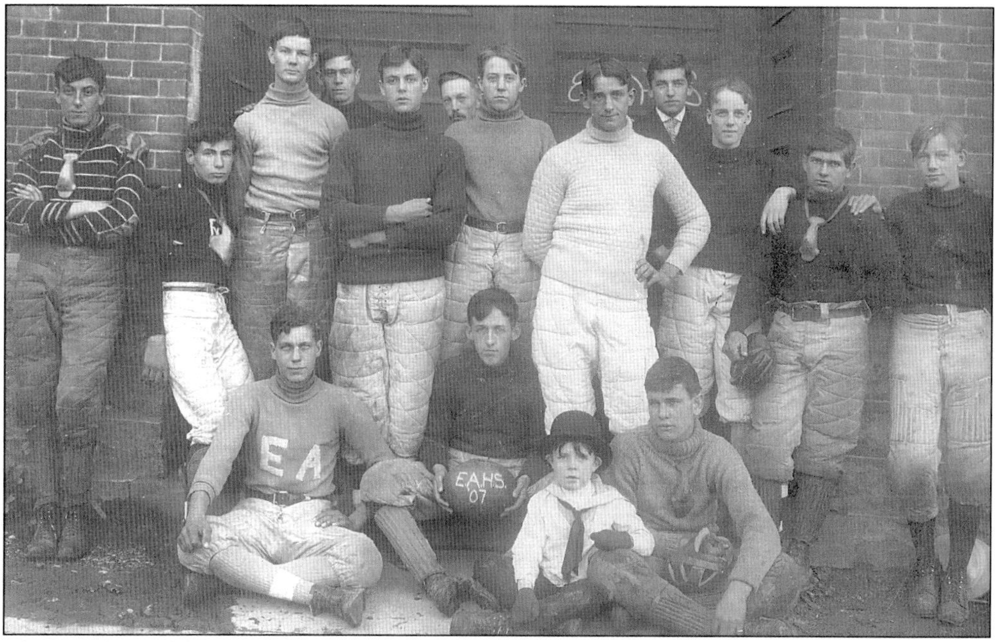

The members of the first East Aurora High School football team in 1907 are, from left to right, as follows: (front row) Stanley Parker, John Whiting, "Sonny" Sutton (mascot), and Harry Whaley; (back row) Howard Eldridge, Charlie "Tom" Perry, Ray Whalen, Lynn "Nip" Brown, Bill Shaffer, Sayles Buffum, Willis Weber, Clayton Beebe, Herbert Cline, Walter Killian, and Bill Persons.

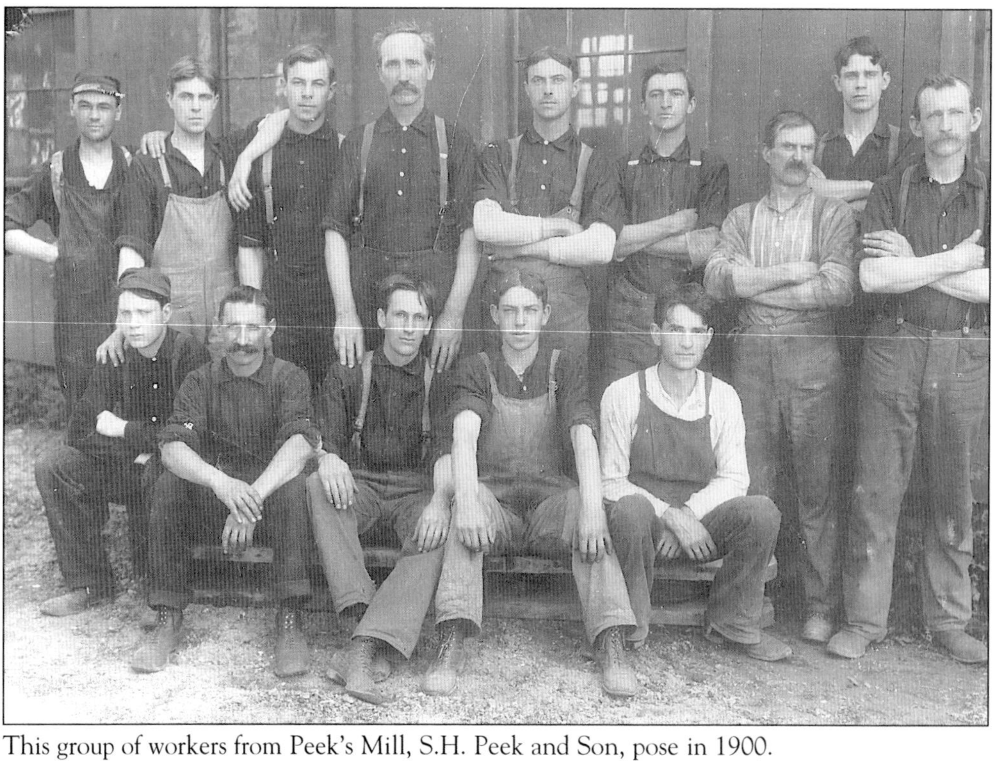

This group of workers from Peek's Mill, S.H. Peek and Son, pose in 1900.

Four

Horse Farms

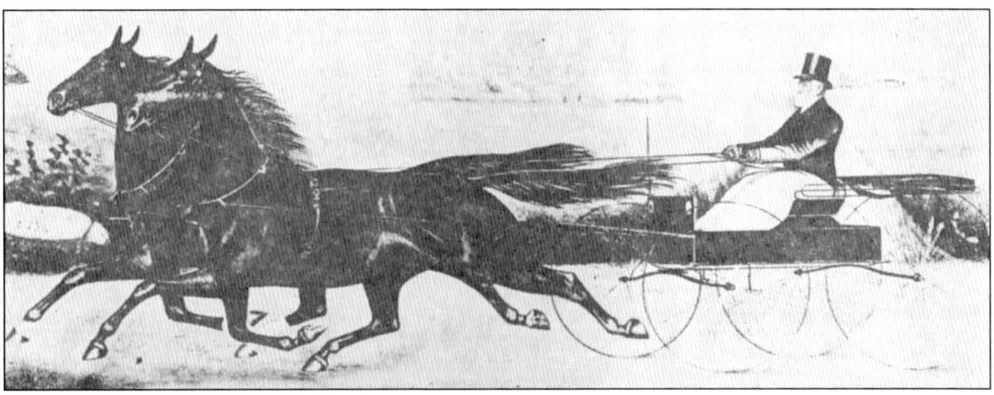

Cicero J. Hamlin is shown driving Belle Hamlin and Justina to the world record of 2:13. The efforts of men like Cicero Jabez Hamlin fostered a reassertion of the spirit of amateurism in the sport of harness racing. In the 1860s and 1870s, the sport had become so corrupt that it faced a crisis, as many races were framed. Drivers, track owners, and even judges fixed the races. Harness racing was losing the support of respectable and influential patrons. Action was taken in 1870 by a group of new patrons—businessmen who trotted their horses not for money, but for pleasure. This group promoted the formation of the National Trotting Association, which became a vehicle for the correction of many of these abuses.

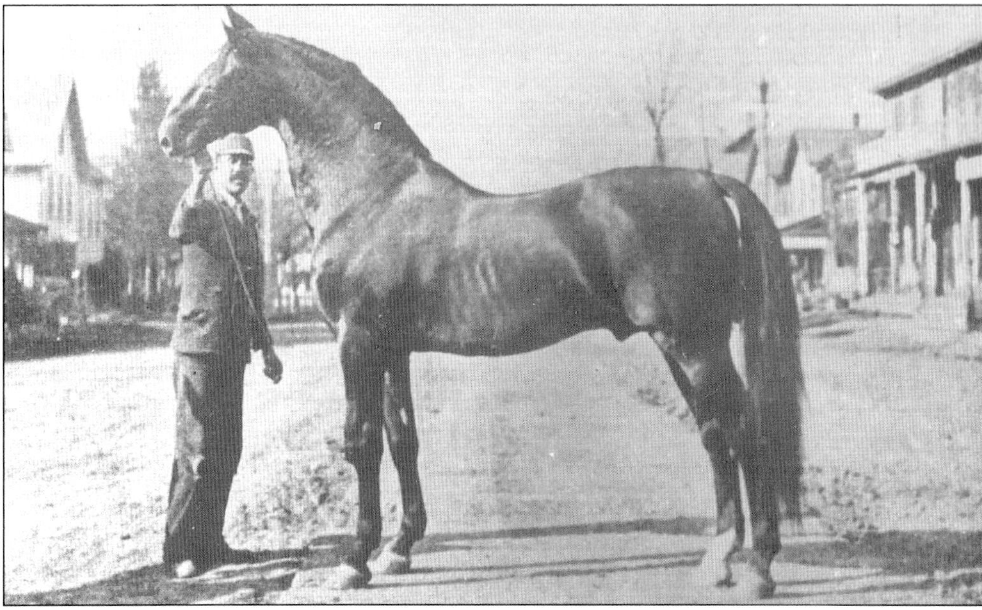

Mambrino King was bought by Hamlin in 1882 for $17,000. He was the most famous show-ring champion known to trotting-horse history. He was judged to be "the Most Handsome Horse in the World." Hamlin stated in 1884 that no fewer than 16,000 people had called to see and admire this chestnut horse, 10-hands high, foaled in 1872. On December 5, 1899, Hamlin ordered Dr. R.C. Bowman to chloroform Mambrino King. It has been reported that "Dr. Bowman has a shoe that was removed from the horse's hoof." The horse was buried in what is now the front yard of the residence at 100 North Willow Street.

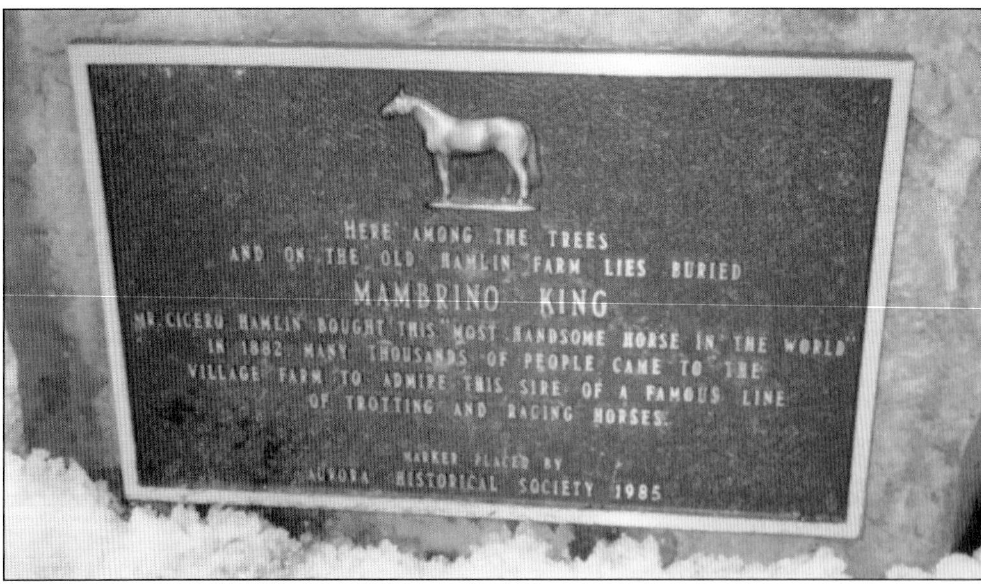

The Mambrino King burial site marker is at 100 North Willow Street in East Aurora. The marker reads, "Here among the trees and on the old Hamlin Farm lies buried Mambrino King. Cicero Hamlin bought this 'Most Handsome Horse in the World' in 1882. Many thousands of people came to the Village Farm to admire this sire of the famous line of trotting and racing horses." The marker was placed by the Aurora Historical Society in 1985.

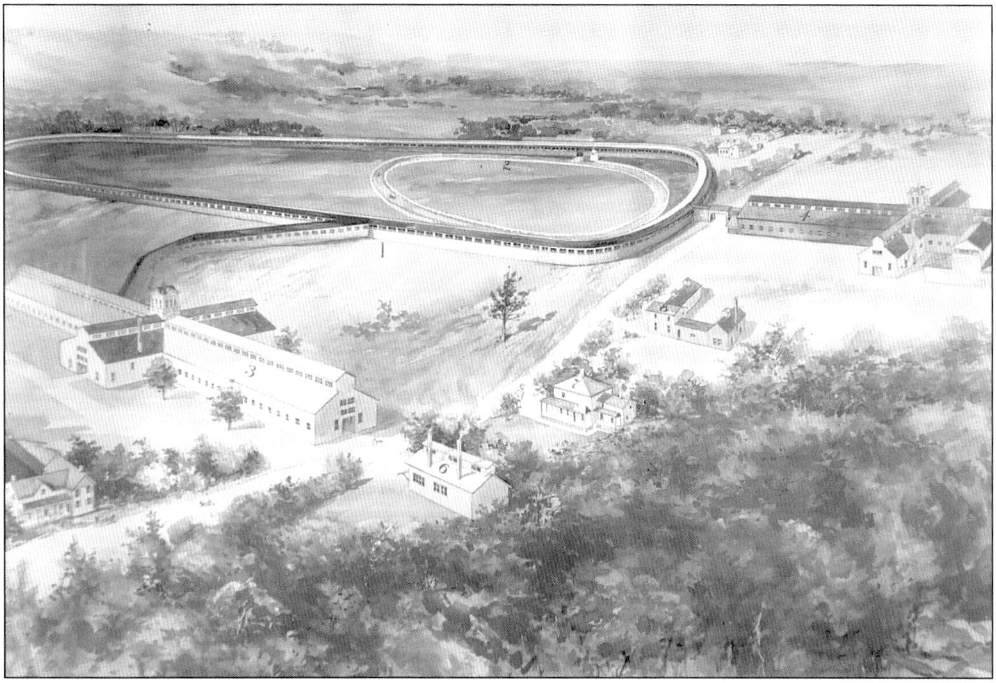

The covered mile track, the only one in the world, was constructed in 1885 on the Jewett Stock Farm. It was 30 feet wide with glass windows on both sides. Young horses and those brought in by owners were trained there. The track was dismantled in 1918, and the large farm was divided.

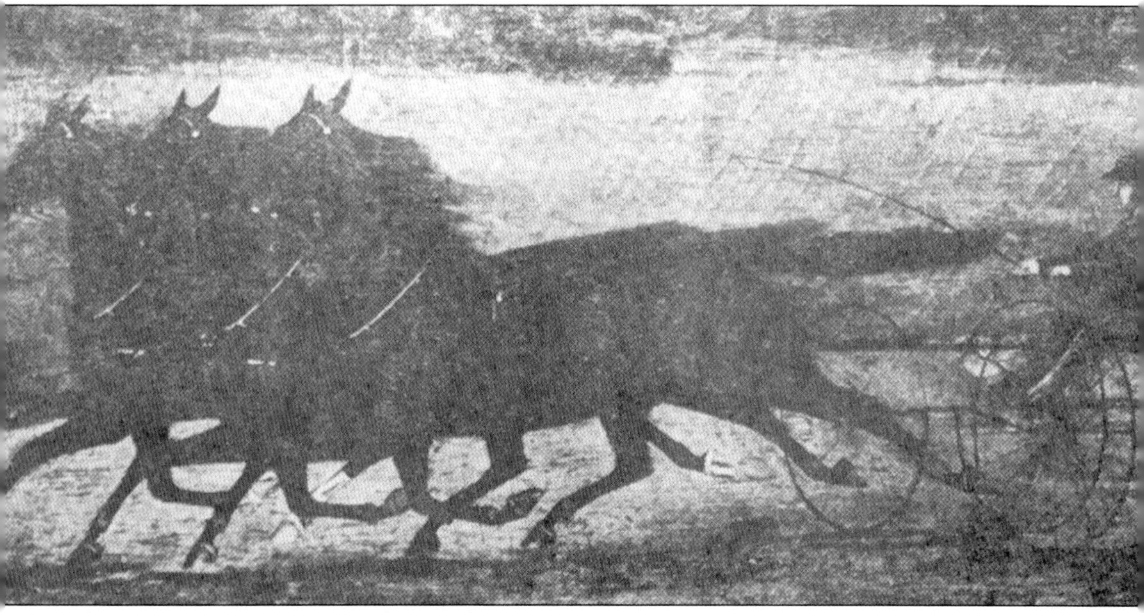

Ed F. Geers drives Belle Hamlin, Globe, and Justina, setting the world record mark of 2:14. In 1892, Harry Hamlin and his father, Cicero J. Hamlin, had signed Ed Geers to a ten-year contract at the sum of $10,000 per year as driver and chief executive of the racing department. On September 3, 1924, Geers was killed in a race as he was rounding the third-quarter pole at a meet in Wheeling, West Virginia.

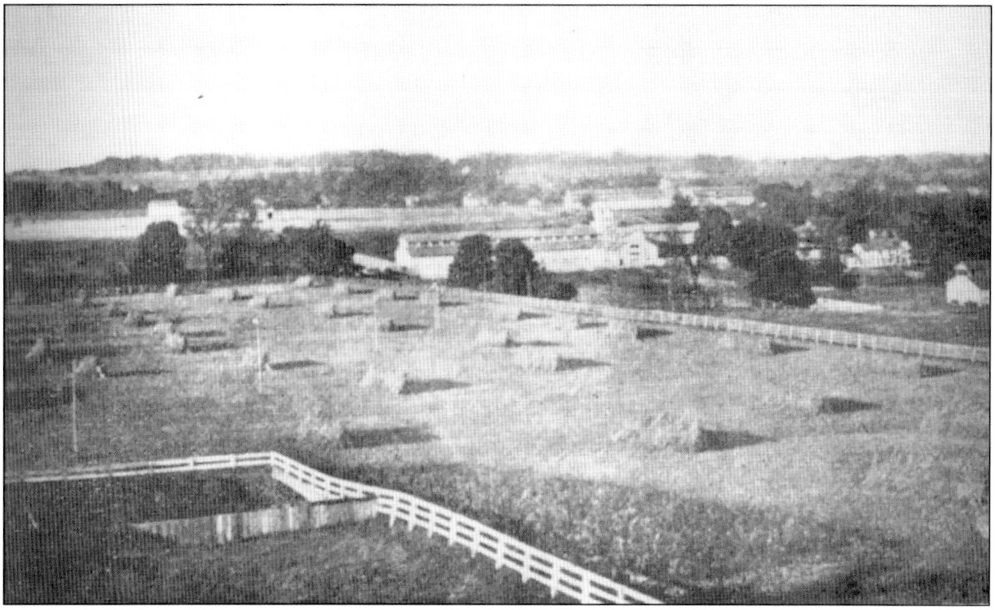

Brothers Henry C. and Josiah Jewett founded the Jewett Stock Farm in 1878. It was located on the banks of the Cazenovia Creek about a half mile west of East Aurora. Josiah withdrew and was succeeded by his father, Sherman. Among their horse holdings was Jerome Eddy, purchased in 1882 for $25,000. The Jewetts bred 71 famous performers and 41 dams of fast performers. This farm was the first in the United States to import Holstein cattle.

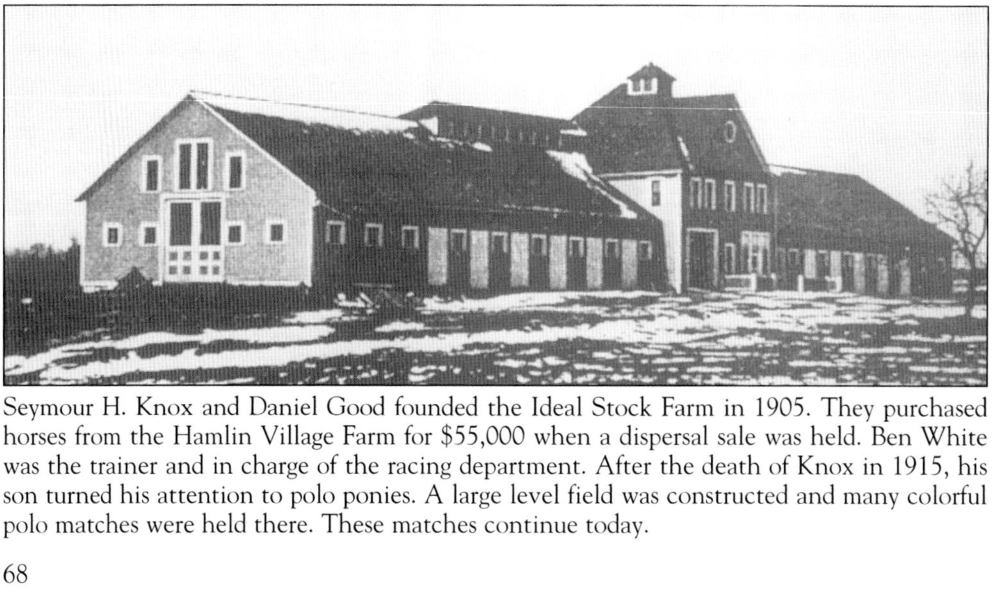

Seymour H. Knox and Daniel Good founded the Ideal Stock Farm in 1905. They purchased horses from the Hamlin Village Farm for $55,000 when a dispersal sale was held. Ben White was the trainer and in charge of the racing department. After the death of Knox in 1915, his son turned his attention to polo ponies. A large level field was constructed and many colorful polo matches were held there. These matches continue today.

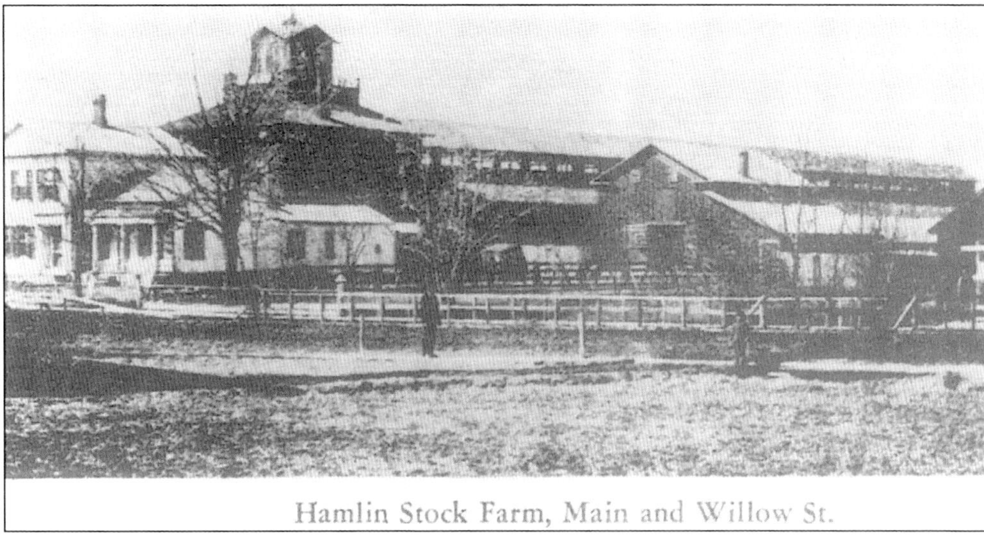

The Hamlin Stock Farm in East Aurora was on the north side of Main Street between Tannery Brook and almost to Buffalo Road. The Village Farm was founded on May 1, 1855, when Hamlin purchased 66 acres of land for $1,200. He immediately began the construction of many barns, sheds, and a training track. The big barn, 2.5 stories high and over 800-feet long, was located at the end of a drive, which is now Willow Street. There were more than 600 box stalls in the building. There was a blacksmith's shop that spanned Tannery Brook, a superintendent's office, homes, a boardinghouse, and many small buildings. The houses and fences were painted white and the barns red. The narrow end of the track bordered Main Street, and people used to stand at the fence to watch trainers exercise the horses.

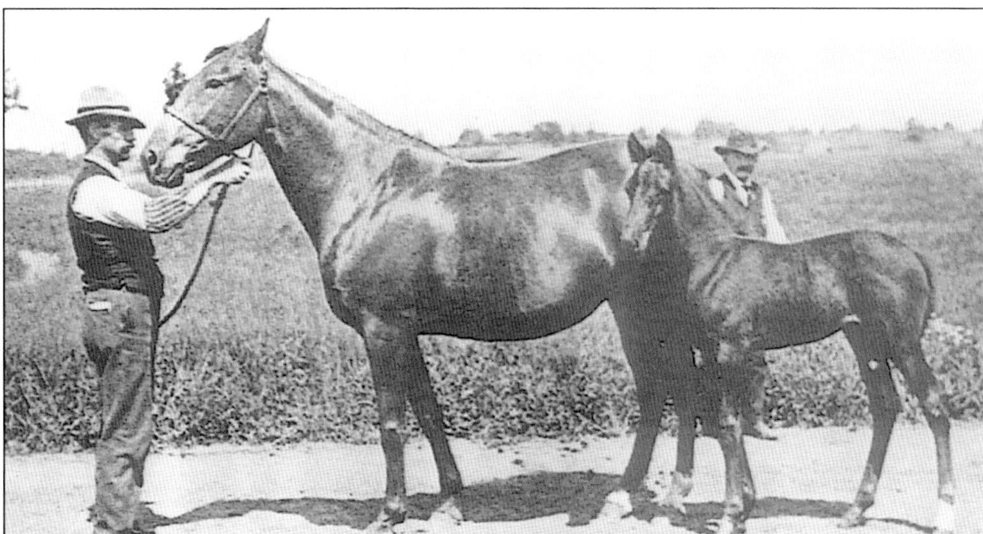

In 1881, Hamlin purchased Nettie Murphy for $250 from Thomas J. Murphy of Buffalo. Bred to Mambrino King, she produced Nettie King (2:20.25), dam of the Abbot (2:03.23), and the Abbot Ideal (2:15.5), as recorded by John Bradburn, superintendent of the Village Farm in East Aurora.

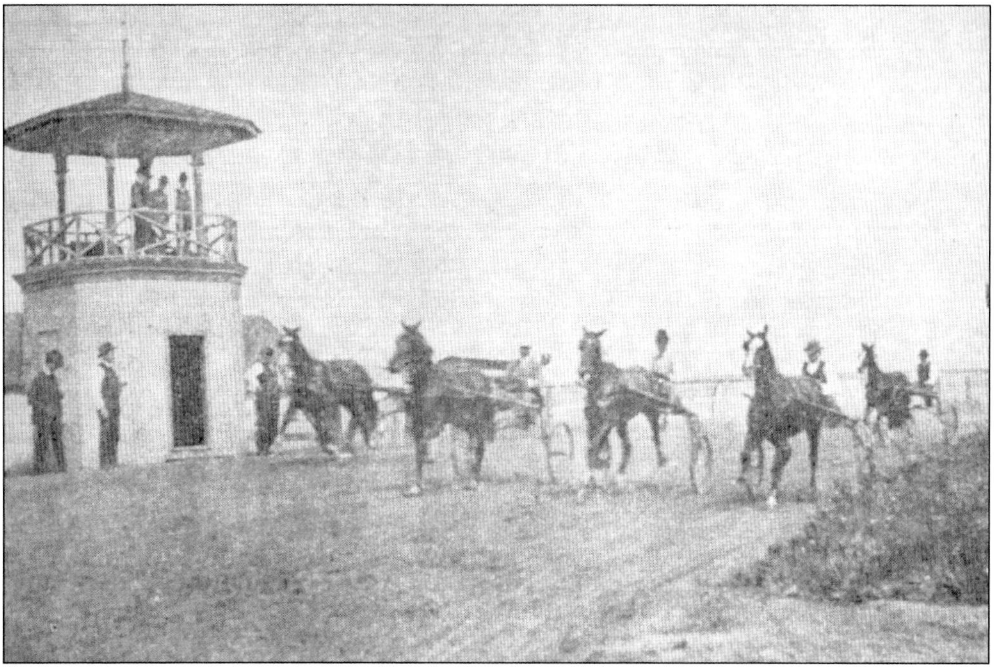

The judges' stand was at the 5/8-mile track on the Hamlin Farm. The upper structure of the stand is now on the grounds of the Aurora Park Health Care Center, Main Street, East Aurora.

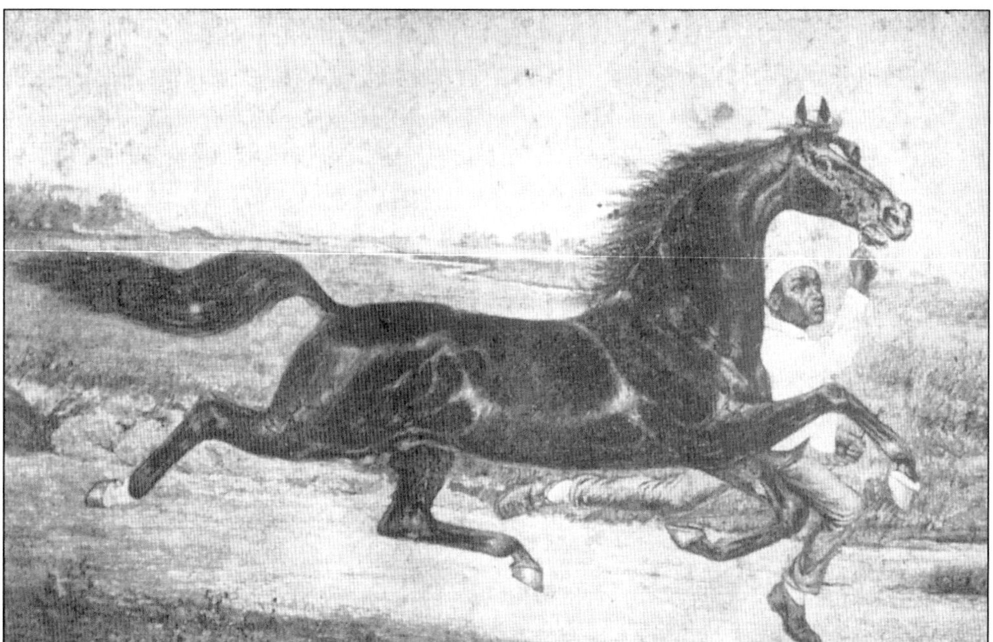

This artist's conception portrays the famous Mambrino King.

Five

Fire Companies

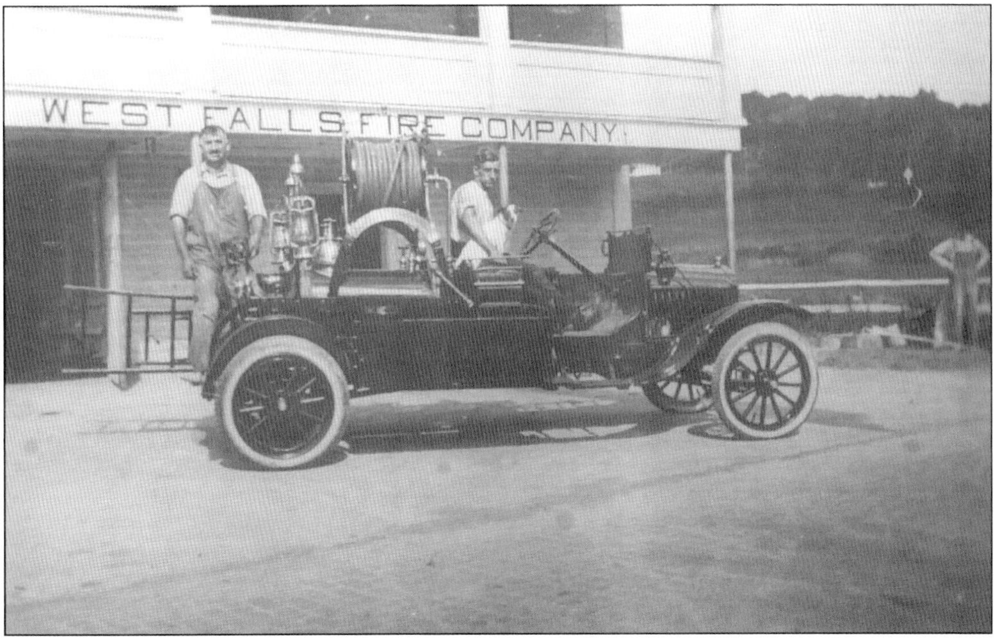

This photograph of the West Falls Fire Company was taken in 1925. On the left, at the back of the truck, is Dick Miller. Walt Reader is standing by the steering wheel of a 1921 truck, his arm around a dog.

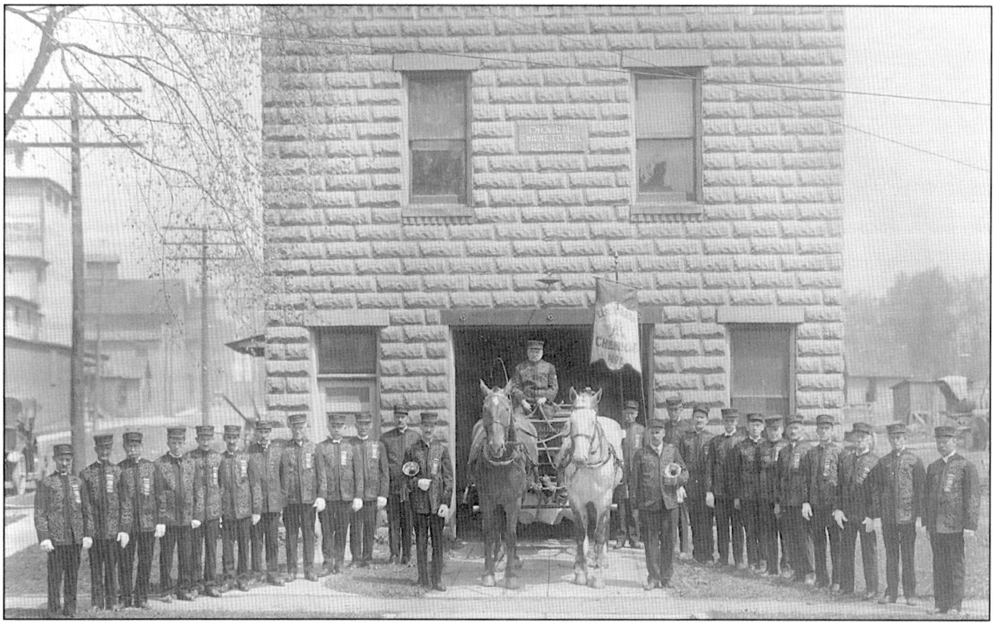

The East Aurora Chemical Fire Company No. 1 was organized in 1885 by the German Singing Society of the Immanuel Lutheran Church. The members shown, from left to right, are as follows: Billy Letson, Francis Fisher, J.J. Marshall, George Geib, Clarence Killian, William Reimer, Frank Heim, John Marshall, Phillip Bodimer, George Bender, Harry Heller, William Miller (chief), William H. Geib (sitting), George Barnhart, George Heim, George Lippert, Louie Boise, Henry Killion, Albert O. Zink, Alvin Offhaus, Leonard Ernst, Edward Ball, Theodore Baethold, Henry Reuther, and Chris Dahlman. The two horses are John, the bay, and Nell, the gray. The two-cell jail was housed in the left corner of the building.

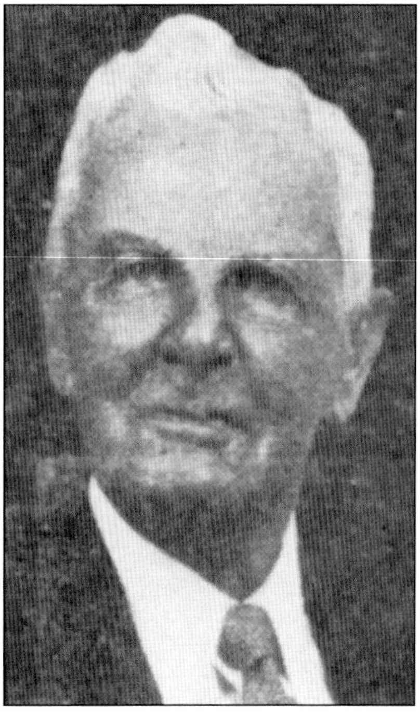

Charles Lamb was an organizer of the Cazenovia Fire Company in 1877. He was born June 23, 1853 in the town of Aurora. Before his death on July 13, 1940, he was the oldest active fireman in New York State and a life member of the Southwestern Firemen's Association.

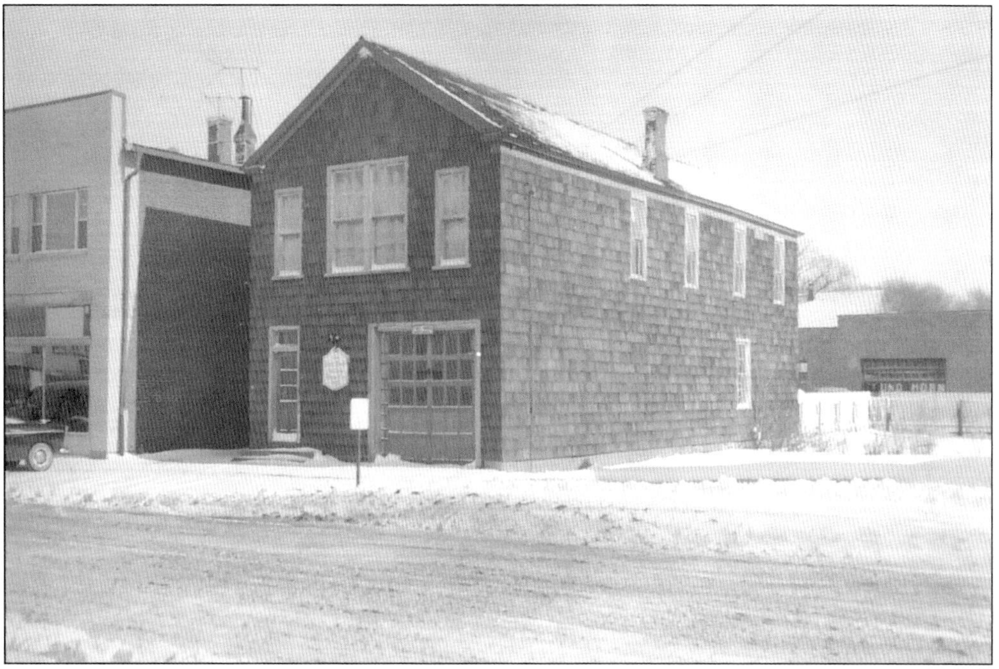

The East End Active Hose Company was organized in 1887, with 30 members. Among the men who made up the first company were Marvin Thompson, Charles Deimer, Henry Fuller, James Peek, Frank Spooner, Dwight Spooner, Henry Persons, Albert Lapham, Hiram Kyser, Frank Nye, Joseph McLaughlin, and Charles Peek.

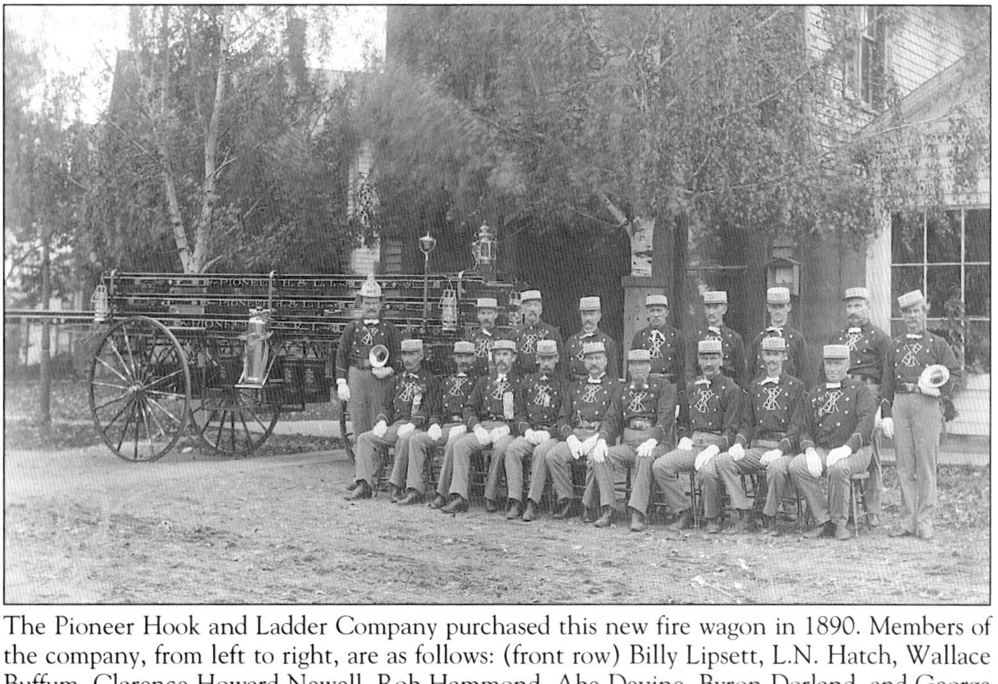

The Pioneer Hook and Ladder Company purchased this new fire wagon in 1890. Members of the company, from left to right, are as follows: (front row) Billy Lipsett, L.N. Hatch, Wallace Buffum, Clarence Howard Newell, Rob Hammond, Abe Devine, Byron Dorland, and George Dick; (back row) Charles Gardner, Charles Finzer, unidentified, unidentified, Rensselaer Thompson, George Hall, ? Damon, Joe Weiser, and Captain Gardner.

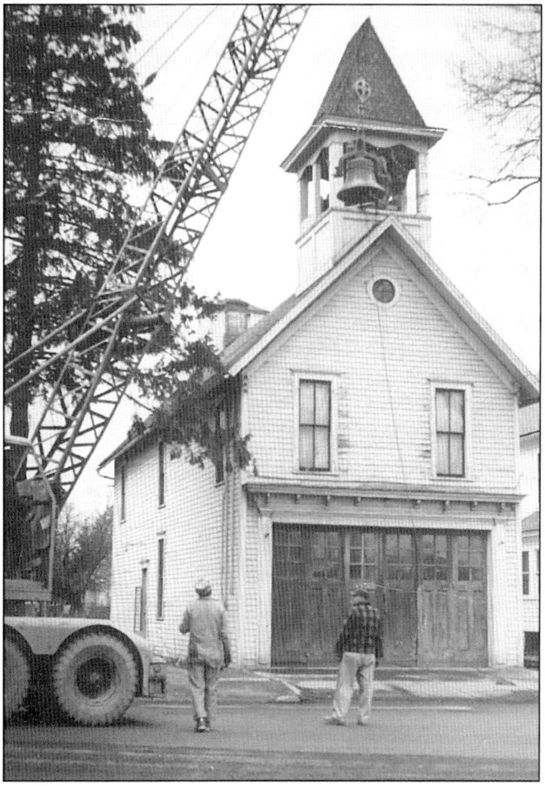

The West End Firemen's Association was formed in 1880 when the Cazenovia and Pioneer Hook and Ladder Companies pooled their resources. One of the first matters of business was the building of a common fire hall. A lot was purchased from Squires for $70. The materials cost $400. It is thought that the members built the firehouse themselves. In 1890, twelve new buckets were purchased for $4.60 (a dozen). On July 4, 1893, a new truck was purchased for $425. In 1915, there was an agreement to pay $2.50 to the owner of the first motorized vehicle to arrive at the fire hall after the alarm was sounded. That person would haul the hose cart to the fire. The Cazenovia Fire Company No. 1 was organized on March 5, 1877. The first fire the company helped to put out was the Cigar and Tobacco Company on Main Street. Pioneer Hook and Ladder Company was organized in 1876. There is proof that the members met as early as 1870, which would make it the oldest fire company in Aurora.

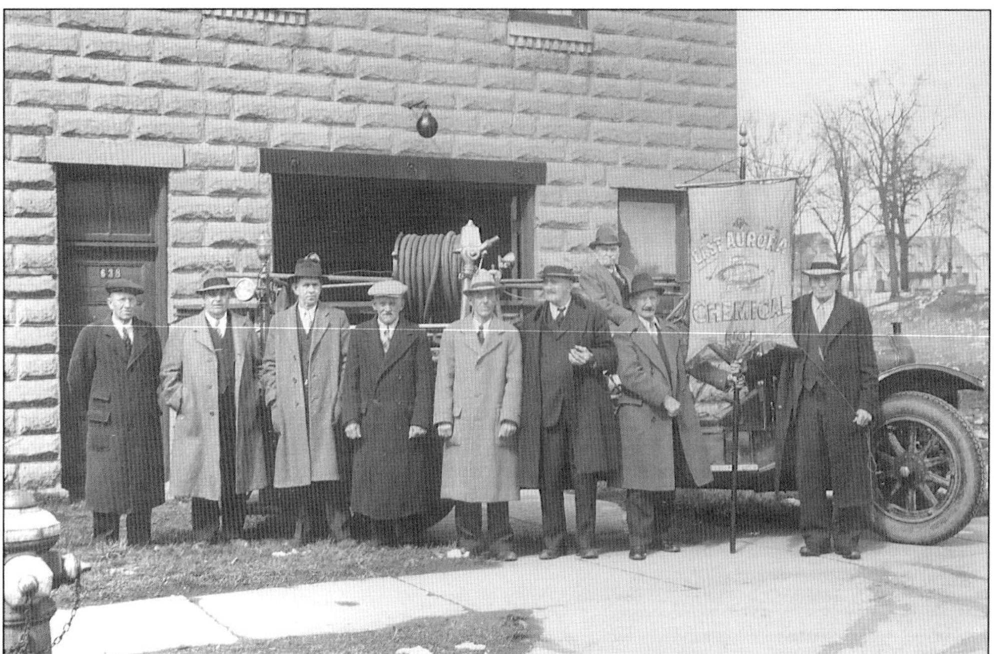

Members of the Chemical Engine Company No. 1 are shown, c. 1920. From left to right are George Geib, George Heim, John Fox, Frank Baitzold, Ed Ball, Henry Heller, Bill Reimer, and George Barnhardt. William Gieb is sitting on the truck.

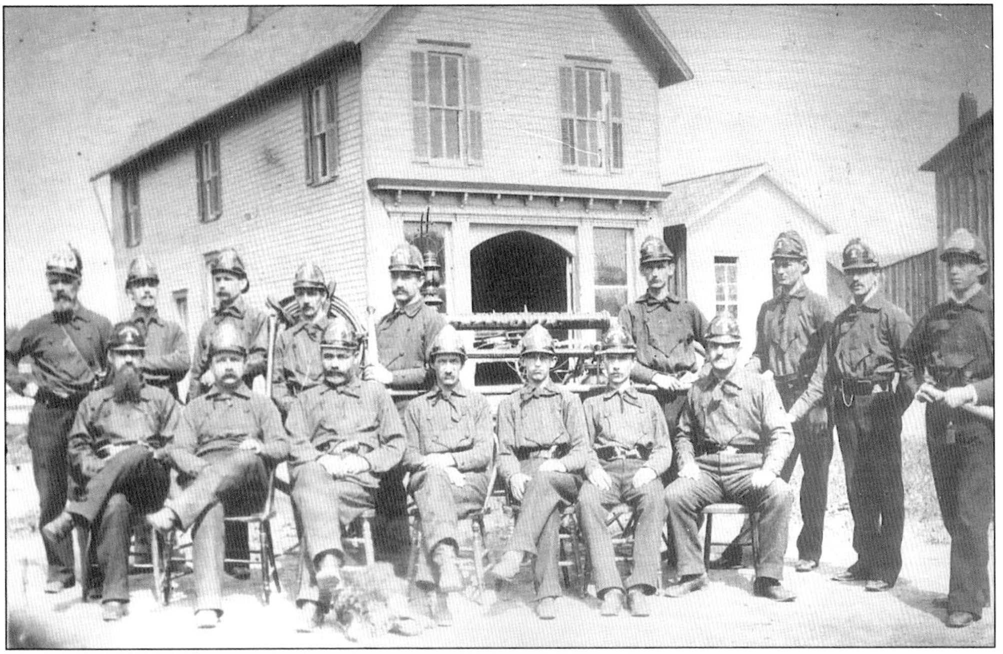

The Pioneer Hook and Ladder Company is the oldest organized fire company in East Aurora. There is proof that the members met regularly as early as 1870, but the company was formally organized in 1876. It is not known where their meetings were held. Their apparatus was kept in Pattengill's barn off Hamburg Street.

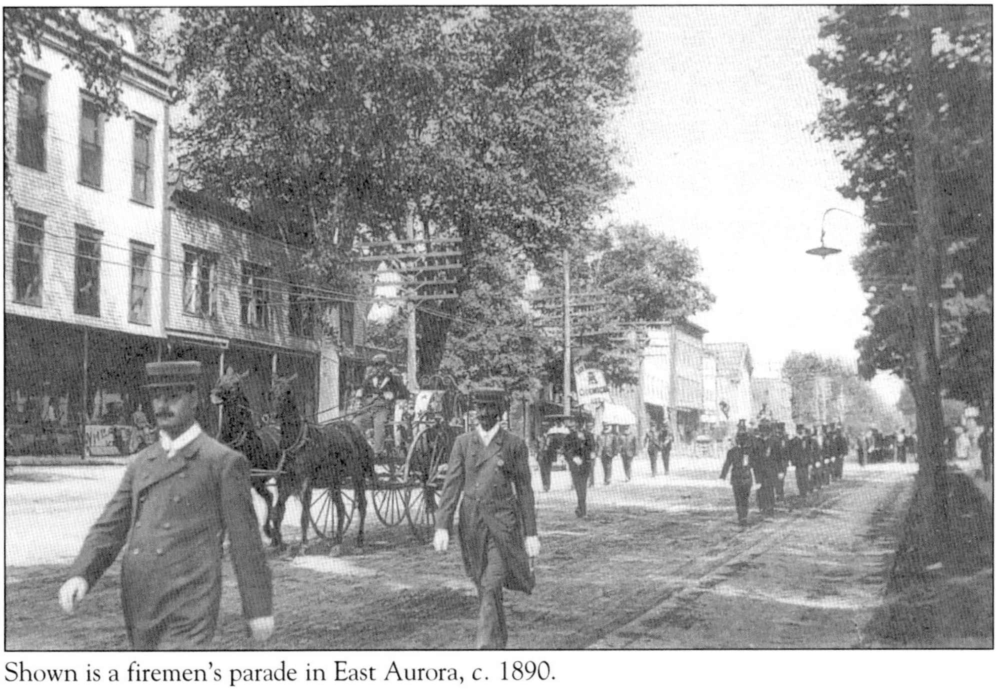

Shown is a firemen's parade in East Aurora, *c.* 1890.

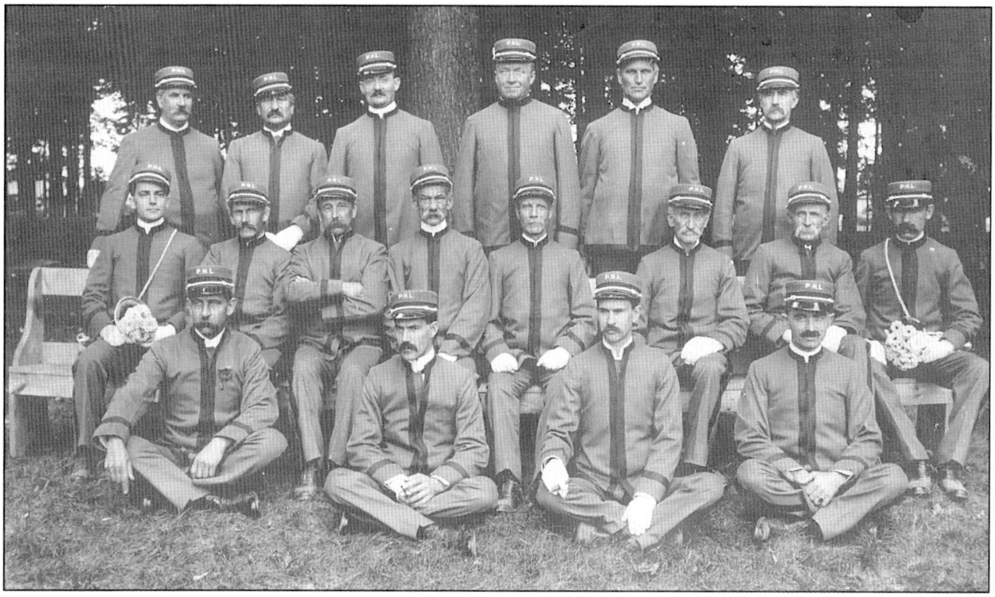

Members of the Pioneer Hook and Ladder Company in the early 1900s, from left to right, are as follows: (front row) Clarence Newell, Herbert Buffum, Merritt Jackson, and Leonard Hatch; (middle row) Dr. Erwin W. Buffum, Charles Finzer, George Edwards, Capt. O.J. Gardner, Eugene Olds, George Hall, Rauselien Thompson, and Lyman Case; (back row) Howard Jackson, Harvey Damon, James Cadzow, George Dick, Abe Devine, and Wallace Buffum.

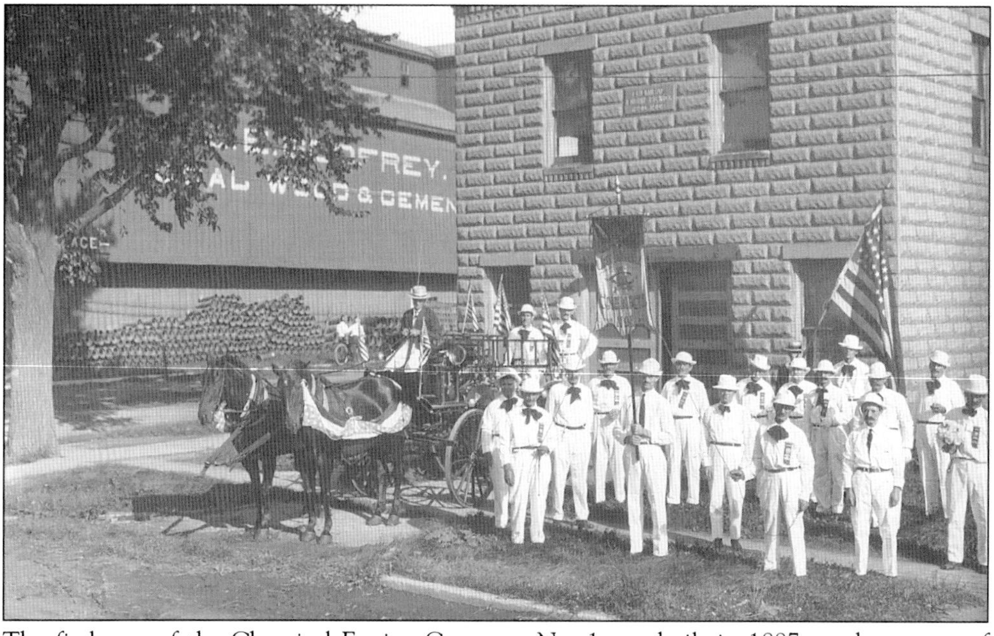

The firehouse of the Chemical Engine Company No. 1 was built in 1887 on the corner of Oakwood Avenue and Elm Street in the village of East Aurora. The fire company was organized in 1885 by the Lutheran Singing Society. Before the erection of this building, meetings were held on the north side of Oakwood Avenue in Wallenwein's Hotel. In 1919, the village was given permission to build two jail cells in this hall. Eventually, in 1954, the Chemical Engine Company joined three other companies to form the East Aurora Fire Department.

Six

SCHOOLS

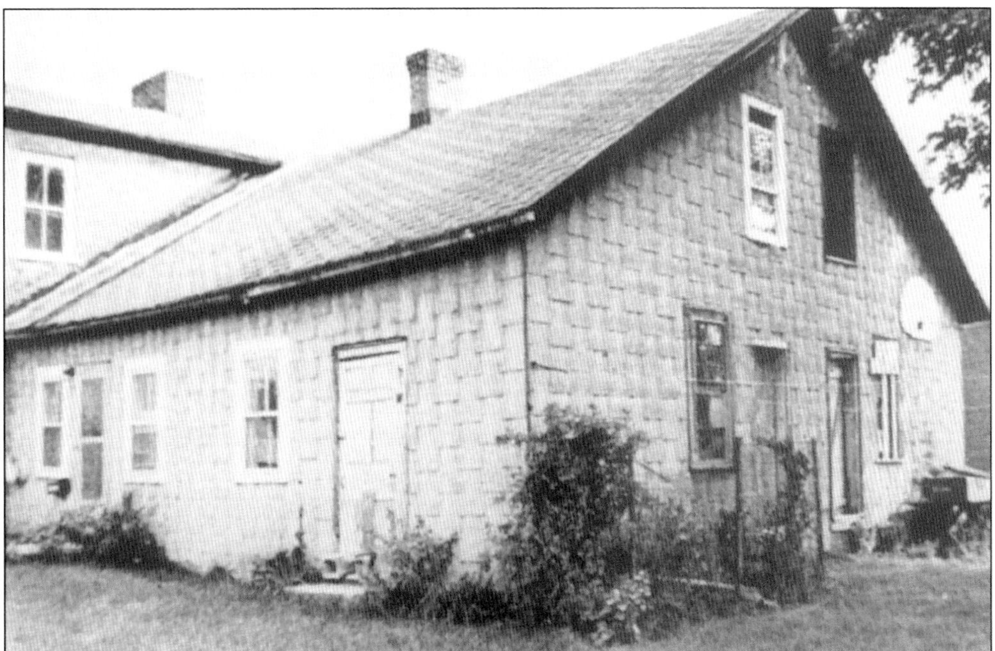

The first schoolhouse was a frame building constructed in 1810 at 39 Olean Street between Main Street and Oakwood Avenue. The following notice was taken from an old record book of October 11, 1811: "Notice—that this schoolhouse be appropriated for all orders of religious worship, when it is convenient and not infringing on the day school." On the same date, this entry appears: "The district agrees to have a school begin on the first day of November next provided they can find a schoolmaster." It was necessary to enlarge this building in 1825 as more settlers moved into the area.

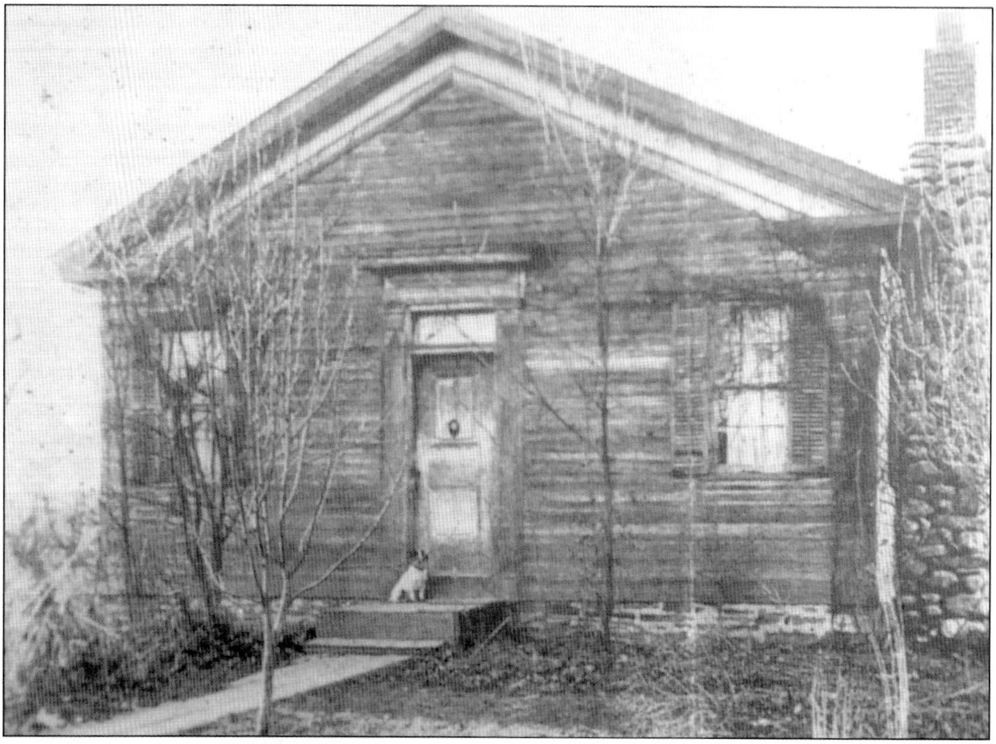

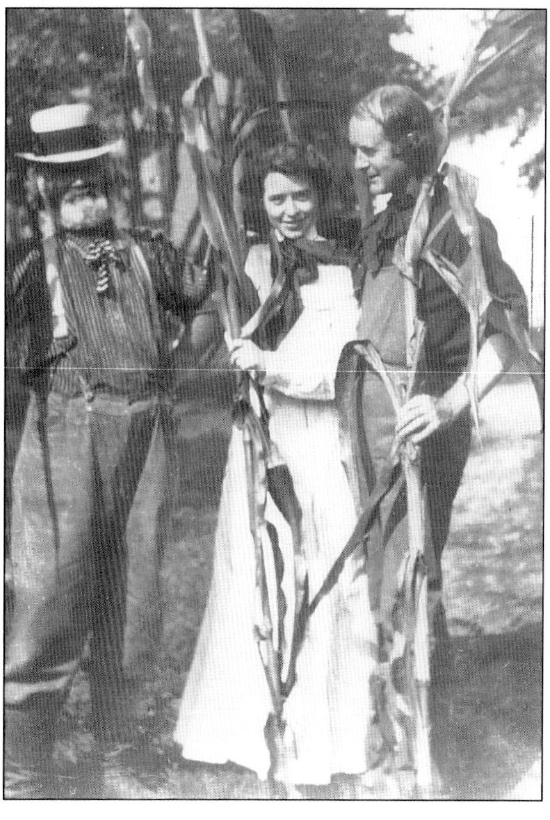

This building, which was the West End Schoolhouse in the 1830s, still stands at 61 Hamburg Street at the corner of Douglas Lane. At one time, it was used as a residence. In the early 1900s, it was occupied by the Taylors, the town's only African American family for many years. Later, Eleanor Douglas, an artist, remodeled it for a studio. The West End Gallery now occupies this building.

In this c. 1900 photograph, Eleanor Douglas poses with Anson Blackman, also known as Ali Baba (left), and Elbert Hubbard (right). Douglas was a Canadian artist who had her studio in the old West End Schoolhouse. Douglas Lane was named for her. (Courtesy of the Roycroft Inn.)

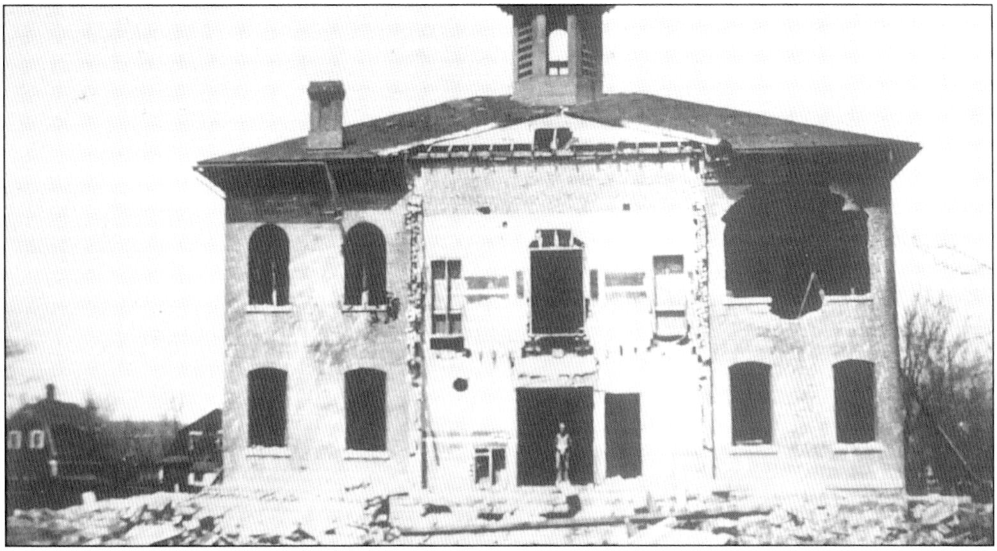

In 1833, the Aurora Academy, a three-story frame building, was erected at the corner of Grove and Main Streets. This land was first cleared by a Mr. Motts who came to Aurora from Vermont in 1806. Calvin Fillmore and his wife, Jerusha, later deeded the site to the trustees of the academy. The only early photograph of the original academy building is of a brick addition being added to the original frame structure. This addition cost $10,000. The new building was directly in front of the old structure, facing south toward Main Street.

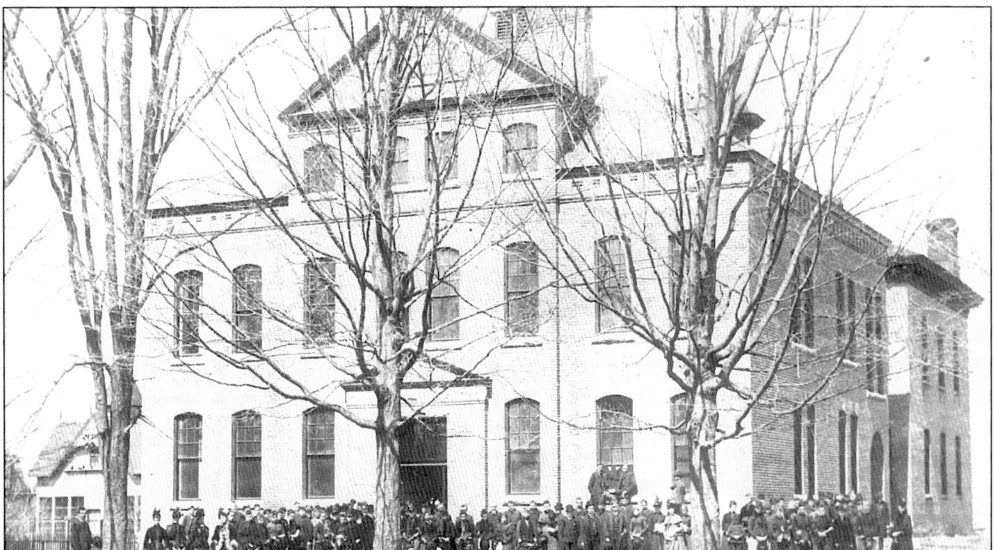

On March 5, 1884, the trustees of the Aurora Academy moved to resign to allow the board of education to assume control of the academy property. The Aurora school was to be known as Union Free School District No. 1. A new addition was built on the front of the academy in 1887 at a cost of $15,000. In 1888, the pupils of old District No. 1 and District No. 10 marched to the new building carrying their books with them. The new part of the building was joined to the old by hallways with coatrooms on either side. In this two-story building, there were five classrooms, a library, and spacious halls. The large bell still hung in the tower of the original academy building.

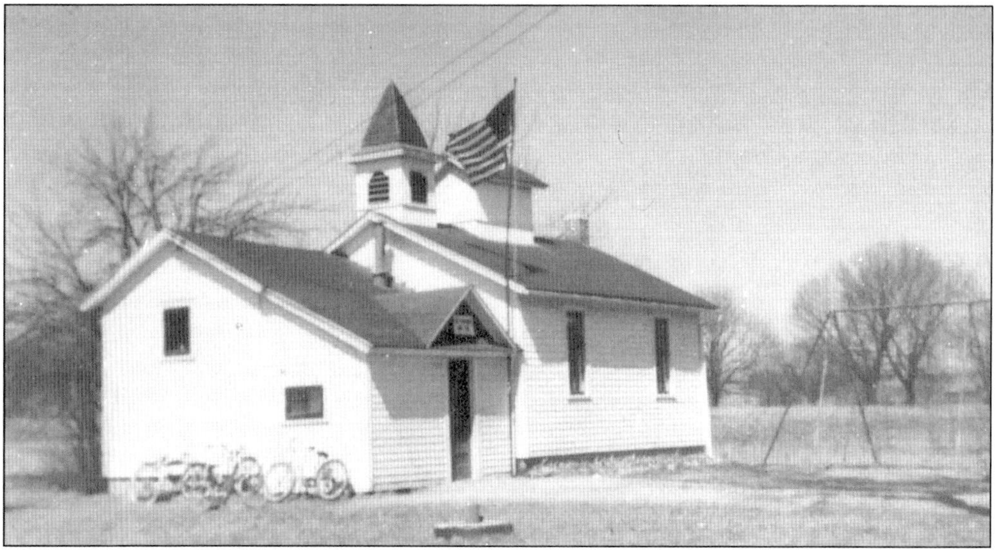

Rural School District No. 11 at Emery and Boies Roads was later used for religious meetings.

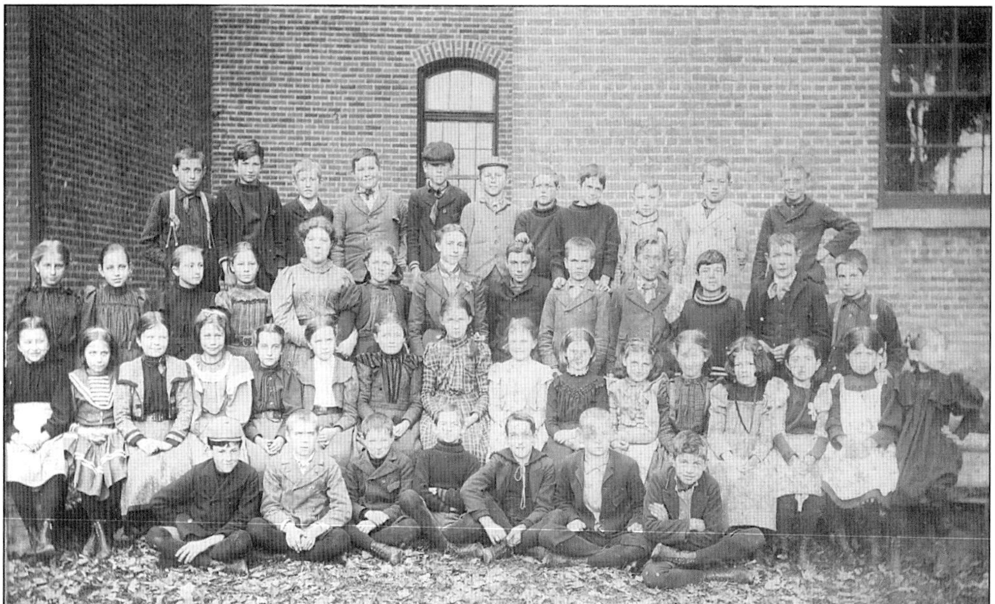

The East Aurora Union School in 1899 included Grace Smith's class. Pictured, from left to right, are the following: (first row) unidentified, unidentified, Clarence Ess, William White, Howard Dorland, Frank Hortman, Burton Bowen, and Sylvanus Freeman; (second row) Florence Rofarge, Florence Kuster, Emma Wise, Elizabeth Perry, Jennie Dick, Mary Green, Mae Wells, Bernice Kelsey, Mildred Hodges, Clara Gerber, Charlotte Houliston, Margaret Marshall, Winifred Ingorsoll, Josephine Youngers, Florence Marshall, and Lydia Hinaman; (third row) Mary Marshall, Evelyn Jarvis, Nellie Below, Dorothea Campaus, Katherine Hoffower, Mary Bodkin, Grace Smith, Frank Burnap, Arthur Wolcott, Leonard Quade, Clem Freeman, James Bodkin, and Frank Shultz; (fourth row) John Shultz, Ray Wigler, Ivan Richardson, William B. Tabor, William K. ?, Jay Perry, Adrian Miller, Lynn Brown, Russell Baker, unidentified, and Elmer Bagley.

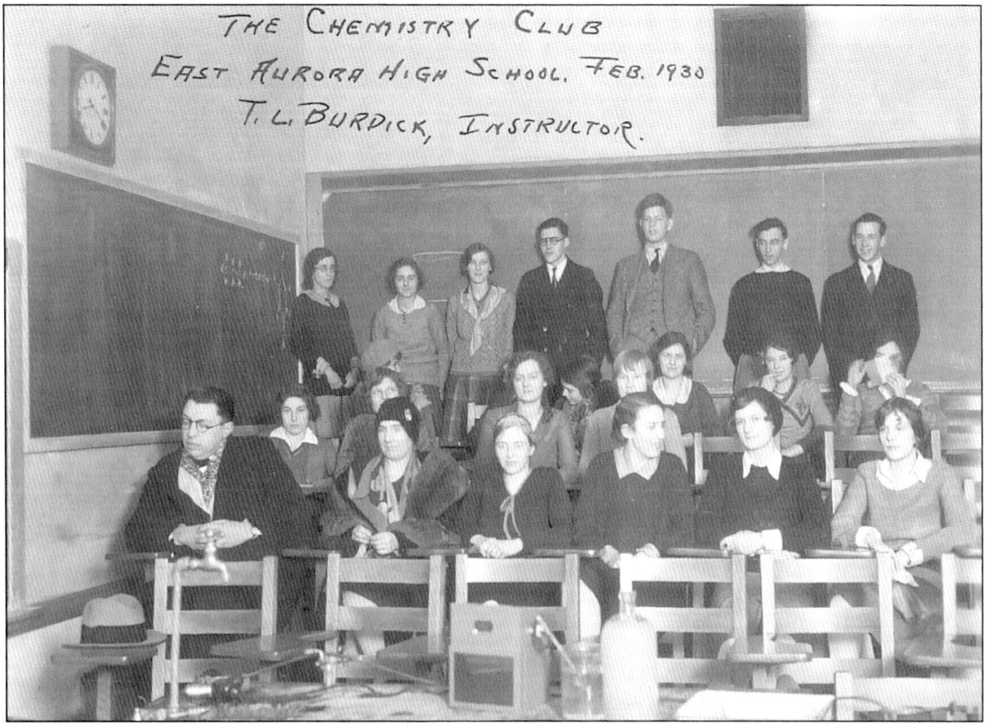

The Chemistry Club of East Aurora High School in February 1930 was instructed by T.L. Burdick. The members of the club are unidentified.

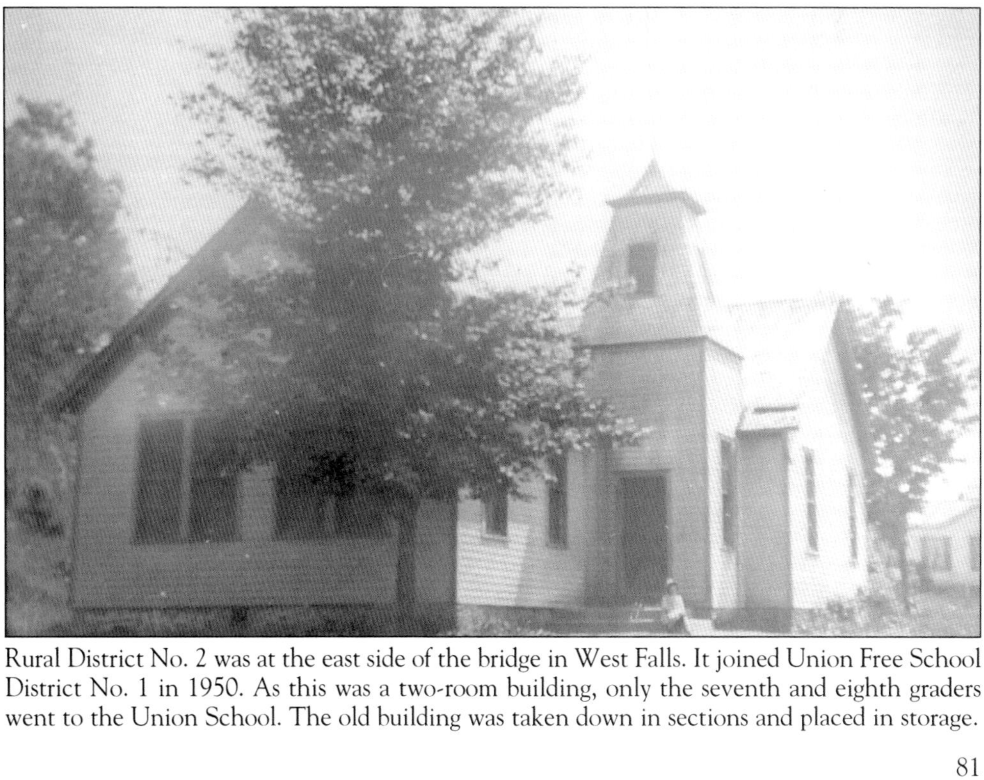

Rural District No. 2 was at the east side of the bridge in West Falls. It joined Union Free School District No. 1 in 1950. As this was a two-room building, only the seventh and eighth graders went to the Union School. The old building was taken down in sections and placed in storage.

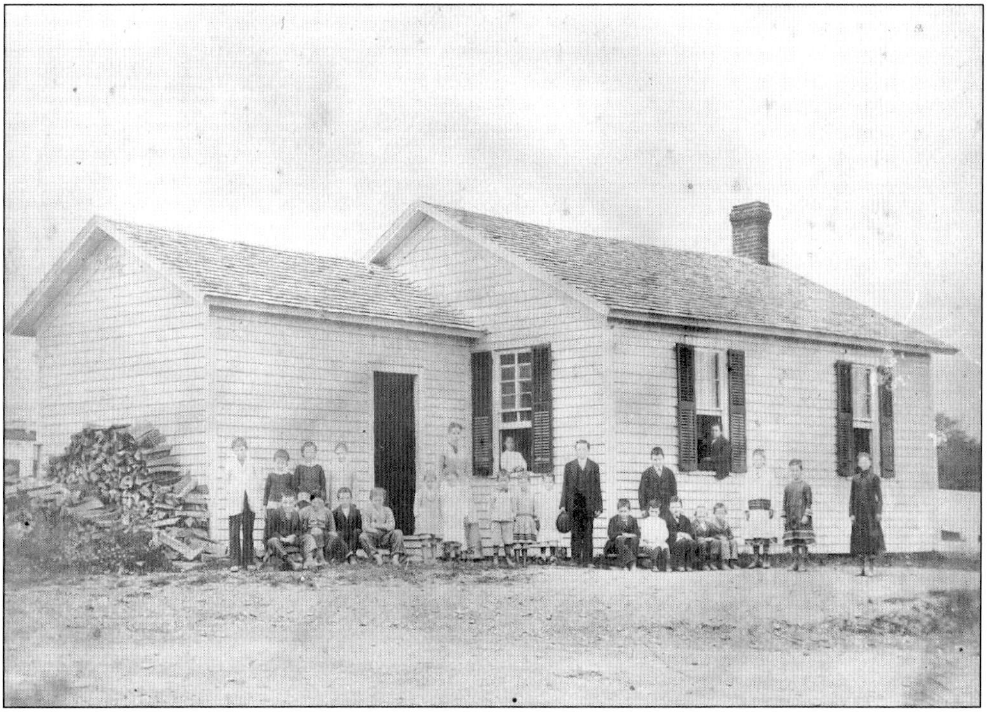

The School District No. 10 building stood at Grover and Jewett-Holmwood Roads in the late 1800s. This building has been sold and made into a private residence.

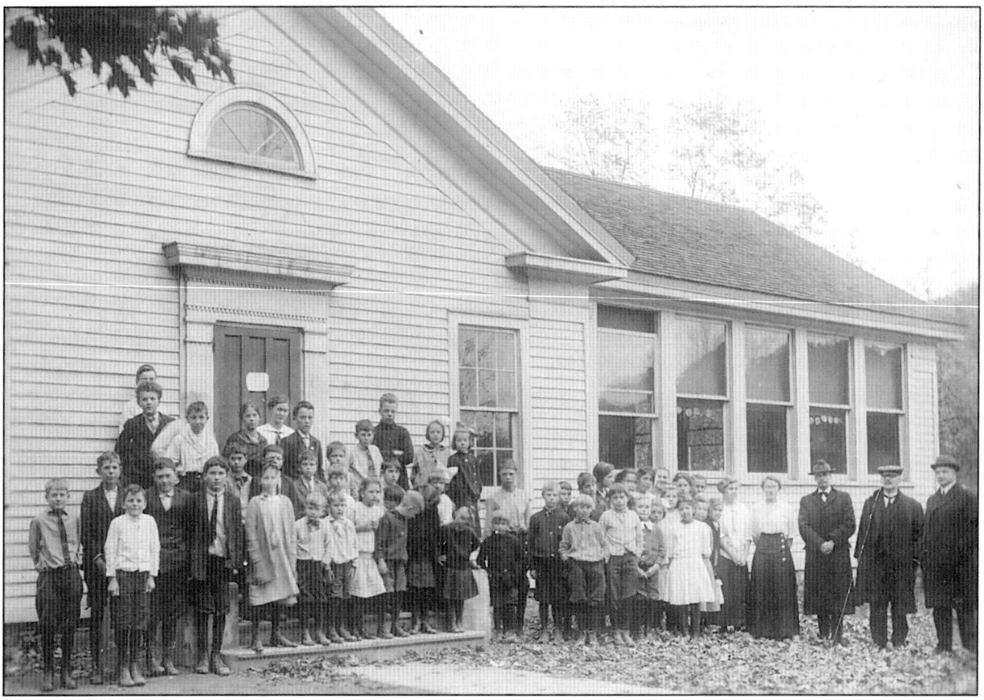

Rural District School No. 8 was a joint district of Wales and Aurora.

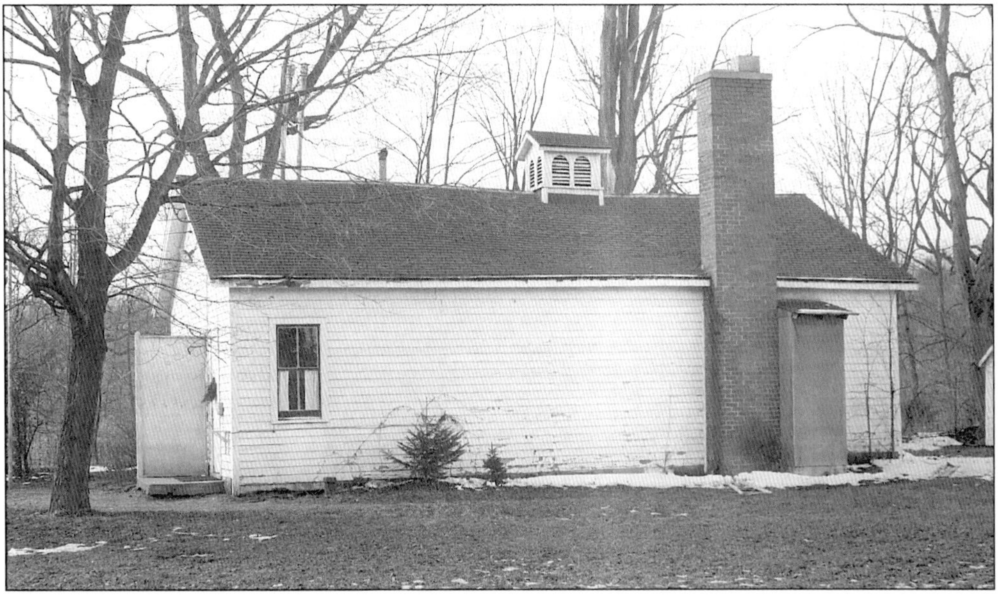

The West Falls one-room schoolhouse is shown in this early photograph.

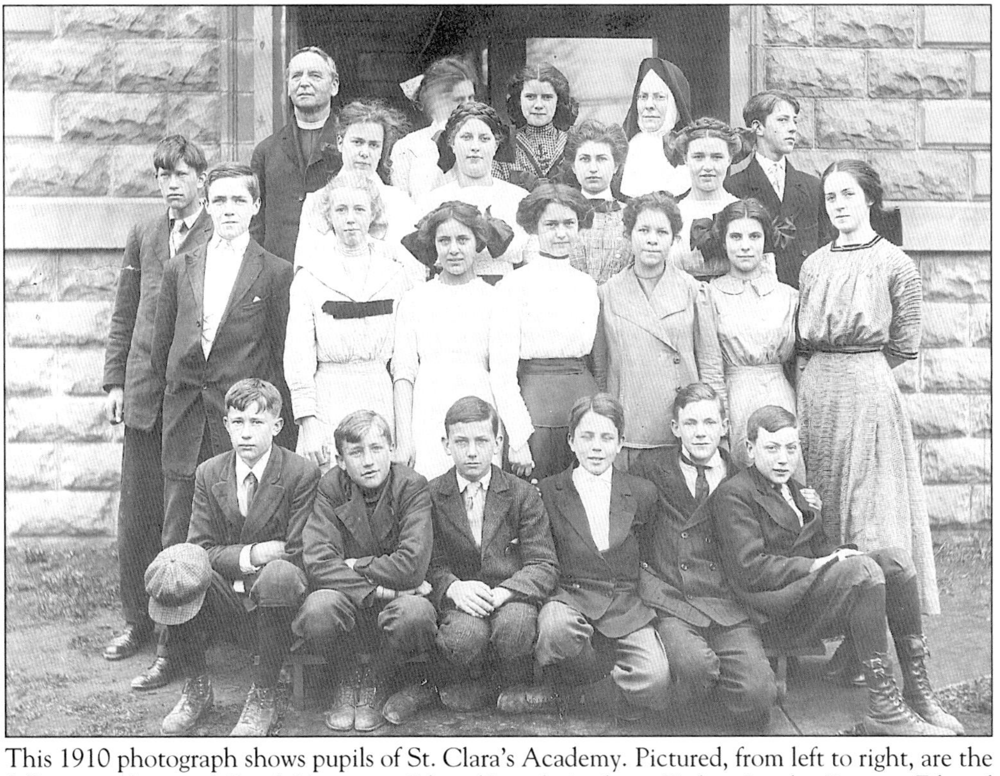

This 1910 photograph shows pupils of St. Clara's Academy. Pictured, from left to right, are the following: (first row) Frank Vigneron, Edward Logel, Anthony Farley, Stanley Persons, Edward Riley, and Floyd Balthazar; (second row) Alphonse Vigneron, Vincent Ragan, Martha Persons, Anna Juenker, Ethel Osborn, Clara Ragan, Maud Ely, and Annabell Hannan; (third row) Henrietta Gardner, Margaret Ragan, Mary Osborn, Juvenille Ragan, and Edwin Marso; (fourth row) Fr. George Zurcher, Gertrude Vigneron, Anna Conley, and Sister Adelaide (principal).

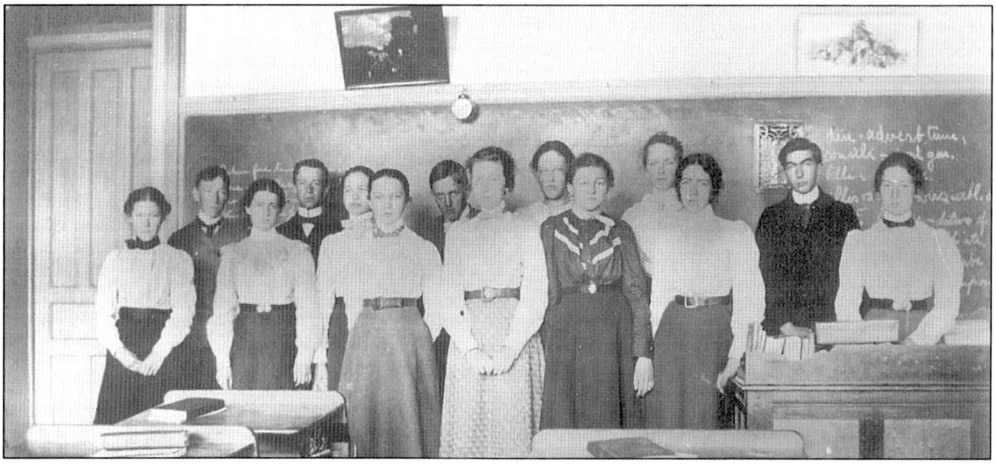

The Latin class of Union Free School is shown in 1898–1899. The teacher was Gertrude Kingman, and the principal was Charles McGavern. Those shown, from left to right, are as follows: (front row) Ina Hopkins, Christine Ross, Flora Wood, Bessie Blakeley, Alice Thomas, Bertha Leigh, Blanche Ingersoll, and Mary Persons; (back row) Andrew Kuster, Ralph Adams, Marian VanVleit, Robert Seyde, Gussie Dorman, and Floyd Richardson.

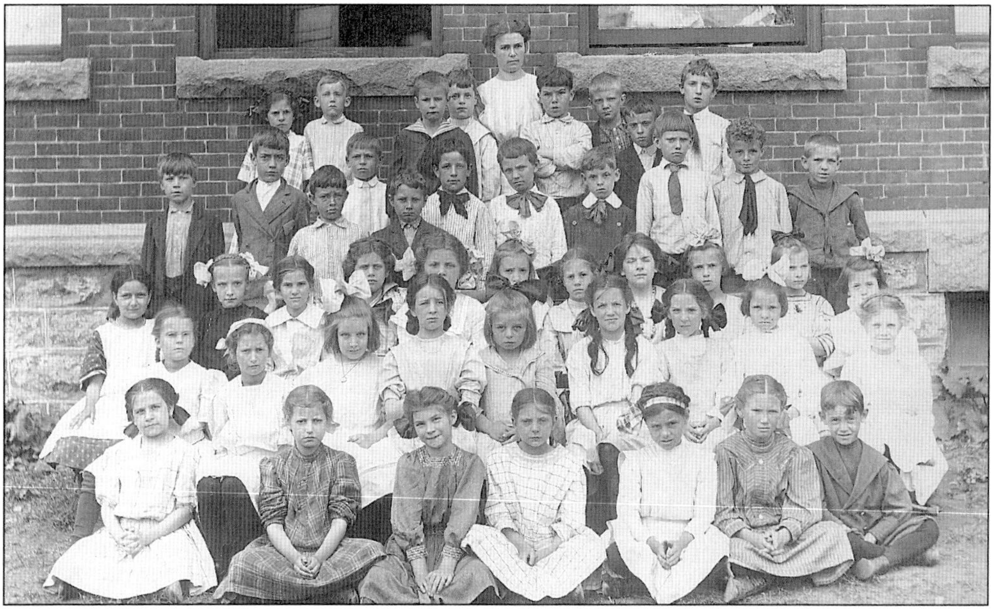

The third-grade class of East Aurora Union Free School is seen here in 1911. Shown, from left to right, are the following: (first row) Susan Branch, Clara Brown, Emma Derby, Elberta Hiles, Helen Wilson Ess, Clara Kelley, and Hayes Ensinger; (second row) Dorothy Smart, Marjorie Hall, Elizabeth Bartlett, Almanza Lewis, Ruth Watson, Mildred Doedema, Daphne Miller, Mildred Rockwood Frantz, and Margery Stocker; (third row) Maude Cotton Squires, unidentified, Alberta Wright, Helen Webster Koenig, Kathryn Perry, Edna O'Neil Fowler, Lorinda Gasmeir Massing, unidentified, Florence Edwards Burnett, Grace Blakeley, and Pansy Claringbold Schang; (fourth row) Clarence Hunt, Floyd Offhaus, unidentified, Carl Kraupcans, unidentified, Saul Bronson, unidentified, Raymond Zink, unidentified, Alvin Karns, and Otto Schultz; (fifth row) Dorothy Roth, Ronald White, unidentified, Carlton Wheeler, Flora Rushbrook Allen (teacher), Ernest Hebdon, George Underhill, Earl Carpenter, and August Avil.

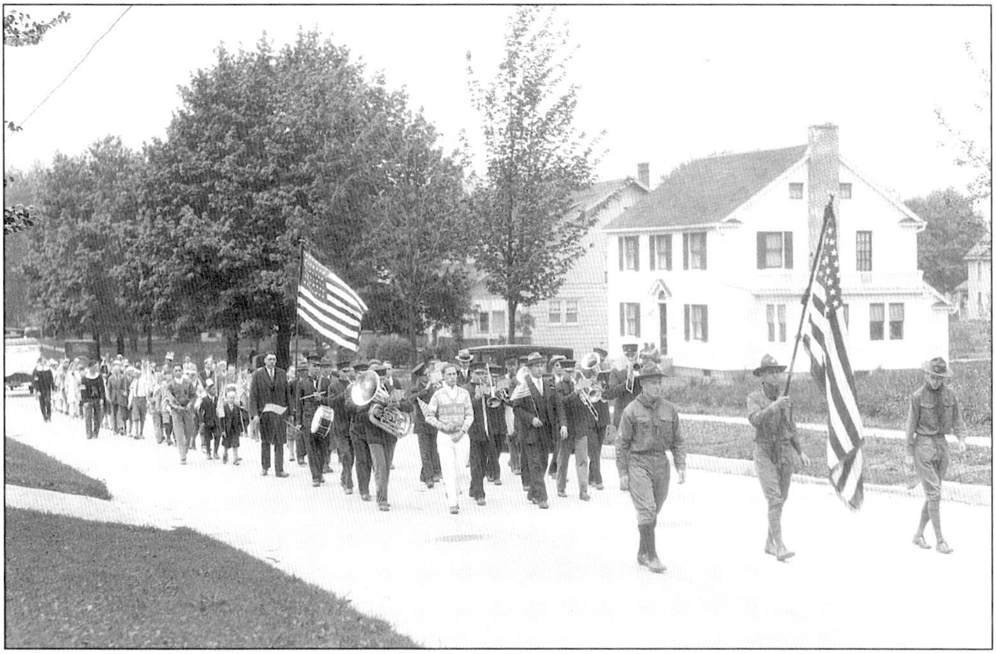

This parade on South Grove Street was part of East Aurora High School Field Day on May 20, 1927. Hamlin Park is on the left side of photograph.

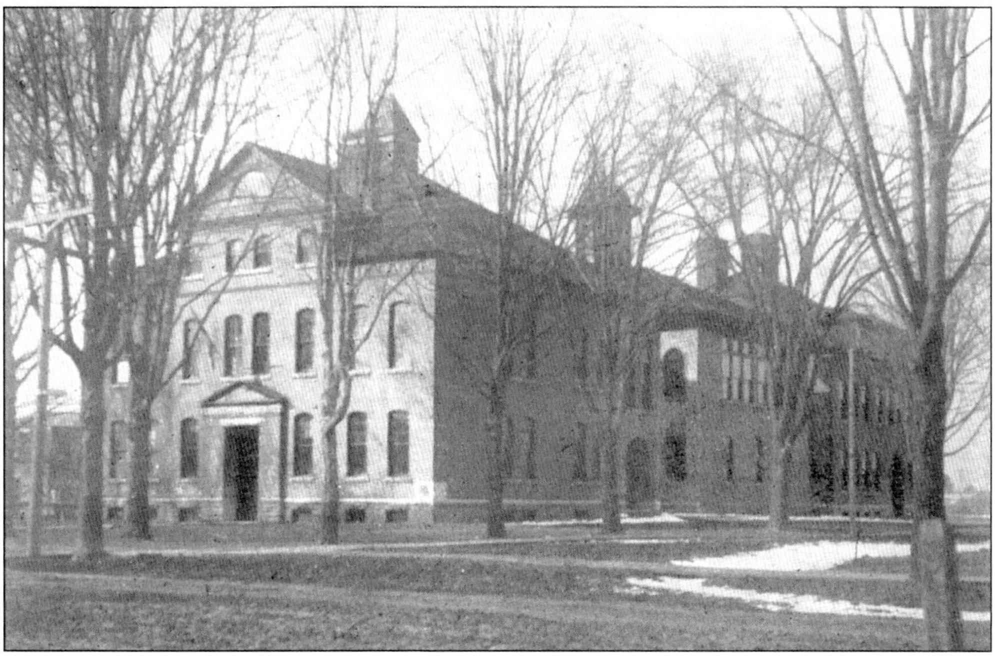

As the population of the village grew, it became necessary for the Union Free School District to build more classrooms. A new building, completed in 1897, was connected to the north side of the old academy building. The outside entrance was on North Grove Street. The second floor of the old academy, now the middle part of the building, became a large study hall for the high school. The study hall had stationary seats; boys were seated on one side, girls on the other, with a wide aisle between.

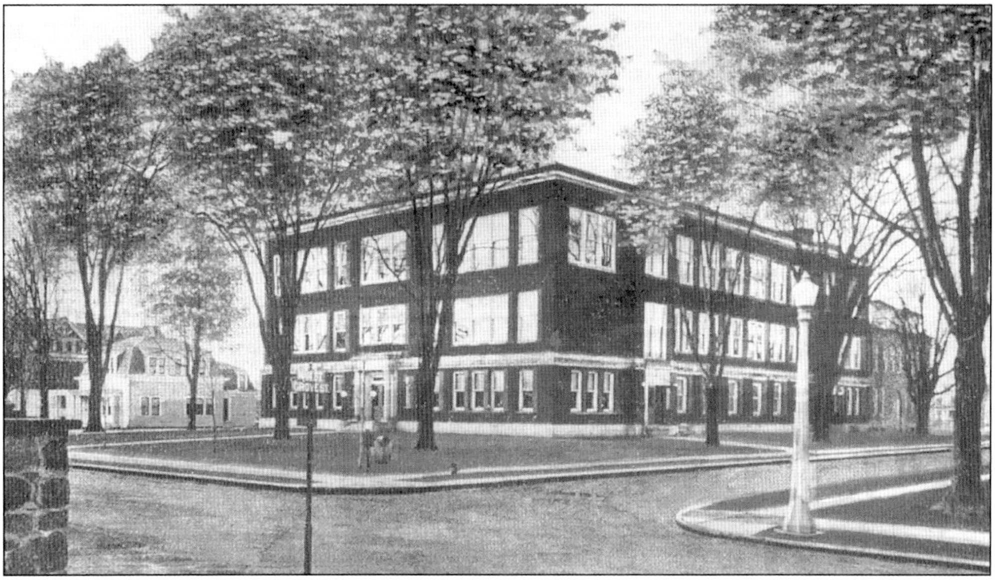

In 1916, there was a need for more space and more modern accommodations. The board of education voted to replace the 1887 addition and the academy building with a larger structure. The two front sections were demolished, and a new brick structure was erected. While that was being built, the high school pupils were moved to Clement Hall, which was set up as a study hall. Classes were held in the basement of the Presbyterian church as well as in the board of trade rooms. The grades continued to meet in the remaining rooms of the school under the supervision of Jennie Rozenkrantz Dewey. The new school was opened in September 1917.

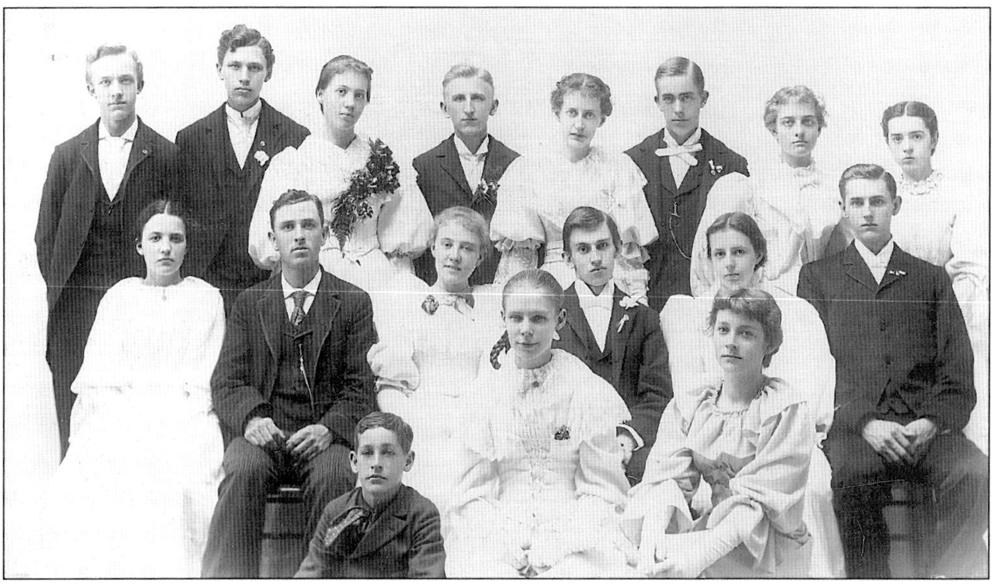

This 1894 photograph shows a group of East Aurora Union Free School students. Included, in no particular order, are the following: Perry Wurst, Eddie Brown, Grace Hansenburgh, Fred Fisher, Nettie Hall, George Vankuren, Grace Billington, Mary Bradburn, Sara Shindler, Harry Kelly, Merti Bush, James Castle, Alyce Pfifferling, James Baker, Wallace Gail, Grace Bowman, and Flora Russell. Charles Gold was not present.

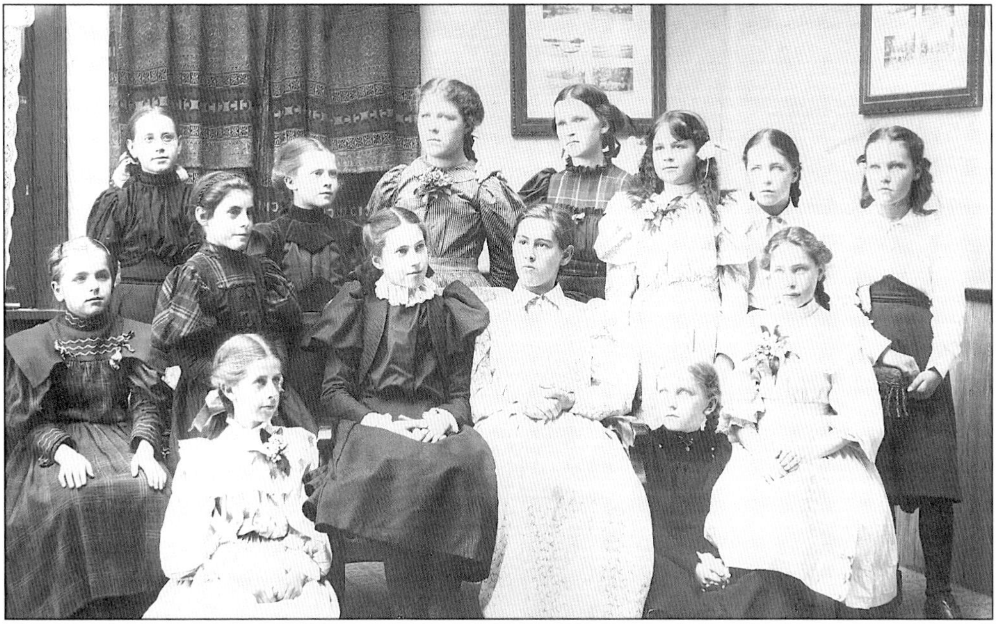

The third- or fourth-grade class of Union Free School is shown in 1898. Pictured, from left to right, are the following: (front row) unidentified, Maggie Curtis, Eloise Longmade, Gussie Dormann, Kate Barnard, Edna Blowers, and Audie Eyre; (back row) Clara Barnhart, Laura Coates, Dolly Hoffower, Ella Cleary, Alida Knights, Ethel Bowen, and Lucy Bowen. The photograph was taken as a gift to their teacher, Ruby Beyers.

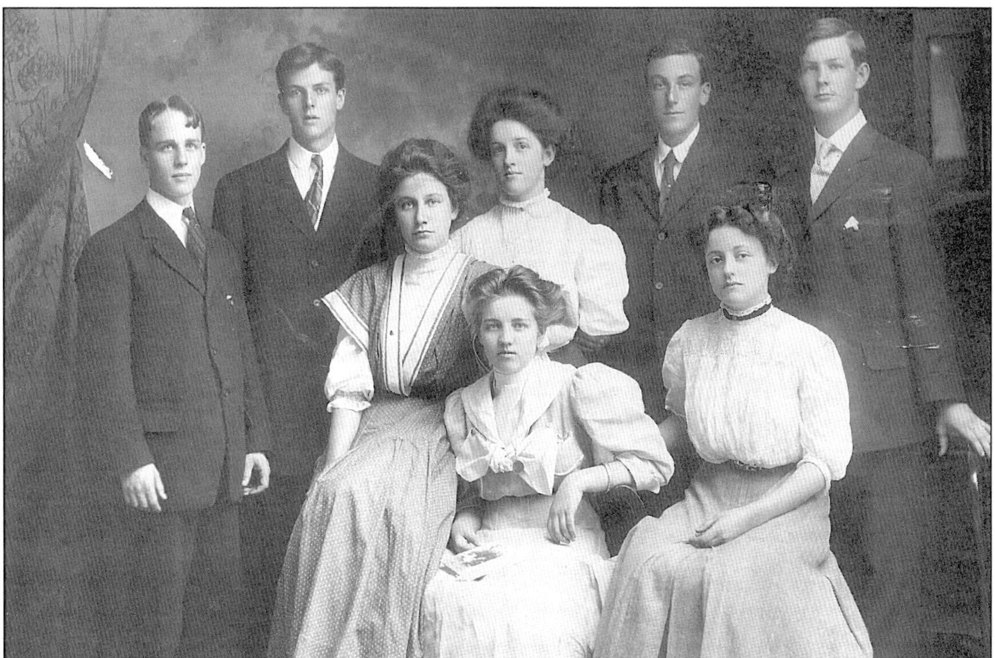

Students of the East Aurora High School, Class of 1908, are shown from left to right: (front row) Florence Lennan, Nora Evans, Vera Miller, and Margery Gregory; (back row) Herbert Cline, Ralph Paul, Howard Eldridge, and Ray Wahlen.

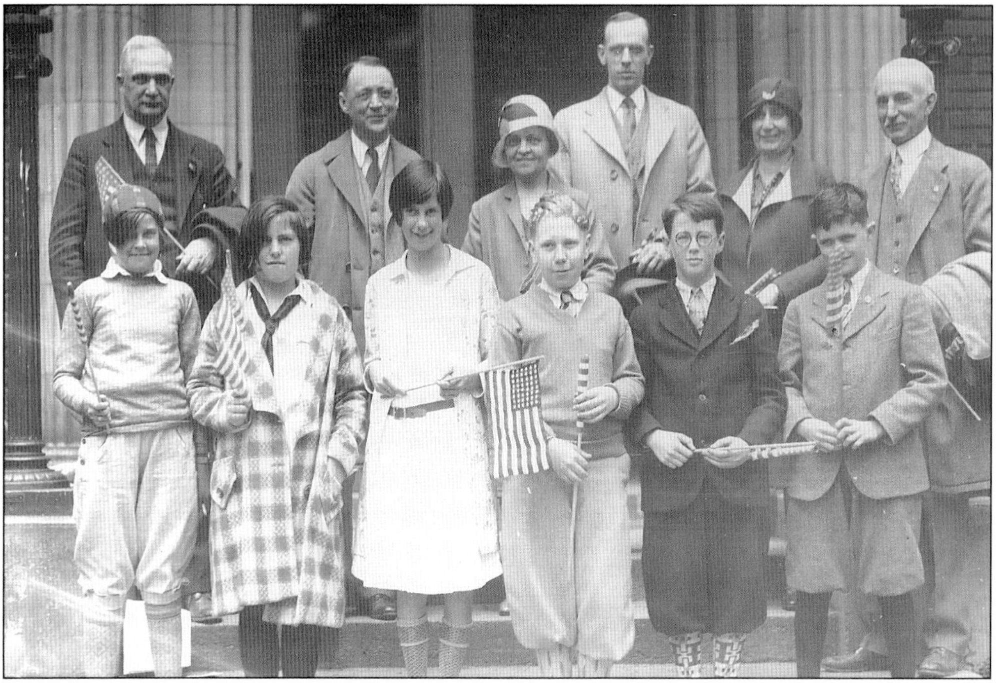

Spelling contest contestants on Field Day, Spring 1929 are pictured, from left to right, as follows: (front row) Lois Zimmerman (Marilla; first place, Rural Division), Arlene Swartz (Marilla; third place, Rural Division), Renee Therion (East Aurora; second place, Grades Division), Lawrence Lipsett (East Aurora; first place, Grades Division), Jasper Frazee (East Aurora; third place, Grades Division), and Eugene Duffy (Marilla; second place, Rural Division); (back row) William Pierce, Harry Mead, Mrs. Harrison Hiles, Walter Bumgardner, Mrs. Andrew Andrews, and George Merrill.

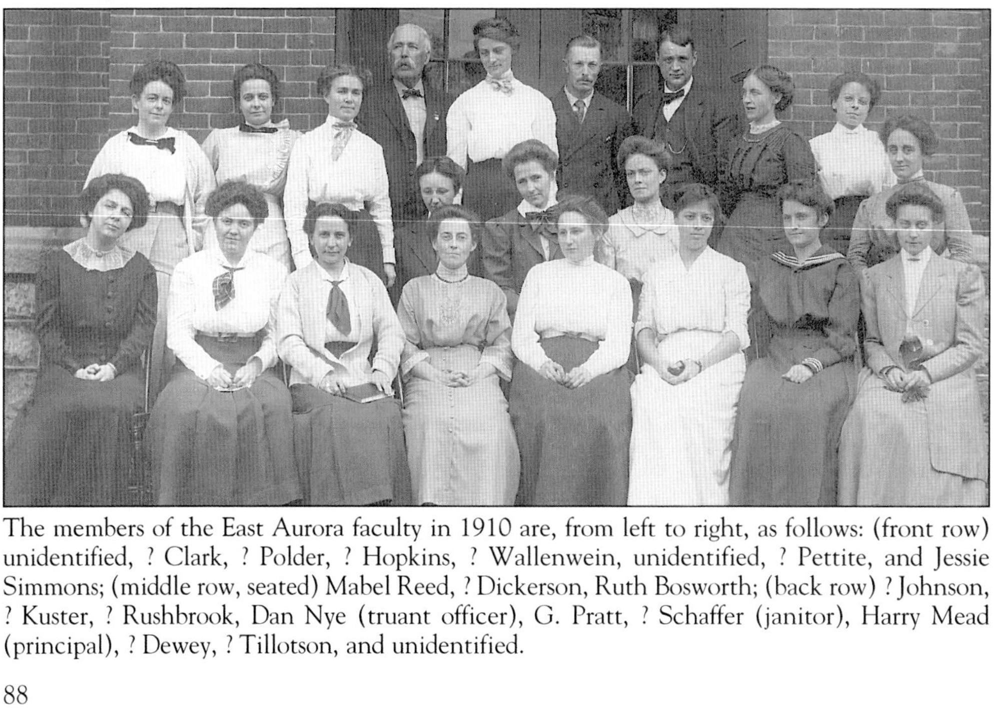

The members of the East Aurora faculty in 1910 are, from left to right, as follows: (front row) unidentified, ? Clark, ? Polder, ? Hopkins, ? Wallenwein, unidentified, ? Pettite, and Jessie Simmons; (middle row, seated) Mabel Reed, ? Dickerson, Ruth Bosworth; (back row) ? Johnson, ? Kuster, ? Rushbrook, Dan Nye (truant officer), G. Pratt, ? Schaffer (janitor), Harry Mead (principal), ? Dewey, ? Tillotson, and unidentified.

Seven

CHURCHES

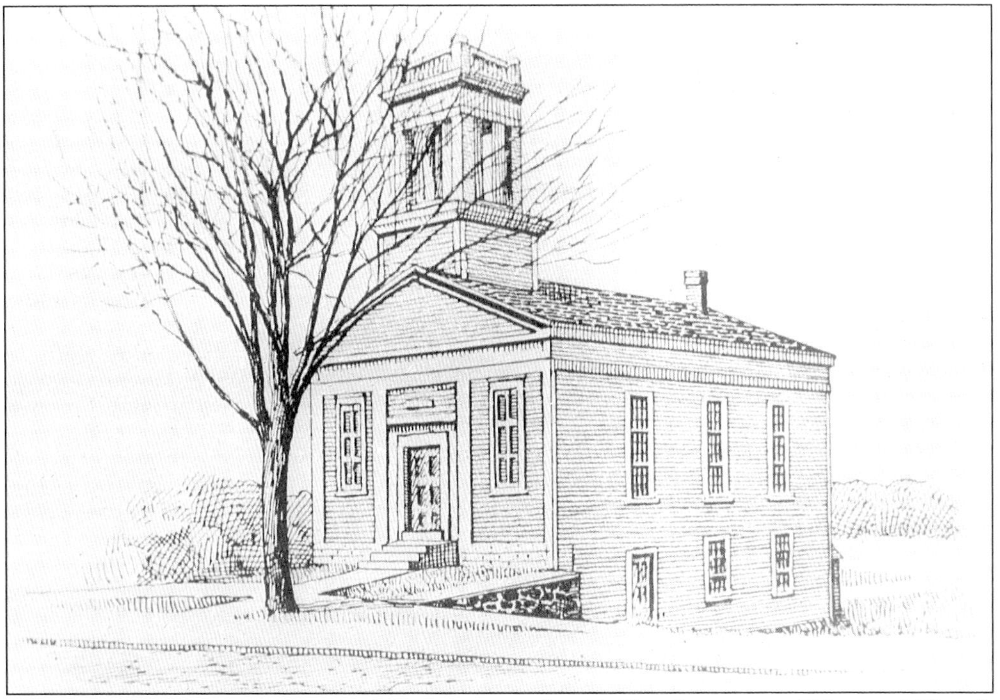

The original Presbyterian church edifice was erected in 1845 at the corner of Main and Church Streets. Before that, gatherings were held in log cabins or sheds. In 1817, a group of ten or more settlers were inspired by the missionary Rev. John Spencer. He had come into this wilderness, which was known then as the Holland Land Purchase. By July 1818, there were 35 members known as the First Congregational Society. On March 3, 1892, a new church building was erected on Main and Paine Streets. The original church building was then renovated to become the East Aurora Opera House.

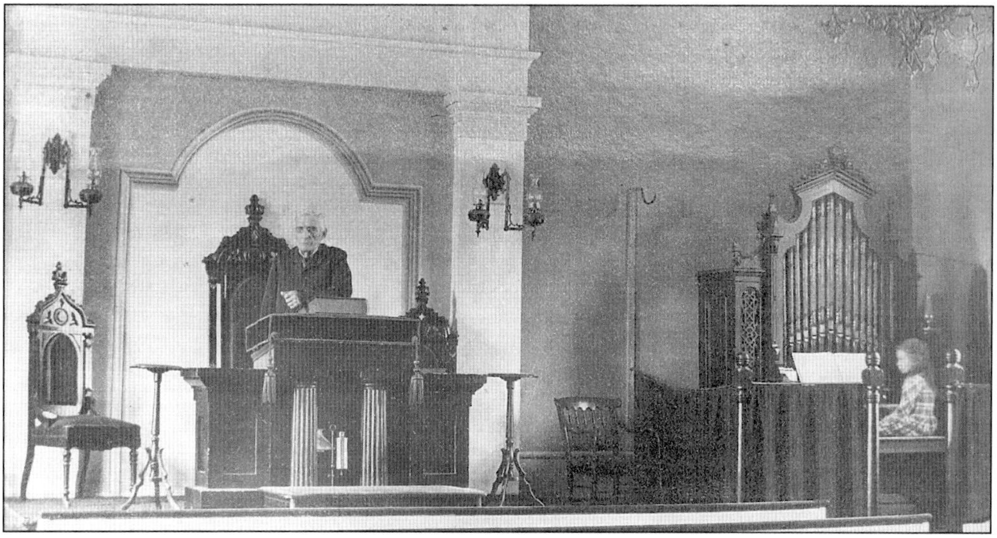

This view shows the interior of the First Presbyterian church, built in 1843 at Main and Church Streets. Standing in the pulpit is Rev. Richard M. Sanford, pastor from 1865 to 1887. Mary Persons is seated at the organ.

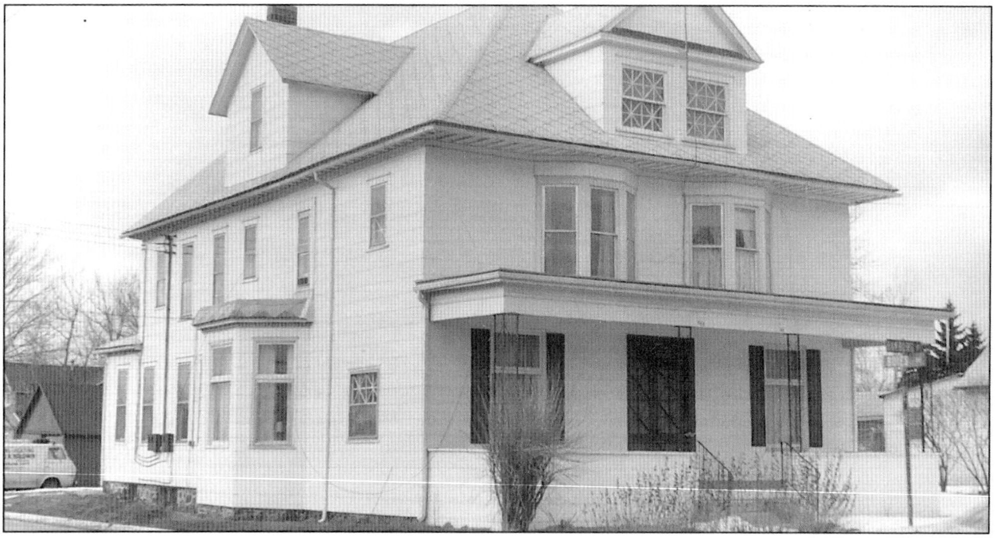

The First Methodist Church Society of the Town of Aurora met at the home of Calvin Fillmore, uncle of Millard Fillmore. On March 2, 1822, they incorporated under the name of the Methodist Episcopal Society of Aurora. In 1826, the name was changed to the First Methodist Episcopal Society of the Town of Aurora. Records name Glezen Fillmore, nephew of Calvin Fillmore, as the first minister. The first trustees were William Allen, Nathaniel Holmes, Samuel Gail, Hauxhurst Addington, Thomas Pratt, Arthur Humphrey, and Daniel Crane. A contract was given to Benjamin Searles to build the first house of worship; it was completed on November 12, 1829. Subscriptions of materials and labor were made, but there were very few contributions of money. Some contributed standing lumber. One gave the use of a sawmill, others gave their horses to haul lumber, while many gave their time. A subscription list made in the spring of 1831 contains the names of 89 people. This building, which was later made into a four-apartment dwelling on Hamburg Street and Boies Alley, was used until 1877, when land was purchased at the corner of Main and Center Streets for a new edifice.

In 1877, the congregation of the Methodist Church purchased land at the southeast corner of Main and Center Streets. The frame building shown in this photograph was erected there with a large auditorium and a basement. At the time, there were 100 members. In 1906, the building was in need of a complete renovation. The horse sheds were reshingled, church and parsonage painted, and the basement enlarged providing for parlors, kitchen, furnace room, and coal bins. New steps, two furnaces, electric wiring and fixtures, and a pipe organ were added.

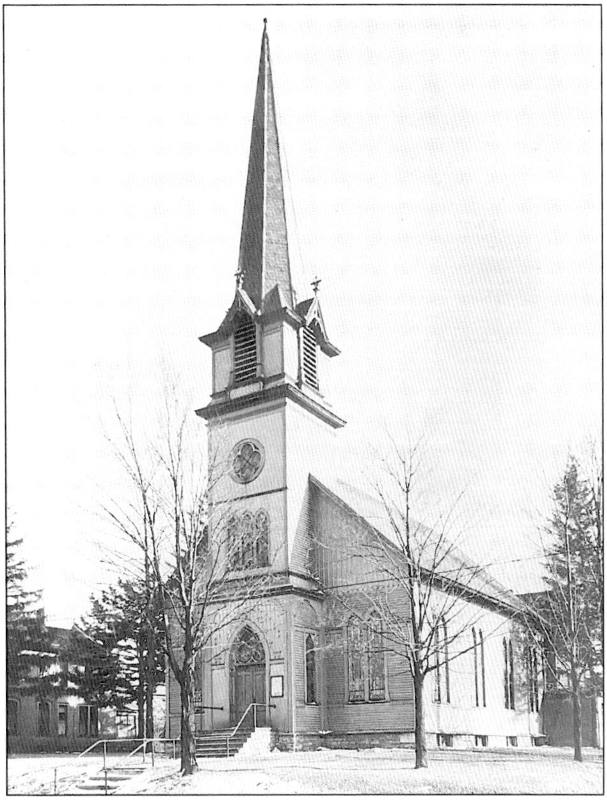

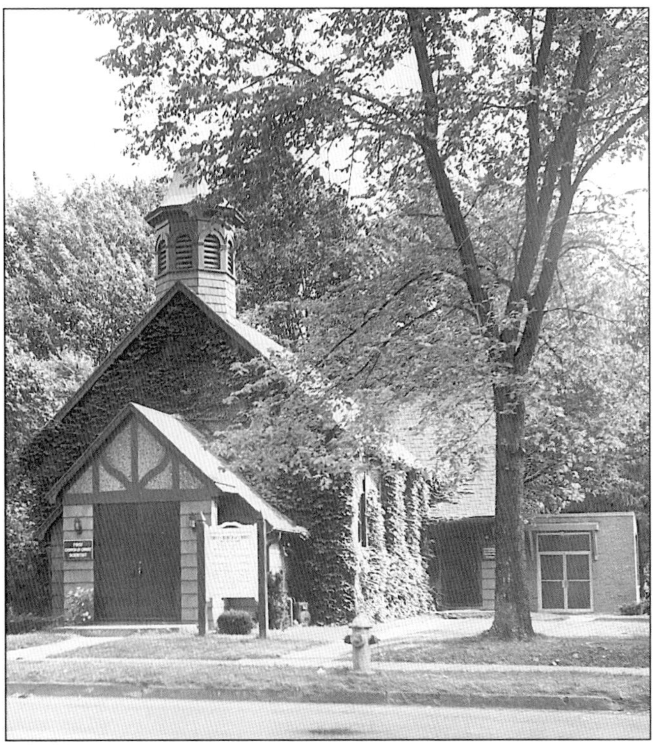

Beginning on August 10, 1902, services of the First Church of Christ Scientist were held in the Roycroft Chapel. Later, Mr. and Mrs. John Fitz opened their home for meetings at 414 Fillmore Avenue. On August 11, 1906, plans prepared by L.P. Eckert for building a chapel, were approved by the Christian Science Society of East Aurora. The cornerstone was laid September 8, 1906, and the church was incorporated on April 23, 1907. Since no Christian Science Church is dedicated until it is debt free, dedication was delayed until August 9, 1925.

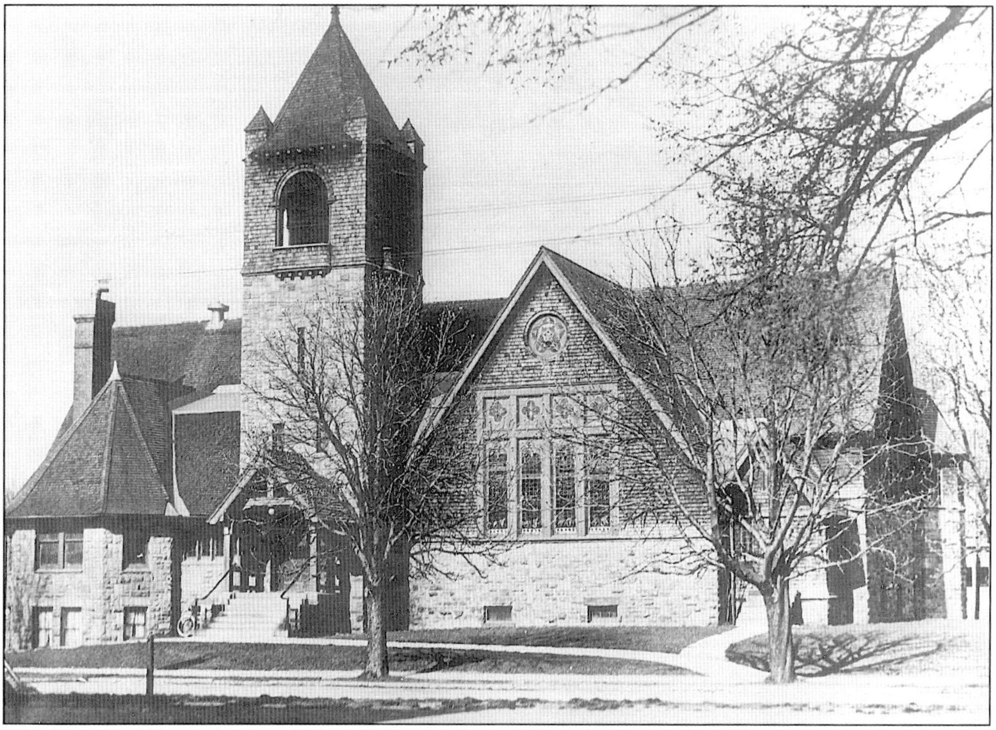

The First Presbyterian church building on Main and Paine Streets was dedicated free from debt on March 3, 1892. It was destroyed by fire on the night of January 24, 1902. A new building was erected on the same site and was occupied on March 1, 1903. Fire struck again on December 27, 1933, destroying both the church and the religious education building. A new church building was dedicated in 1935.

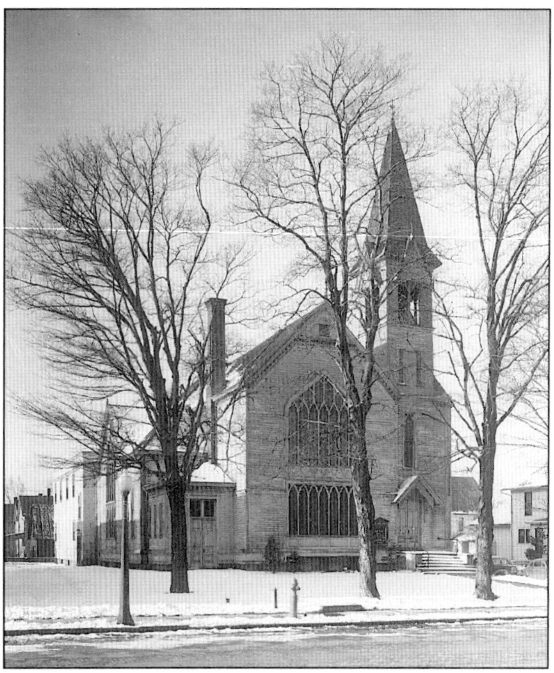

The First Baptist church building was on the corner of Main Street and Temple Place. It was dedicated June 24, 1884 during the ministry of the Reverend Alfred M. Tenent. By 1941, the building was in such need of major repairs that it was demolished. The history of the congregation goes back to 1807, when gatherings were conducted by Deacons Calkins and Rowley. On October 17, 1810, the Baptist Church of Willink was organized.

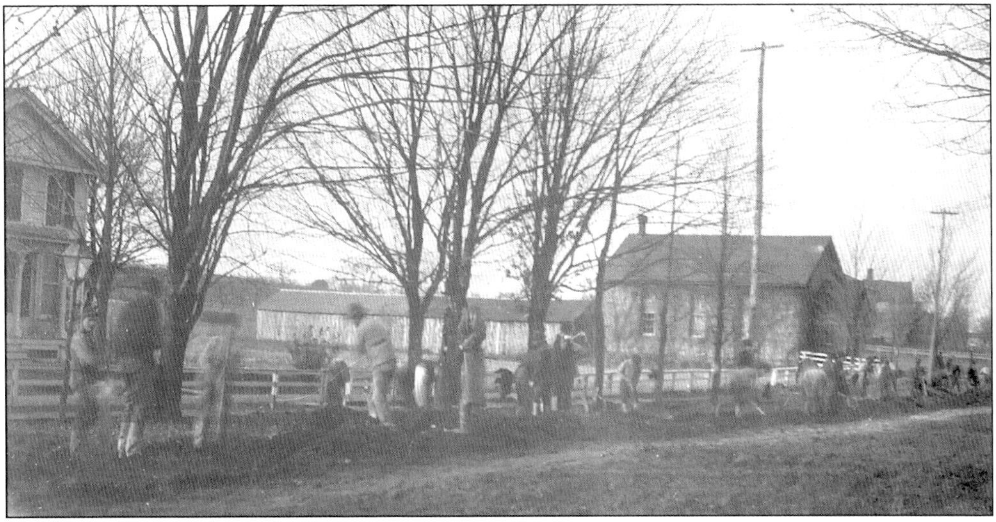

The sanctuary of the congregation of the Christian Church (the name was later changed to Church of Christ) was built in 1866. After 40 years of service, it was razed in the spring of 1906. It is pictured on the right side of the first telephone pole. The East Aurora Christian Church came into being in 1843 with the gathering of 13 people in the home of Hugh J. Minton. The church building was located on the south side of East Main Street approximately halfway between Olean and Elmwood Streets. The one stained-glass window pictured a cross, a crown, and a Bible with the words, "No Cross. No Crown." This structure was abandoned in 1905, when a new building was erected at the corner of Main and North Grove Streets.

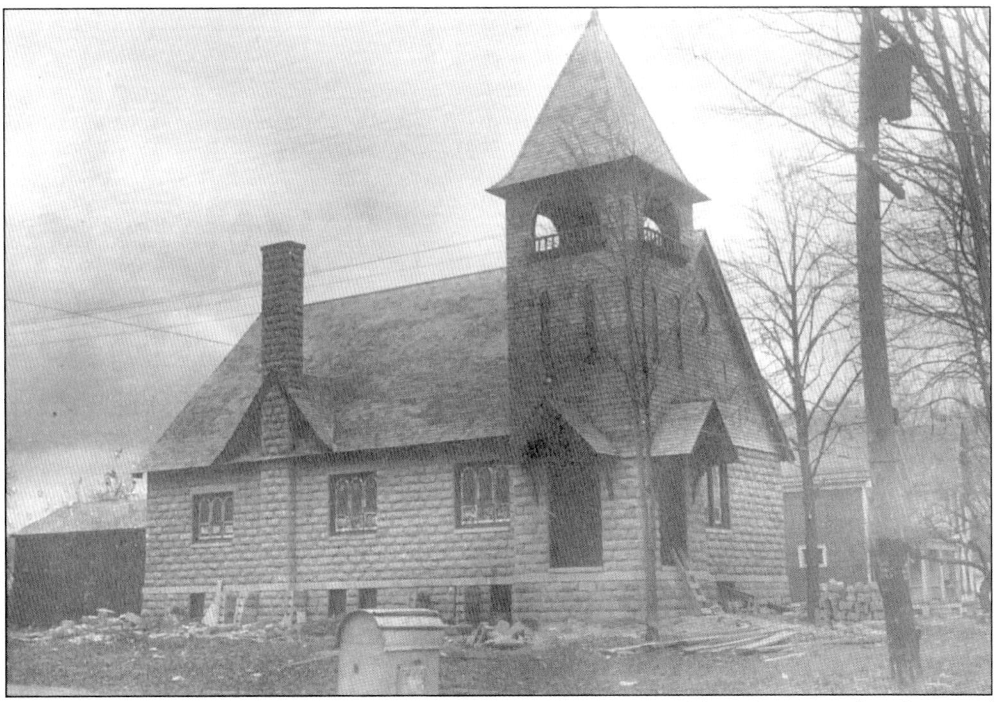

While the Reverend Lewis Cost was minister, the congregation of the Christian Church moved to Main and North Grove Streets. A new and larger church, shown here under construction, was built in 1904 at a cost of $10,000.

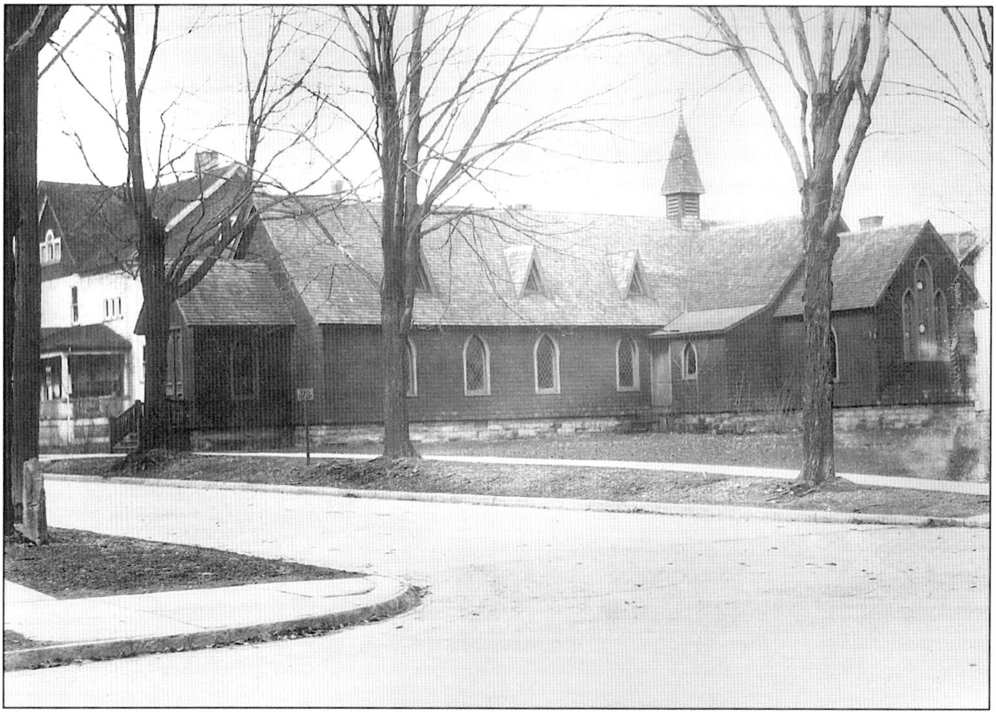

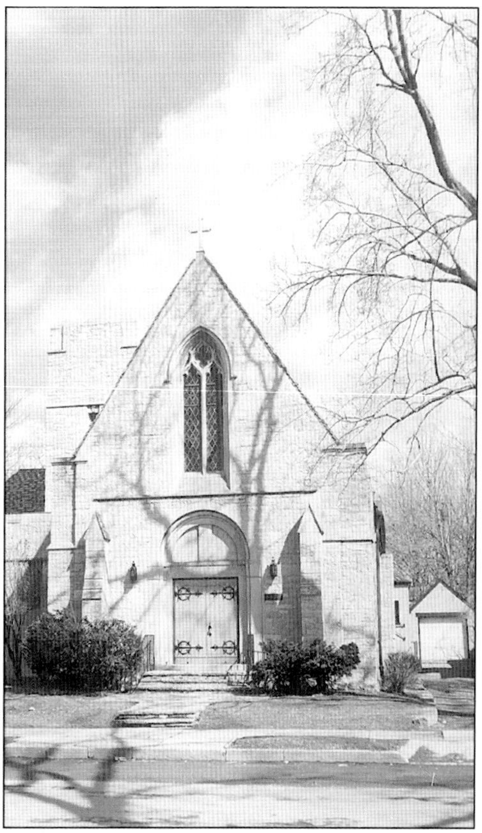

The St. Mathias Episcopal church on the corner of Main and Maple Streets, shown in this photograph, was erected in 1870. The entrance faced Maple Street. The body of the building was parallel to Main Street. The white house, at the left, was the rectory and has since been demolished. An incorporation meeting was held at the Universalist meetinghouse on February 24, 1869—St. Mathias' Day. Six people attended the organizational meeting: Byron D. Persons, Warren S. Rogers, William D. Jones, Thomas Wright, John Townsend, and Clark Bowen. It was agreed that the parish would take its name from the saint whose feast day it was. During the first year as a parish, the congregation rented space for worship at the Universalist meetinghouse.

The cornerstone of this new St. Mathias Episcopal church building was laid on September 10, 1927. The first building, erected in 1870, was sold to the Universalist congregation. It was moved from the east side of Maple Street to the west side. The new church faces Main Street; the old one faced Maple.

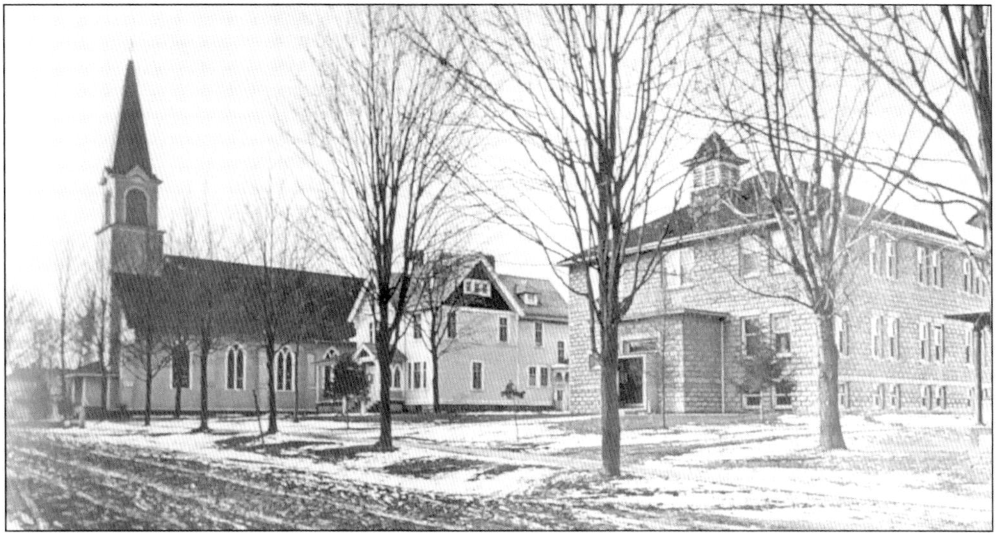

Shown is the Immaculate Conception parish as it appeared in 1906. The buildings shown, left to right, are as follows: the Immaculate Conception church at the corner of Park Place and Oakwood Avenue, the rectory, and the newly built St. Clara's Academy. The site for the academy had been an old sandpit. The parishioners filled the hole, leveled the slight hill along the street, and dug the school basement. The school was completed and dedicated by Bishop Charles H. Colton on November 4, 1906. The Right Rev. Msgr. Nelson A. Baker, the famed Apostle of Charity, of Lackawanna, assisted him.

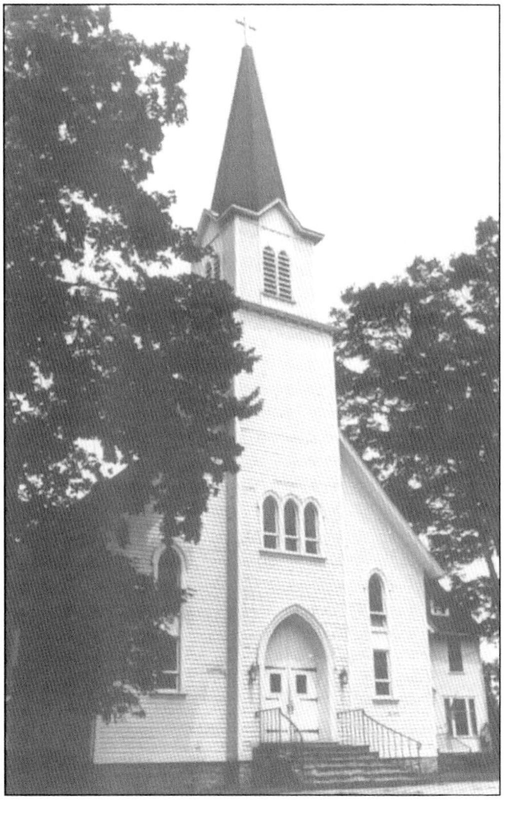

The little white church of the Immaculate Conception Parish was built in 1882. It was enlarged in 1901 to provide more seating space and three altars. Leonard Ernst erected the cross on top of the steeple in 1920 after the original was struck by lightening.

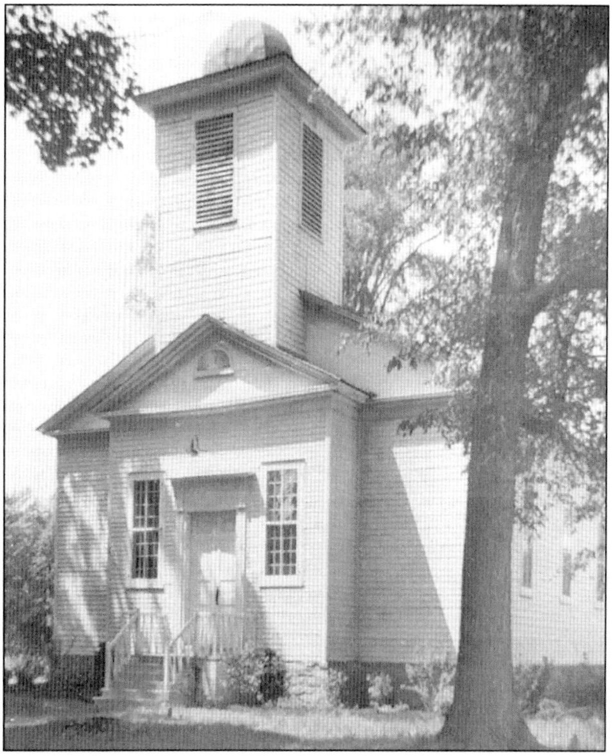

The Griffin's Mills Presbyterian Church was founded on August 18, 1810 as the West Aurora Congregational Church. The building was erected shortly after the War of 1812. As nearly as possible, without sacrificing the comfort of modern conveniences, the church has been restored to its original form.

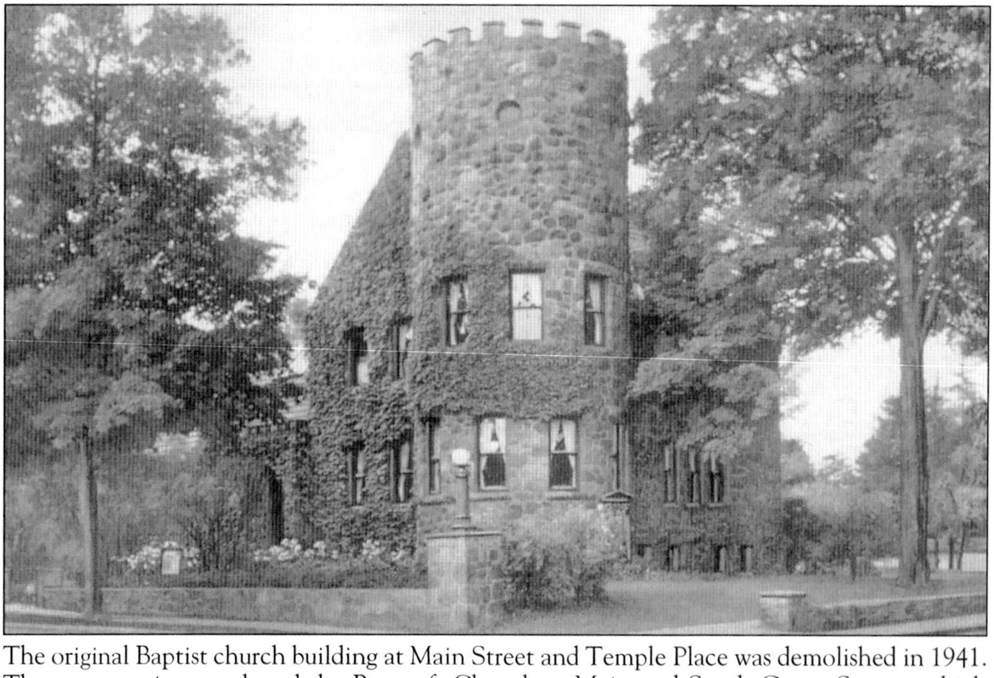

The original Baptist church building at Main Street and Temple Place was demolished in 1941. The congregation purchased the Roycroft Chapel on Main and South Grove Streets, which was their house of worship from 1942 until 1958. The new building, on Porterville Road, was dedicated on January 26, 1958. The chapel, on the Roycroft Campus, was sold to the Town of Aurora for use as the town hall.

The Reverend George C. Knights was the pastor of the East Aurora Baptist Church from 1899 to 1905.

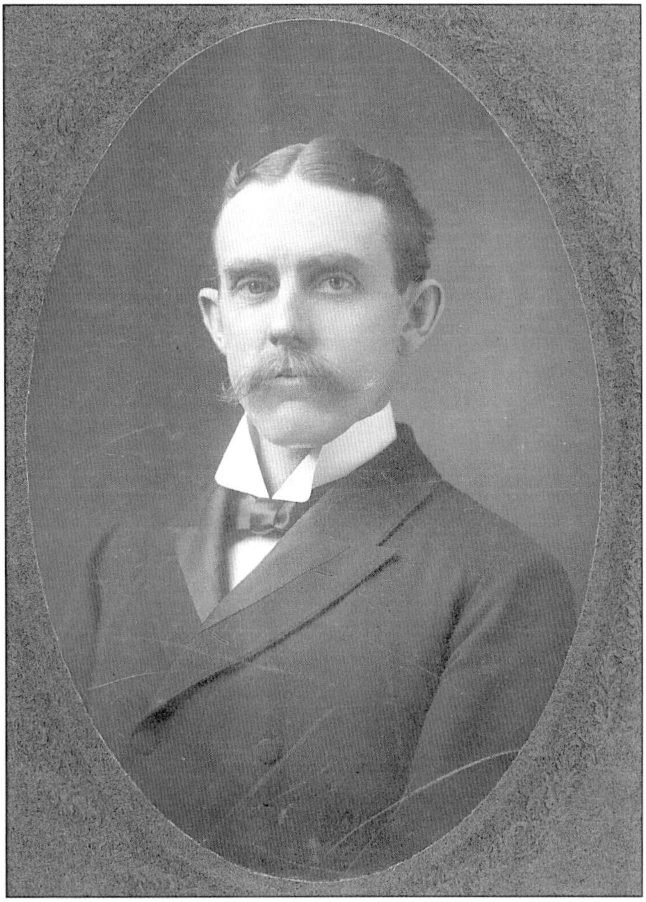

The Assembly of God Church purchased the former powerhouse on the Roycroft Campus in July 1944. The birth of this church in East Aurora was the result of prayer meetings held in the town of Wales. Services were started in July 1932, in the vacant church building owned by the Universalist Church. The tabernacle of this congregation was erected at 54 Elm Street and dedicated January 1, 1933. The powerhouse was purchased when more space was needed for the growing number of members.

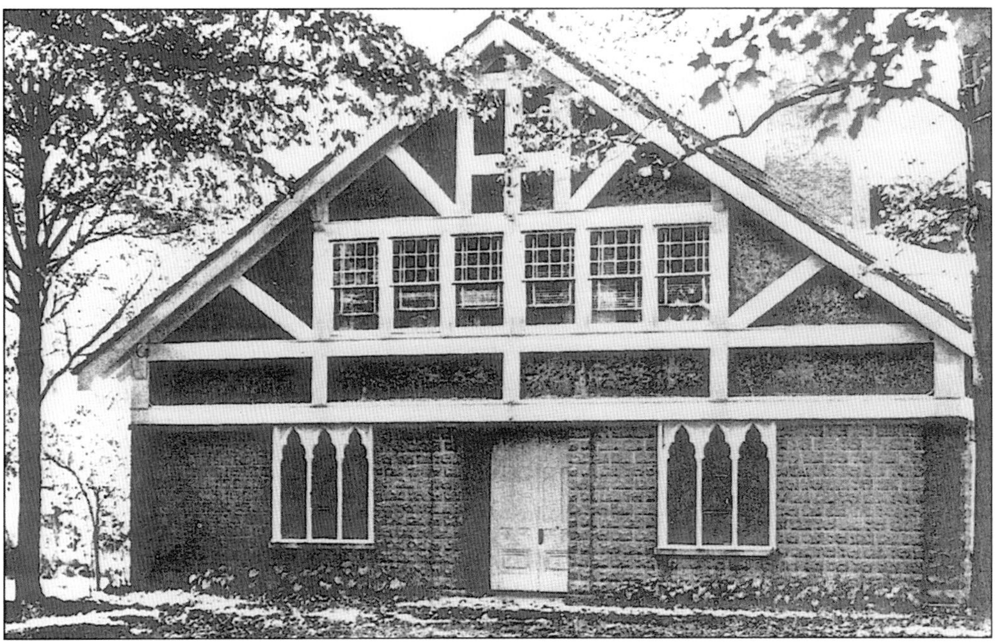

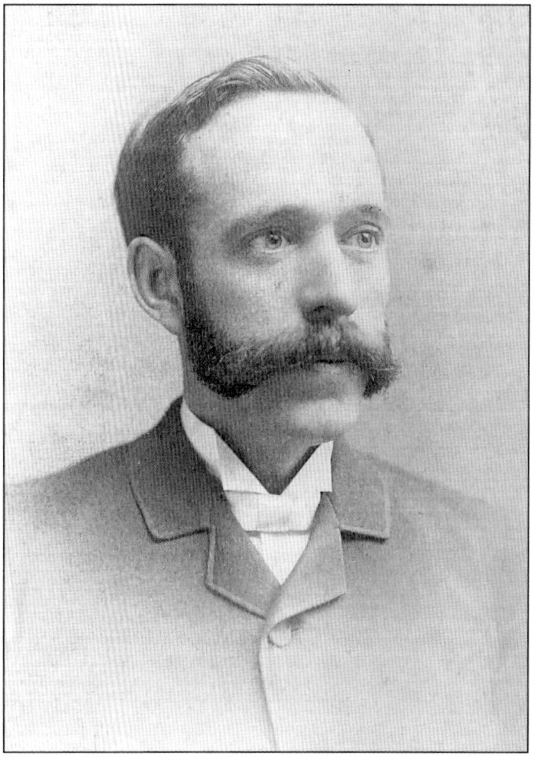

The Reverend J.W. Phillips was the pastor of the East Aurora Baptist Church from 1885 to 1886.

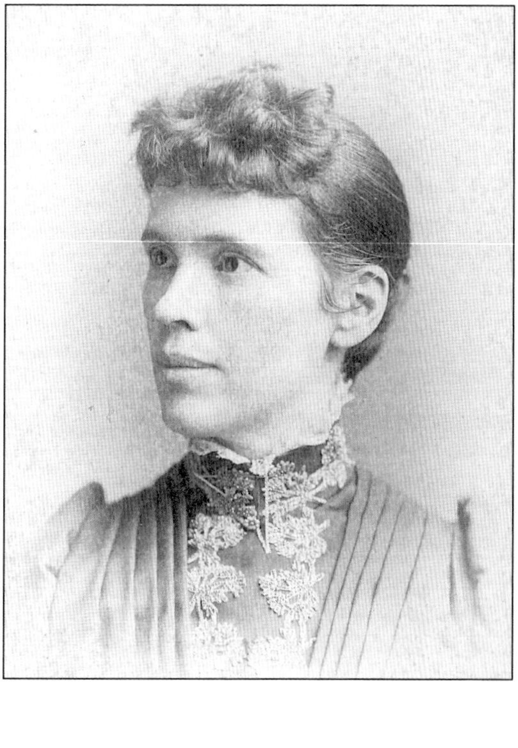

Jennie C. Phillips was the wife of Reverend Phillips, pastor of the East Aurora Baptist Church.

Men work on the steeple of the First Baptist church on Main Street and Temple Place. The building was dedicated on June 24, 1884.

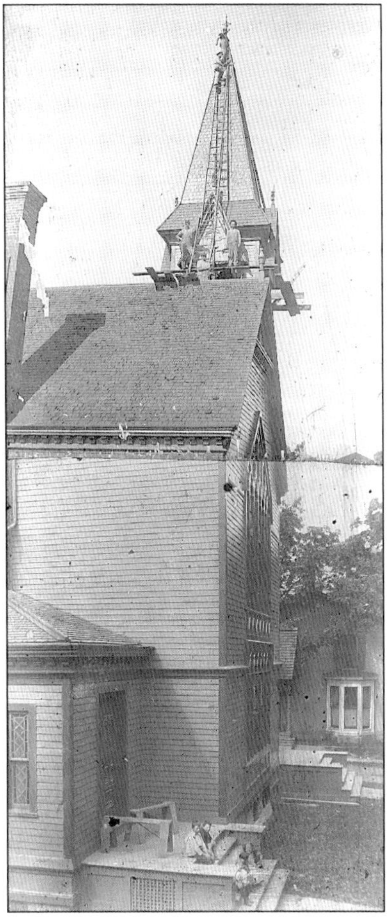

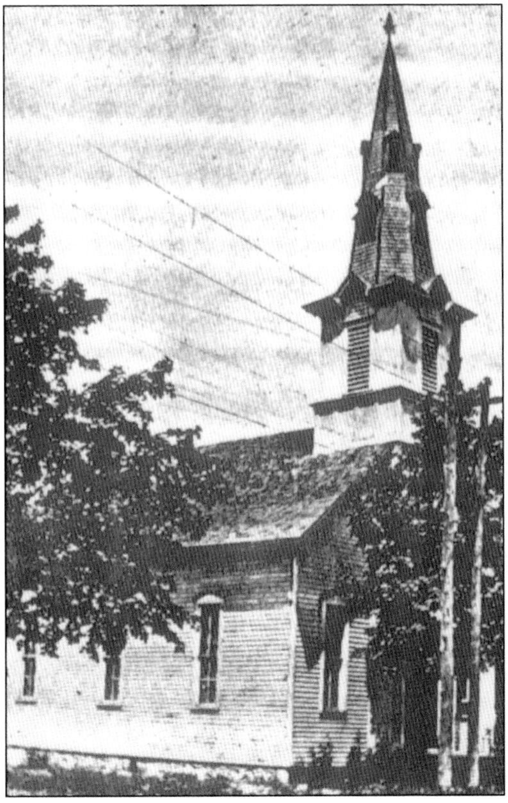

The Immanuel Lutheran Church was organized in 1880 as the United Evangelical Emanuel Congregation. Property was bought on Pine Street and, while this frame structure was being completed, the members met in the basement of the Presbyterian church. The new building was dedicated on March 22, 1881.

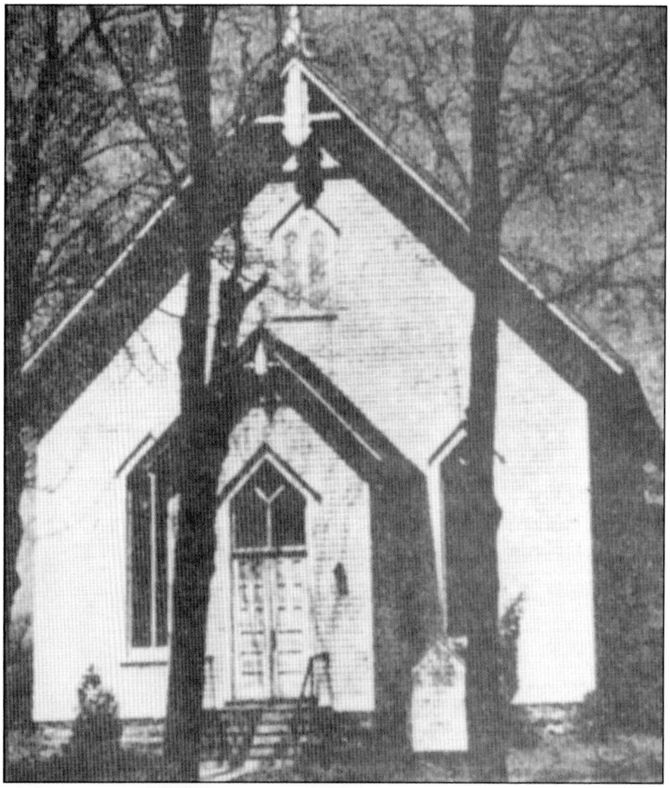

In 1951, the Wesleyan Methodist congregation purchased the former Universalist church building, which was erected in 1844. The supporting timbers of this structure were hewn out of white pine logs with a broadax, and are 40 feet long. The sanctuary contained the first chandelier in East Aurora, a large wheel holding 100 candles, designed by an East Aurora tinsmith. In 1866, the roof was raised, stained-glass windows were installed, and the bell tower was removed. The Sunday school was the original St. Mathias Episcopal church. It was moved across Maple Street (from east to west) and attached to the back of the Universalist sanctuary.

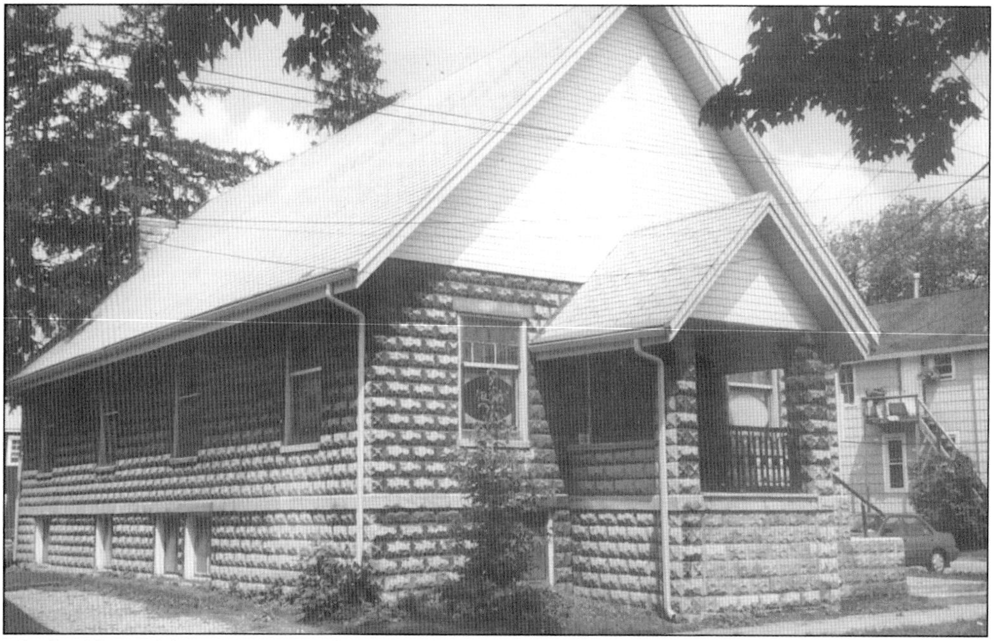

The building of the First Spiritualist Temple was completed in December 1911. H.W. Richardson purchased the land with the legal assistance of Wells Parker. A captain's chair, built in 1852 by Henry Morrow, an East Aurora cabinetmaker, was presented to the society on August 26, 1902. The chair is still used for special occasions. The temple is located on Temple Place.

Eight

HAMLETS

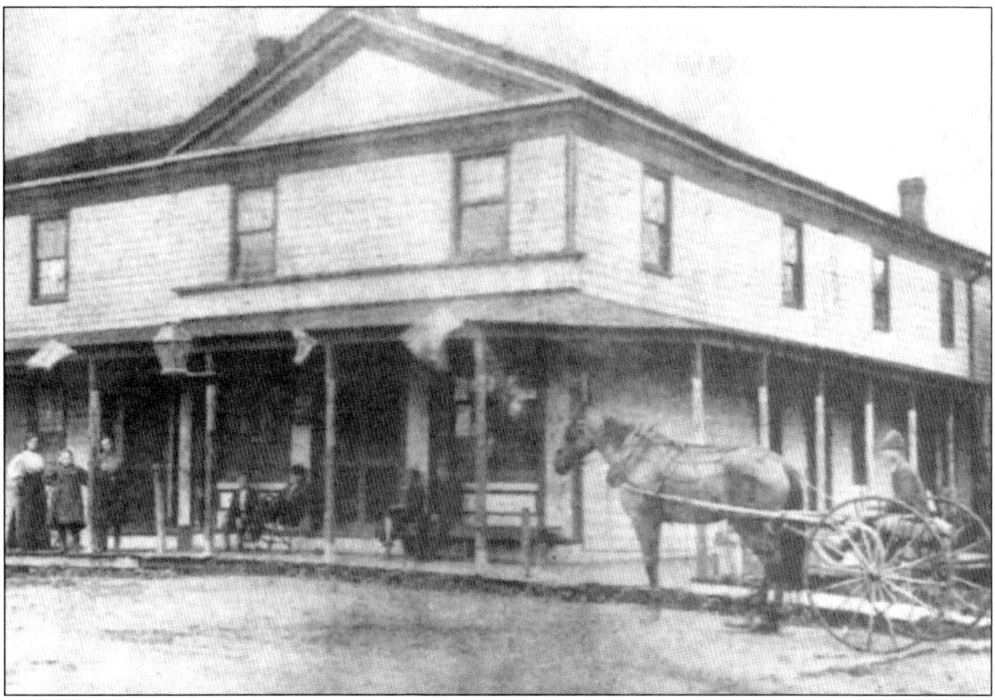

The West Falls Hotel, known later as the Dog Bar, is shown here as it was decorated for the Fourth of July. The date of this photograph is not known, but it was taken from a tintype, which was first used in 1856. The hotel has been operated continuously either as a hotel or tavern since 1809. Note the high-wheeled sulky on the right.

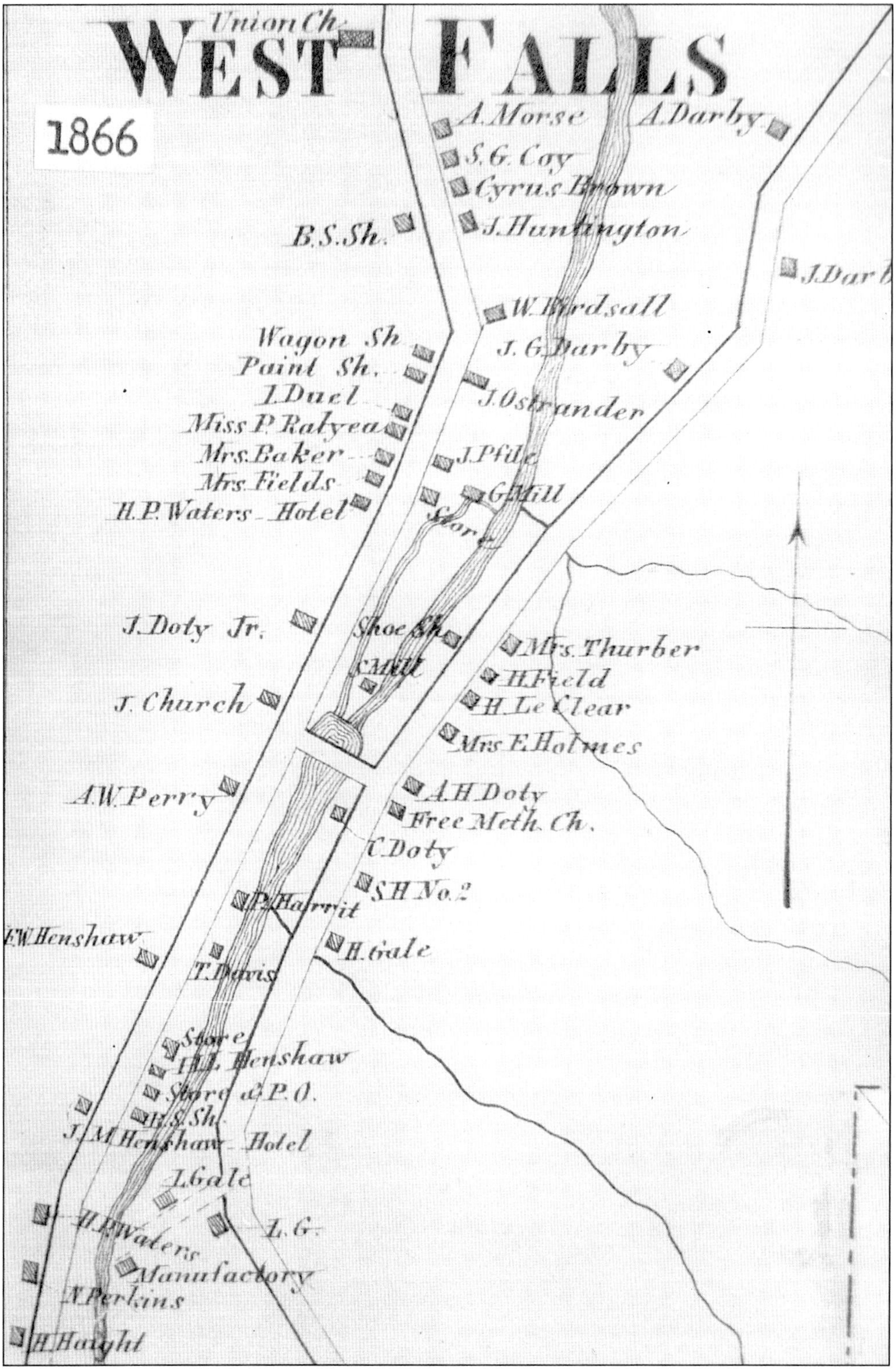

This map of West Falls is from 1866.

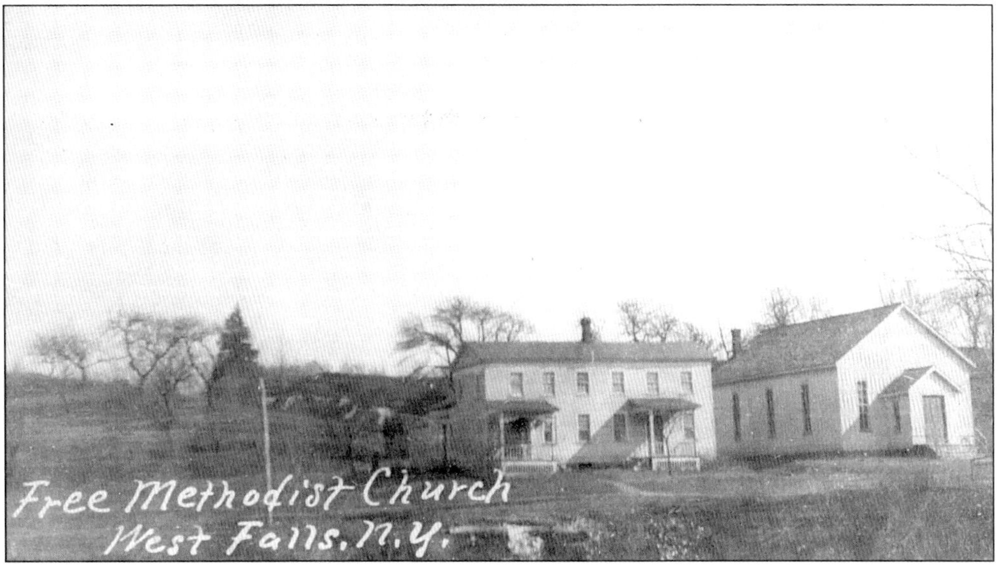

This West Falls Free Methodist church was demolished *c.* 1910.

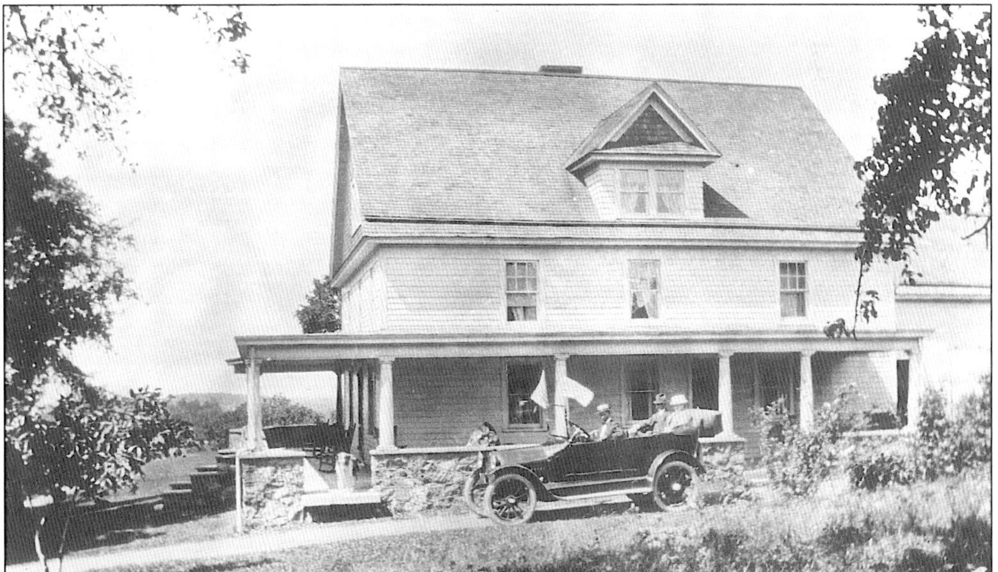

In 1831, Richard Reading and his son traveled from England to West Falls via the Erie Canal and bought 375 acres of wooded land, which they cleared. Over the past 169 years, the farm has produced oxen, vegetables, milk, grain, and eggs. It is now operated by Linda Reading Jackson and her husband, Mark; they raise hay and breed thoroughbred horses. Their daughter, Holly, is the seventh generation to live in this original farmhouse. (Courtesy of Richard Reading.)

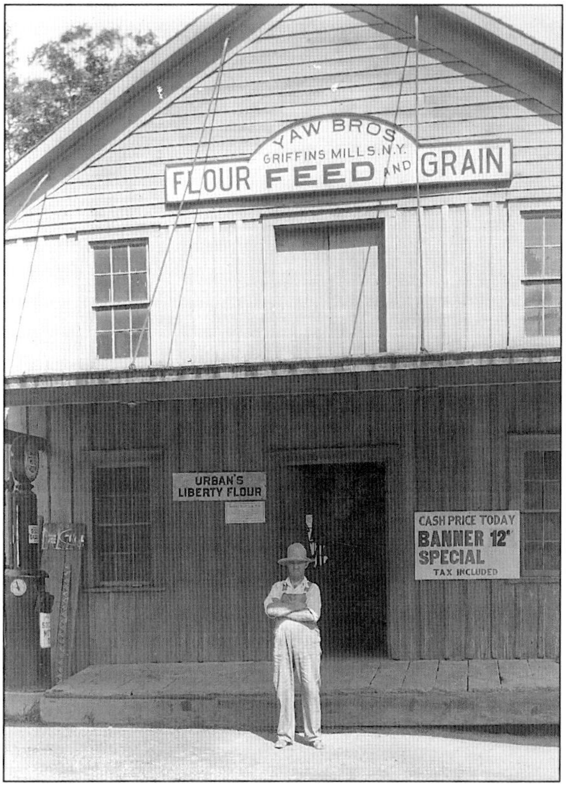

Frank Yaw stands in front of the Yaw Brothers feed mill in Griffins Mills.

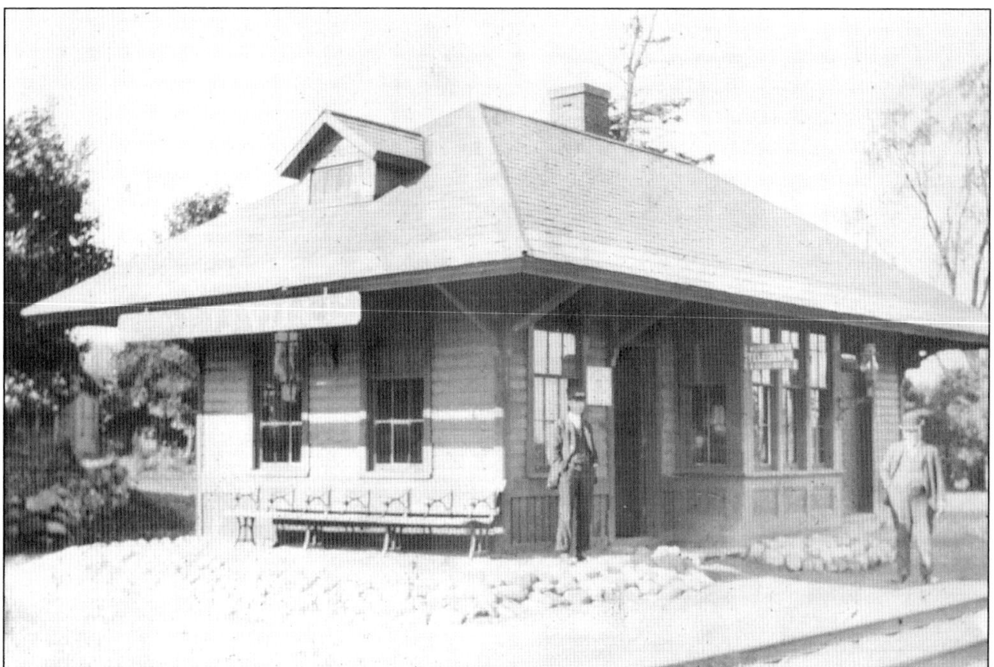

Around 1887, the Jewetts built this Jewettville Railroad Station in order to ship their famous horses. The station was torn down in 1963.

This is an 1880 map of Griffins Mills.

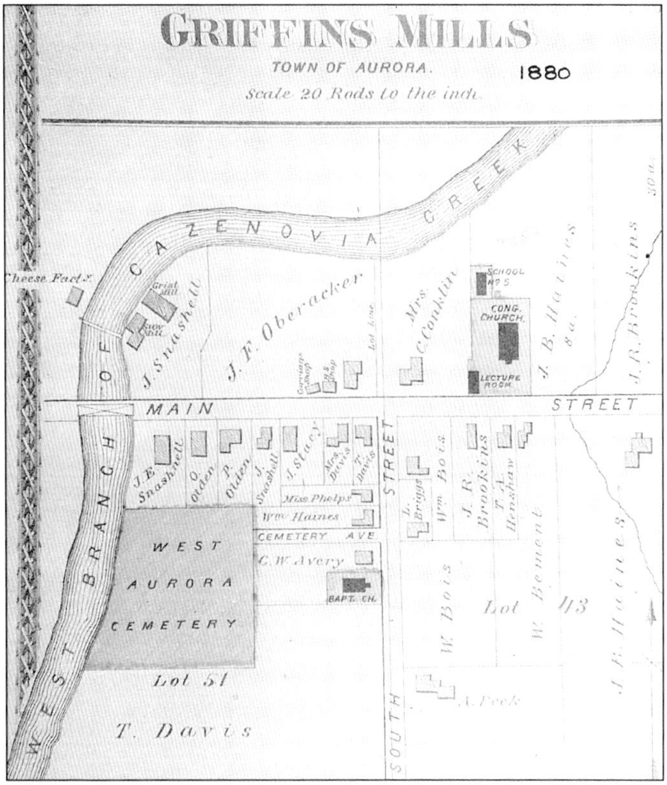

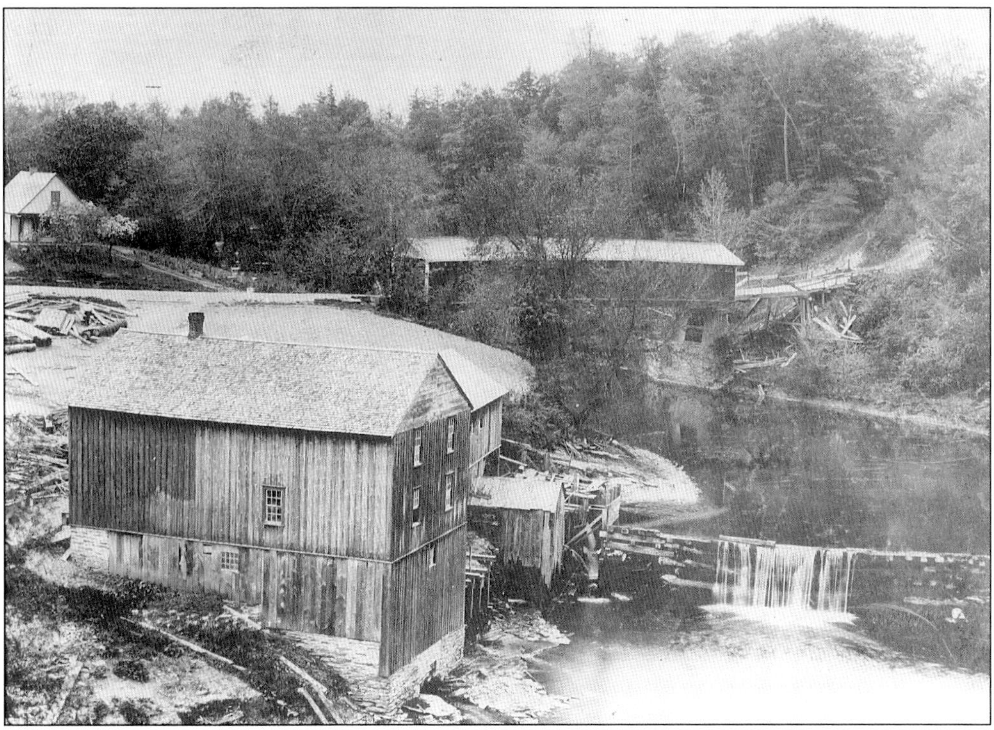

This gristmill and sawmill was established in Griffins Mills c. 1809.

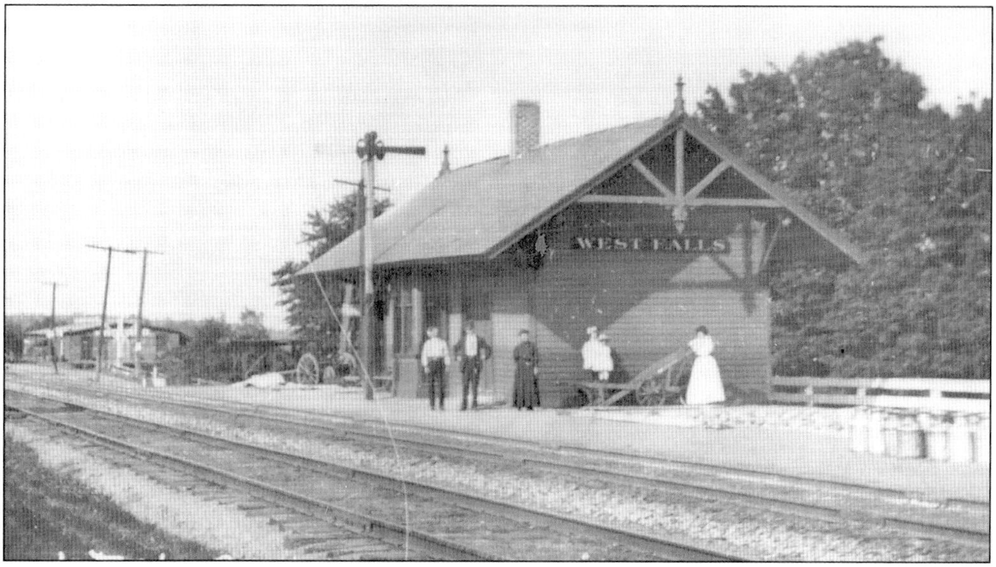

The Rochester and Pittsburgh Railroad established the first railroad station in West Falls in the early 1800s. George Dascomb, the stationmaster, came to work in West Falls in 1882. He lived at Mrs. Woods's boardinghouse. The station burned in 1915.

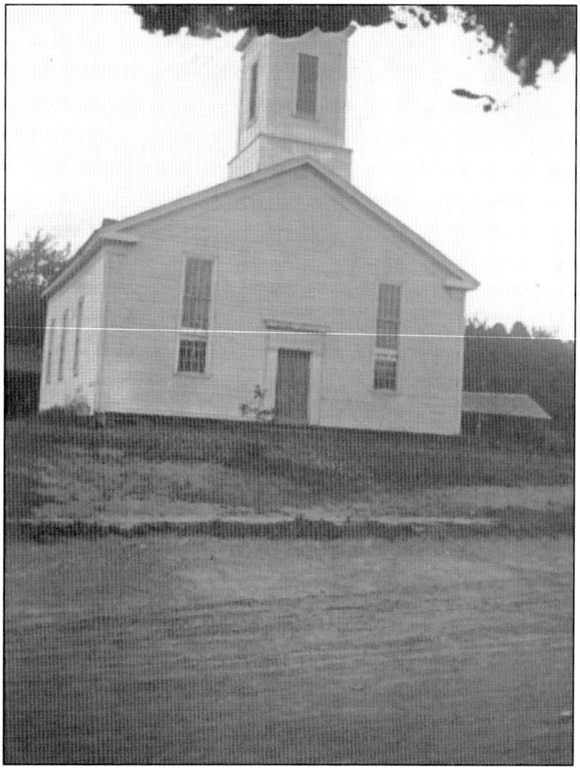

This postcard shows the Union Church of West Falls. The message written on the back of this card reads, "Here, over forty years ago, Kendall held a revival fruitful in spiritual results, some of which abide to this day." The people of West Falls organized and built one church building. For Sunday services, the Baptists met in the morning and the Methodists in the afternoon. The Methodist minister preached in Boston in the morning, in West Falls in the afternoon, and in Colden in the evening. His salary ranged from $100 to $200 per year, plus donations of farm produce.

The Presbyterian Church in Griffins Mills was founded on August 18, 1810, as the West Aurora Congregational Church. This building was erected shortly after the War of 1812. The church has been restored to its original form. The "whiskey" tree rules the churchyard. Legend has it that this tree was purchased as a sapling for a pint of whiskey.

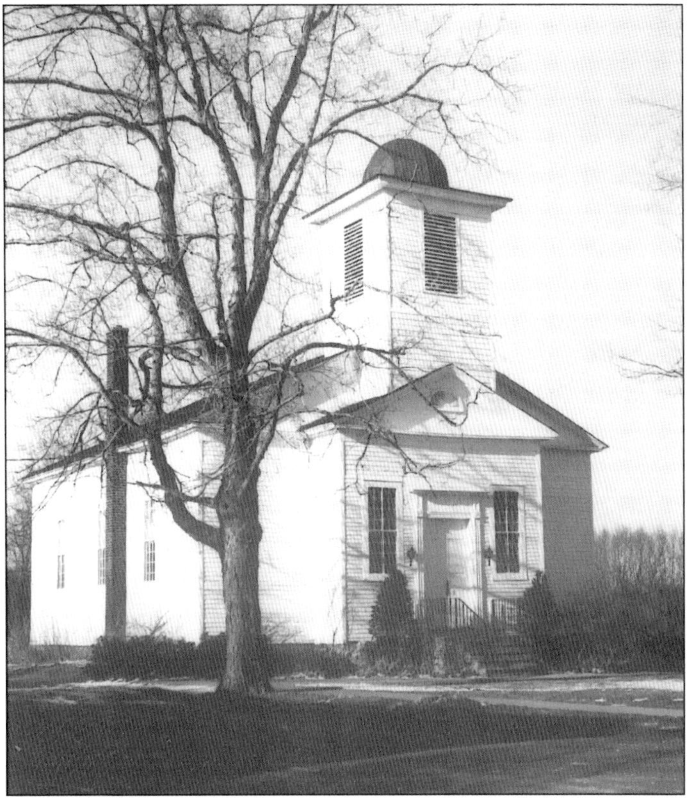

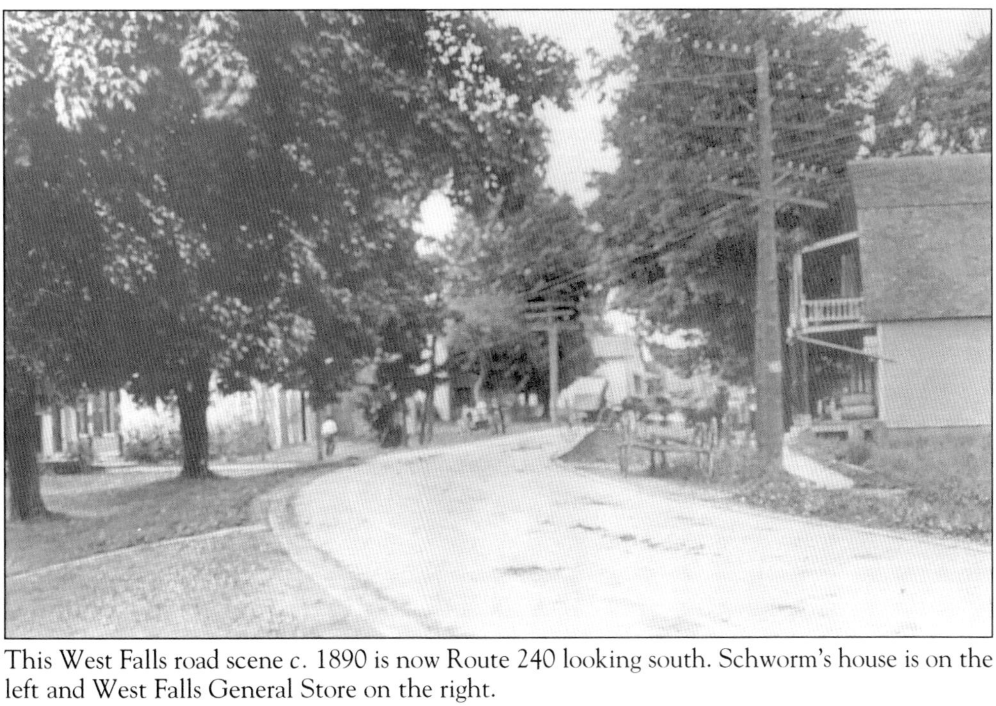

This West Falls road scene *c*. 1890 is now Route 240 looking south. Schworm's house is on the left and West Falls General Store on the right.

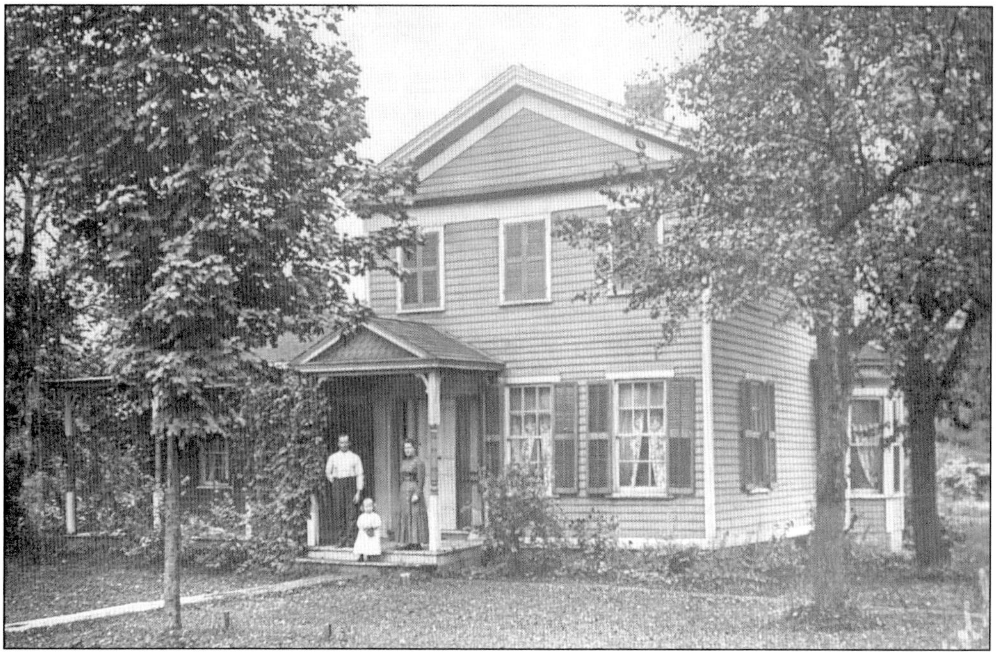

Here we see the three-year-old Katherine Schworm standing in front of her family home in West Falls *c.* 1911. The house is across the street from the West Falls General Store, where Katherine clerked from 1920 through the 1940s. She never married. During the war, she kept area service men in touch with each other through monthly letters. There were 50 service men in the group.

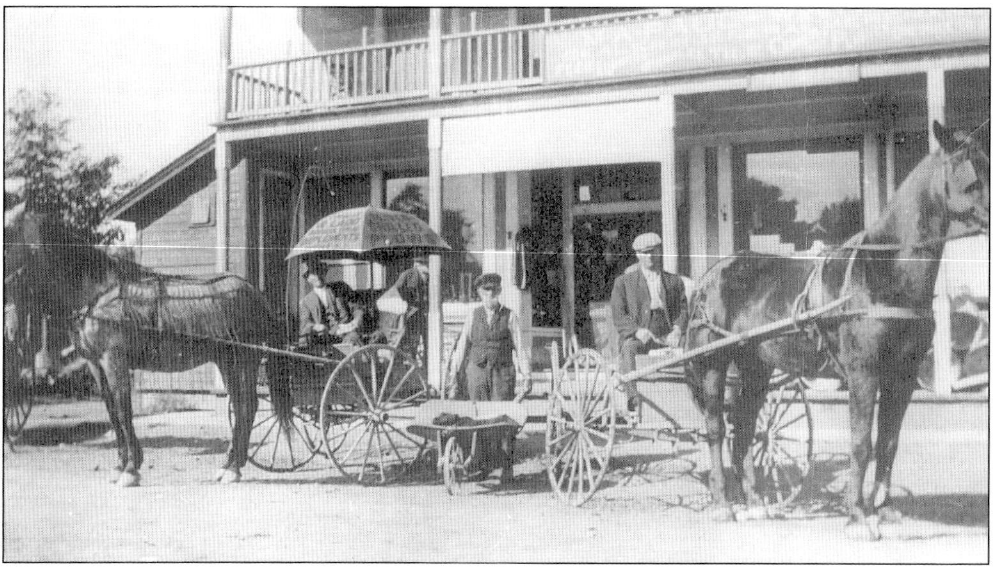

Shown is W.A. Paul's store in West Falls. The note on the back of this photograph reads, "Grandpa Fred Darbee with wheelbarrow—sometimes he took the mail to the train in his wheelbarrow so he could bring a bag of feed home for the cow and chickens; otherwise, he took a little pack of mail on a cane over his shoulder."

In 1914, this brick road was built between East Aurora and South Wales.

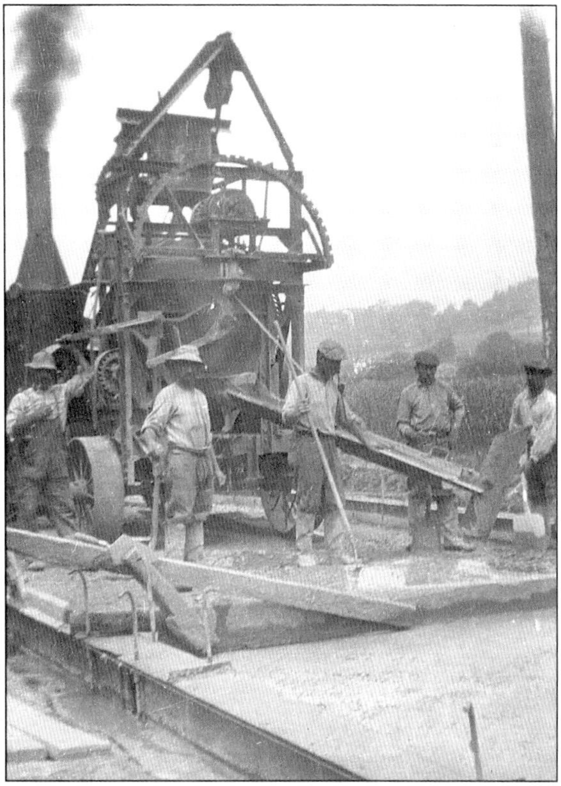

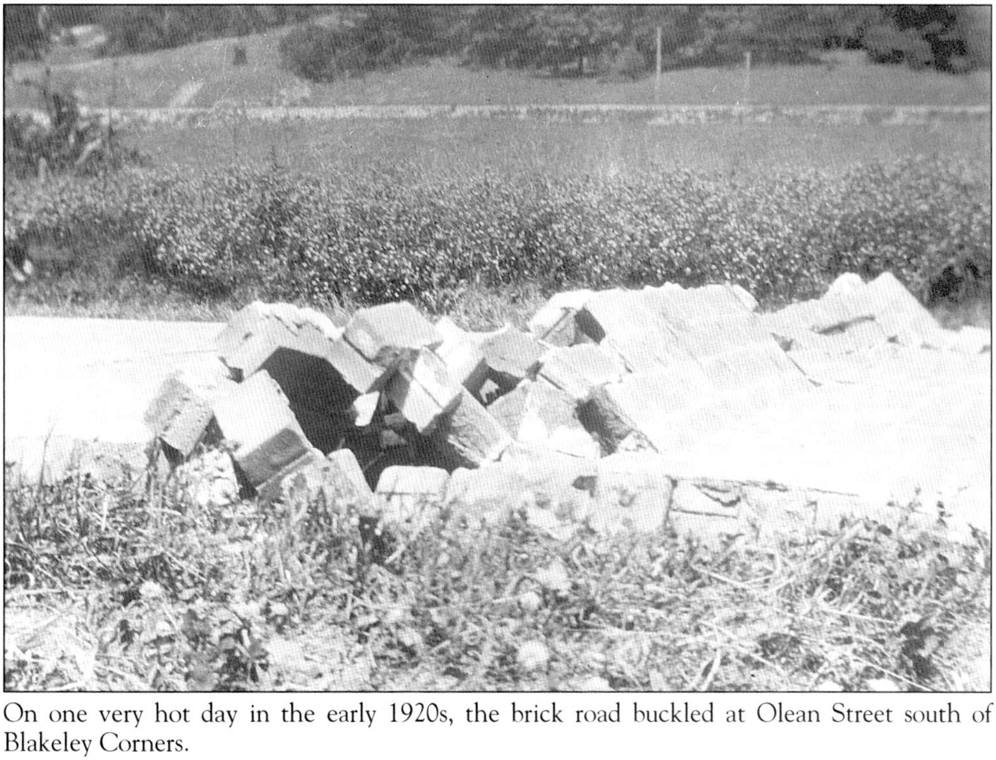

On one very hot day in the early 1920s, the brick road buckled at Olean Street south of Blakeley Corners.

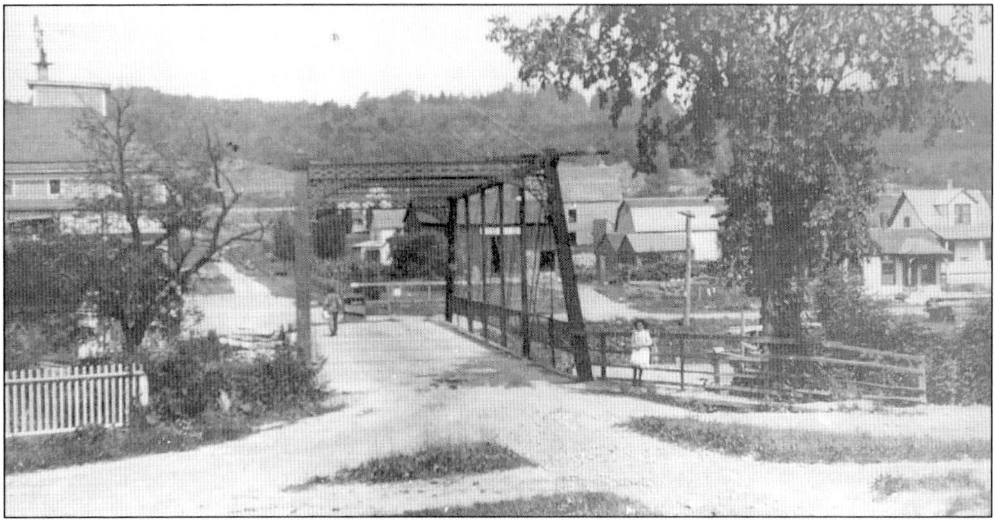

This view, looking west from the Free Methodist church, shows the West Falls bridge. When the bridge was torn down in 1920, a group of teenagers spent a Saturday night moving the steel to Mr. Snyder's driveway. They thought they could keep him from driving his Model T. They watched Sunday morning from the bushes. When Snyder came out of his house, he looked at the steel and then walked to church, as his Model T was at a local repair shop. The boys then put the steel back! On the back of this postcard sent to Mrs. O.T. Brown, 506 Swan Street, Buffalo is written, "The weather is perfect. Just like summer. Everybody well. Am having a wonderful time. Clara."

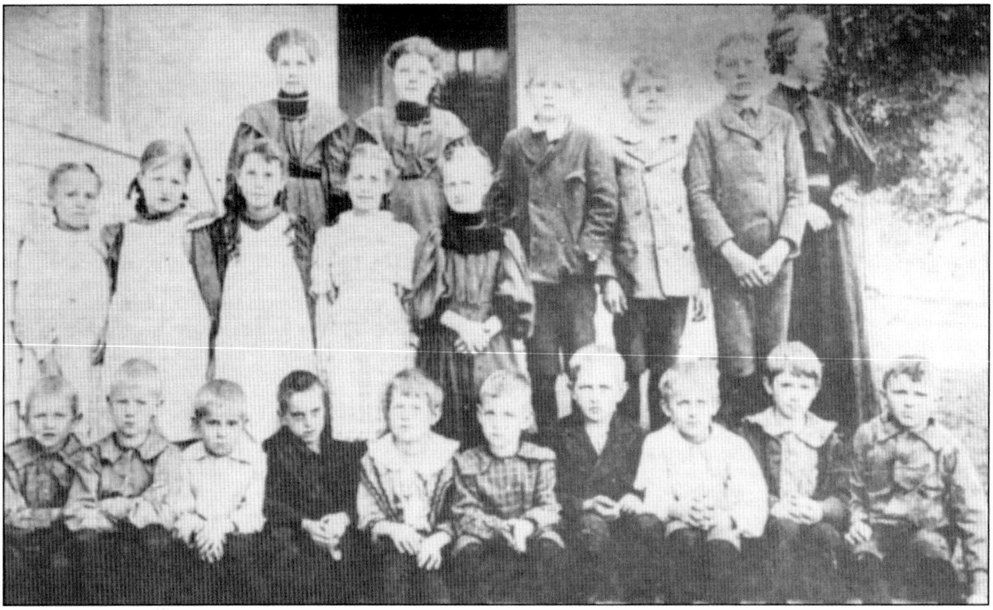

The children of the 1897 West Falls School are, from left to right, as follows: (front row) Andrew Vanderlin, Otto Stockman, Howard Henrich, Clarence Thurber, Arthur Perkins, Frank Stockman, Allen Holmes, Elmer Heinrich, Oakley Creedeman, and Fred Haas; (middle row) unidentified, Jessie Darbee, Lillian Ritter, Sarah Reading, and Helen Van Armin; (back row) Ida Perkins, Marcia Perkins, George Decker, Frank Moore, Clarence Gerstung, and the teacher, Miss Franklin.

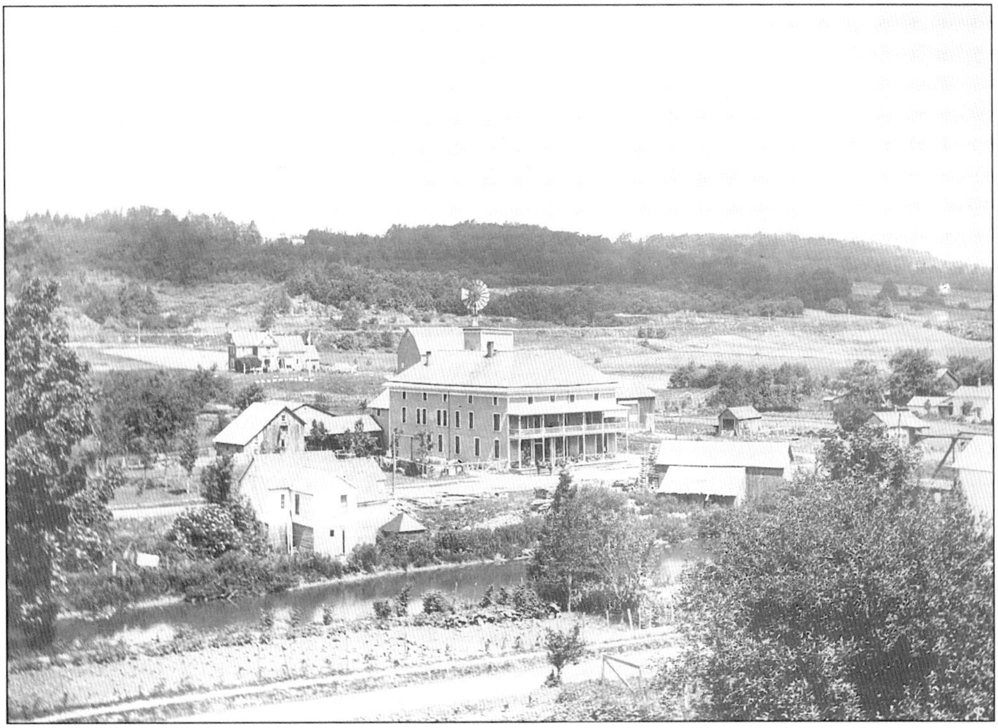

Myron Paul's store is visible in the center of this picture. At the extreme right is a portion of the steel bridge at the intersection of Route 240 and Bridge Street, West Falls. (Courtesy of Richard Reading.)

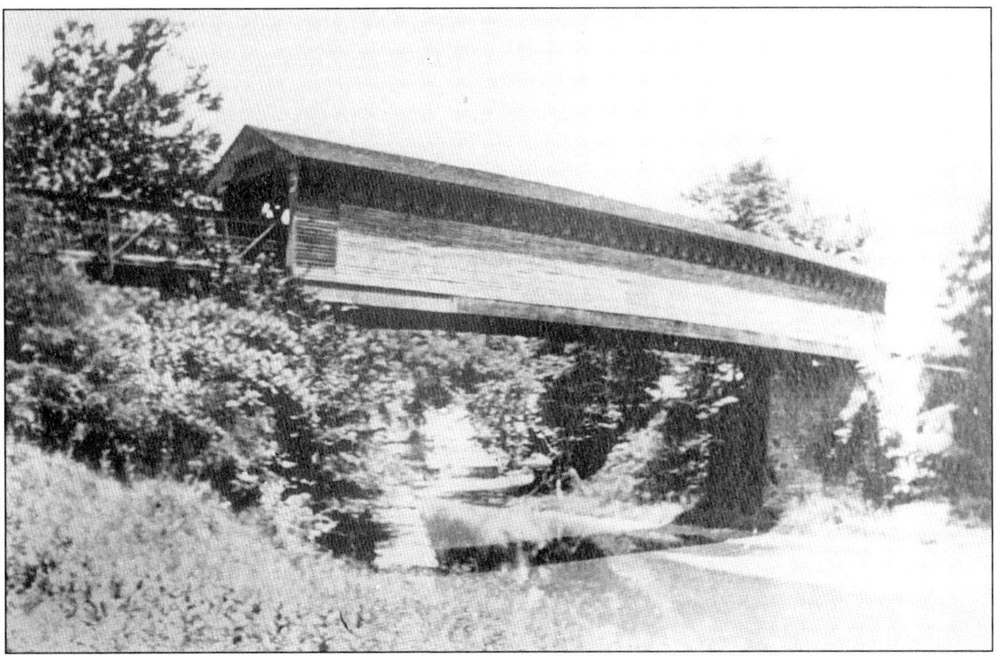

This covered bridge over the West Branch of Cazenovia Creek in Griffins Mills was built in 1867. It was painted red. The bridge was torn down in 1924 and replaced with a steel structure.

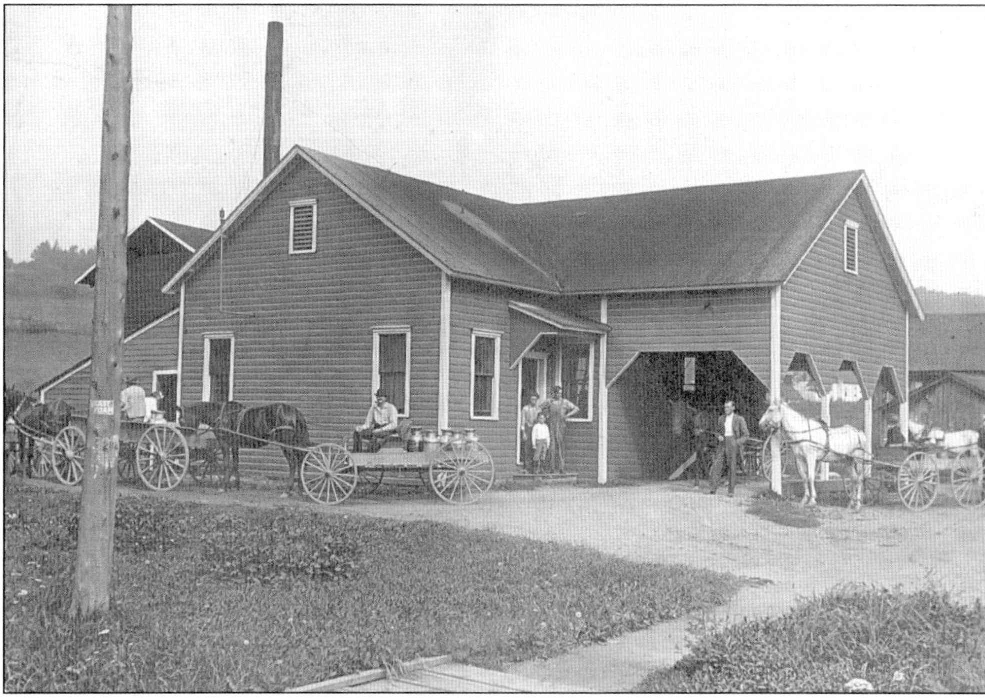

This creamery, or butter factory, in West Falls was the place farmers brought their excess cream to be made into butter and cheese. An old story tells of a farmer who brought in his cream and asked to have it made into butter. He mentioned that a mouse had fallen into the cream so he would appreciate it if the butter made from it would be exchanged for that of someone else. The management agreed, but without telling him, gave back to the farmer the butter made from his own cream. (Courtesy of Richard Reading.)

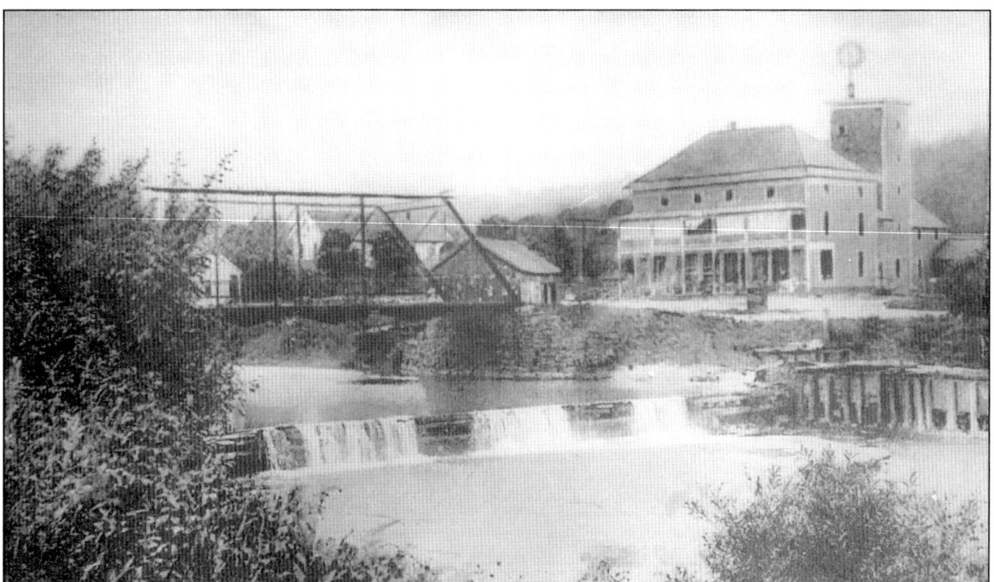

At the intersection of Route 240 and Bridge Street, this view looks across Cazenovia Creek to Myron Paul's store. The blacksmith shop stands beside the store.

Nine

AROUND TOWN

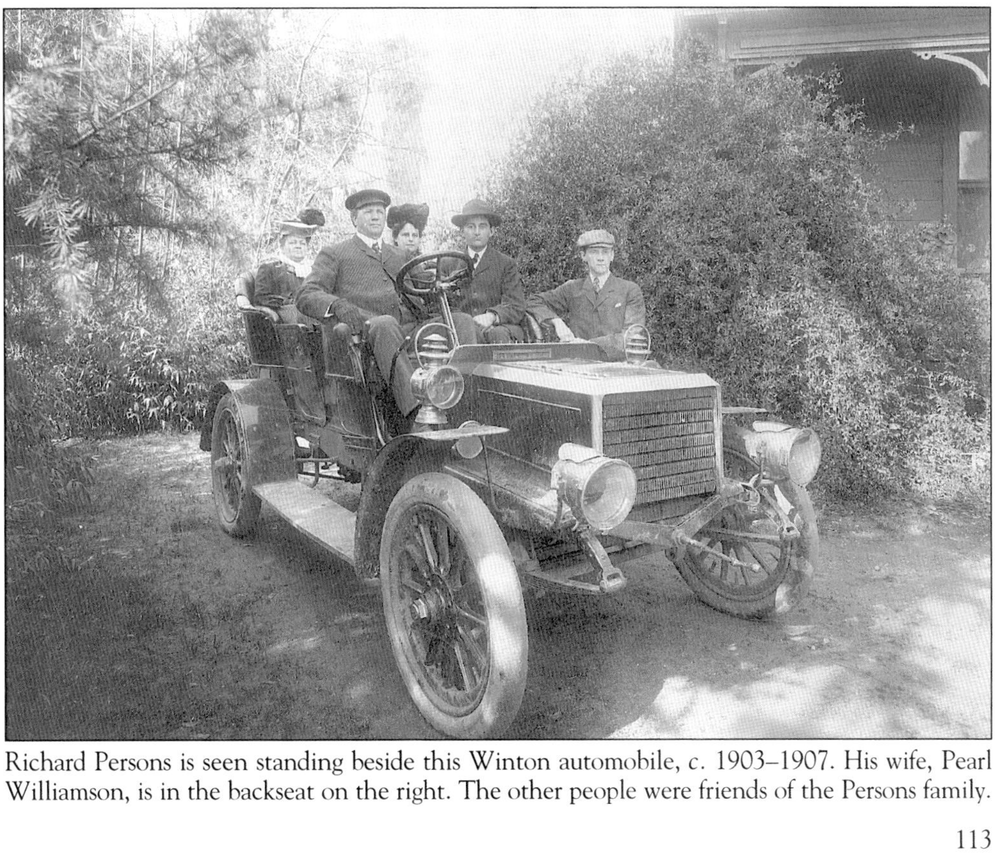

Richard Persons is seen standing beside this Winton automobile, *c.* 1903–1907. His wife, Pearl Williamson, is in the backseat on the right. The other people were friends of the Persons family.

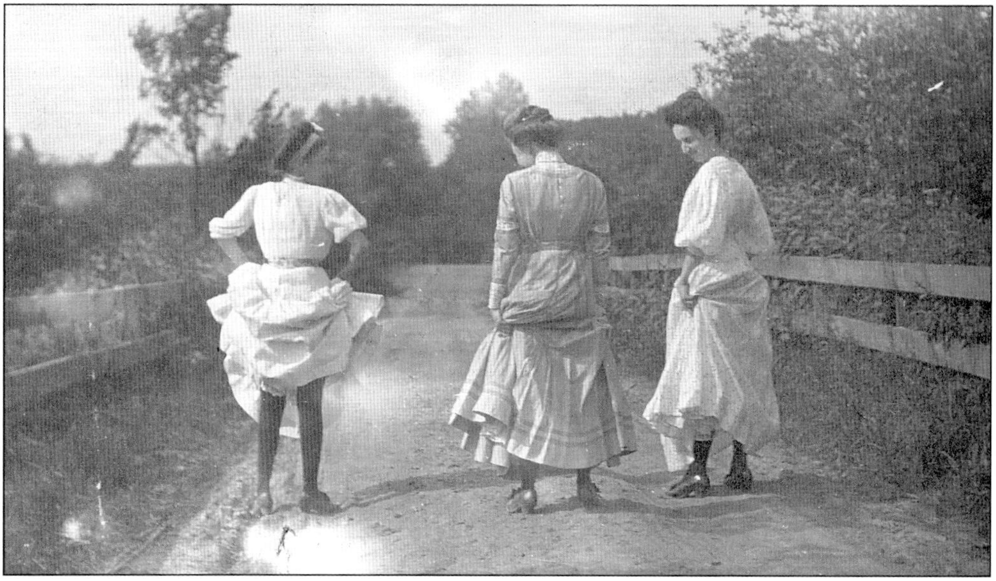

Mary French Tackbary, at the far left, is seen walking with friends down a road at Sinking Ponds in East Aurora.

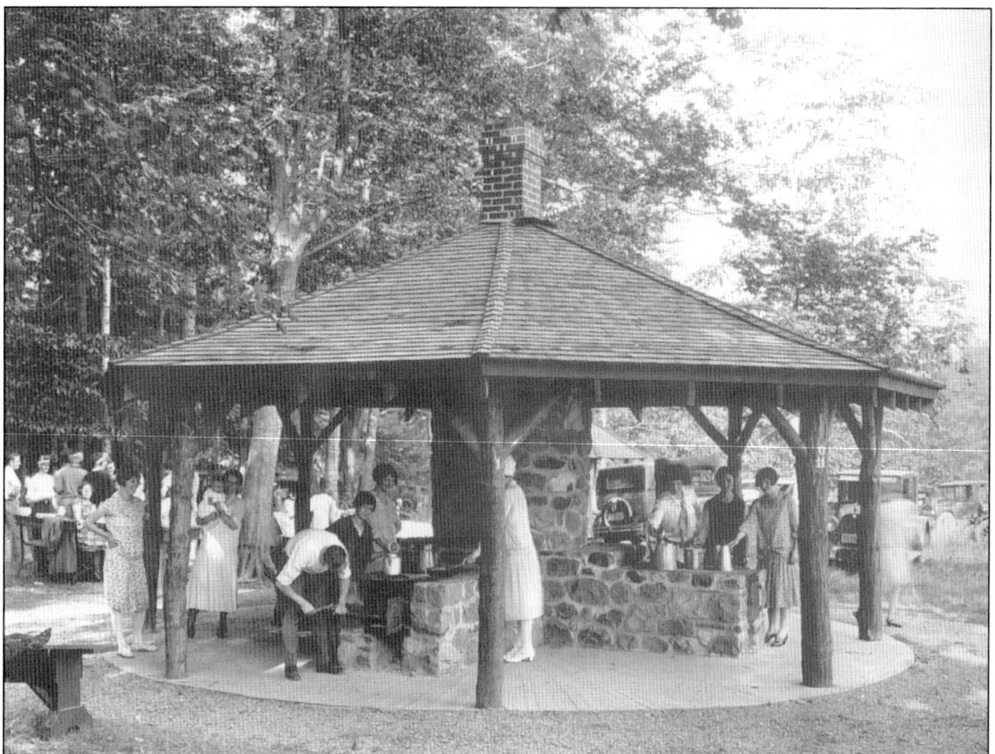

Colony Oven at Emery Park was developed as an all-season park. There are many pieces of play equipment for children, a ski lodge with a ski tow, and tennis courts. Many picnic areas were built throughout the 481 acres. It has been a favorite recreation area for Aurora citizens since 1924.

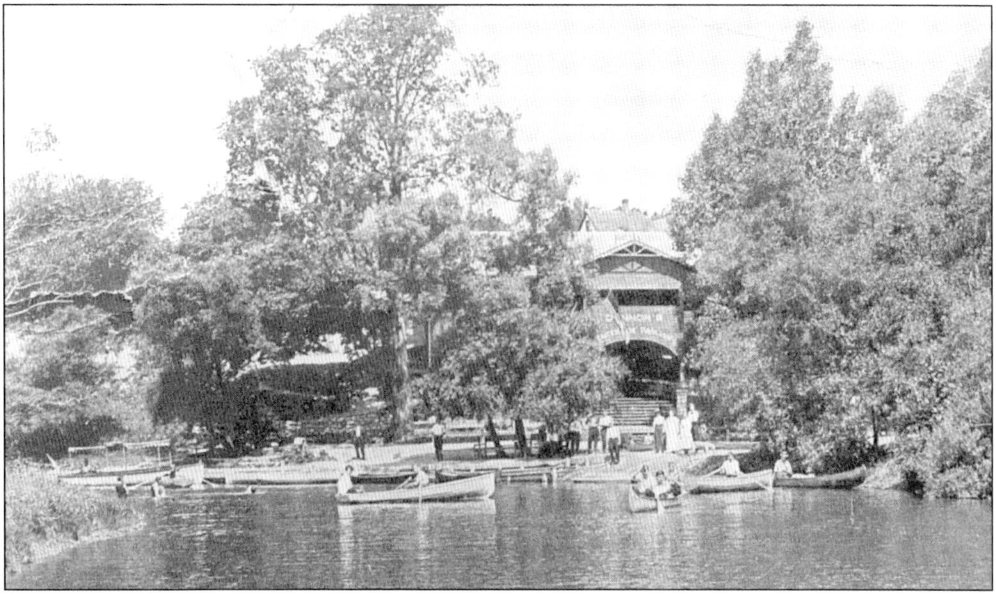

Donnor's Creekside appears in this 1900 image. In 1896, Mr. and Mrs. Robert J. Donnor bought land from Harvey W. Richardson on South Street, where they built Creekside Park. Cazenovia Creek was the southern boundary. A large pavilion was built into the hillside. The dance floor was considered one of the best in the area. On Sundays, there were hundreds of people at the park from East Aurora, Buffalo, and all of western New York. It was known as "the place to be." Canoeing and boating were also popular attractions.

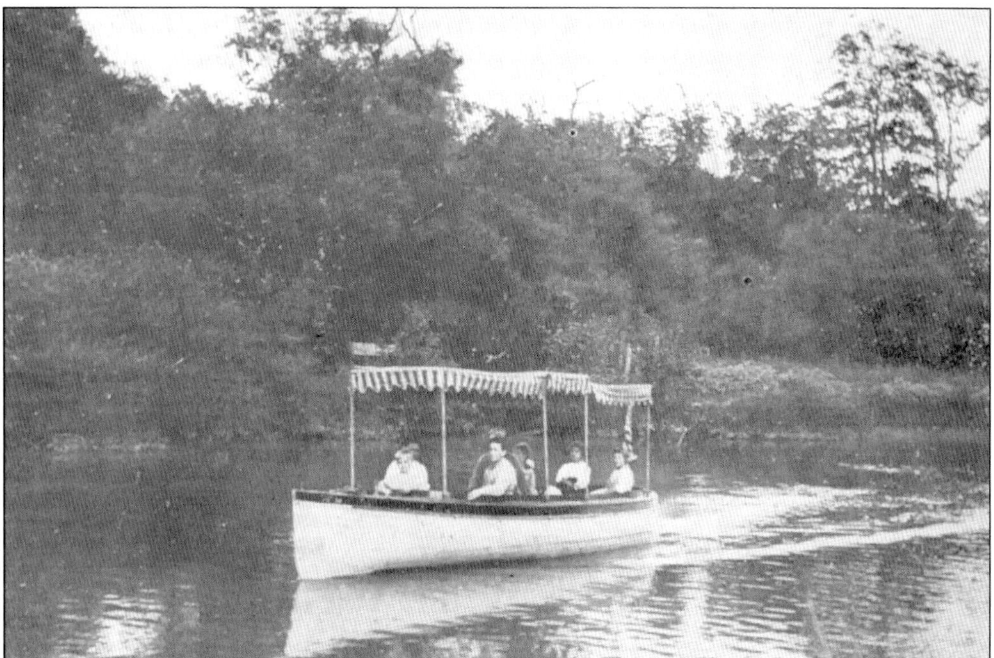

The "Arrow" was a pleasure boat for rides on Cazenovia Creek. This image appears on a postcard mailed from East Aurora on July 7, 1913 to Mrs. Grace Zimmer, Sardinia, New York. It is signed, "Nellie."

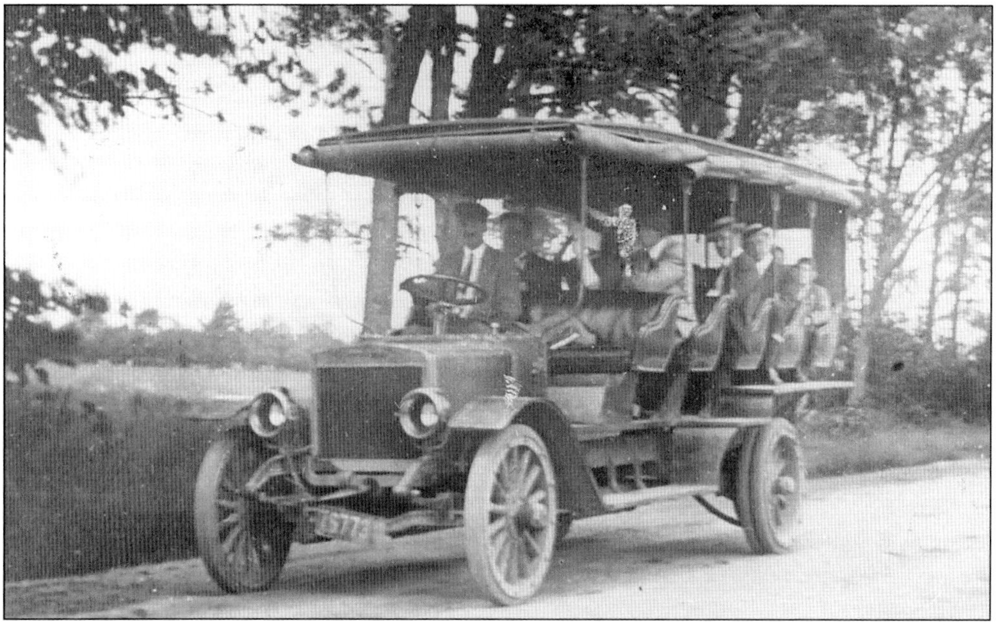

Pioneer bus service between East Aurora and Buffalo was provided in this vehicle. The ride was neither fast nor comfortable. Passengers were protected from weather only by the canvas drop sides. The passengers, from left to right, are Irving Ogilvie, Edward Cummings, unidentified, and William Quade.

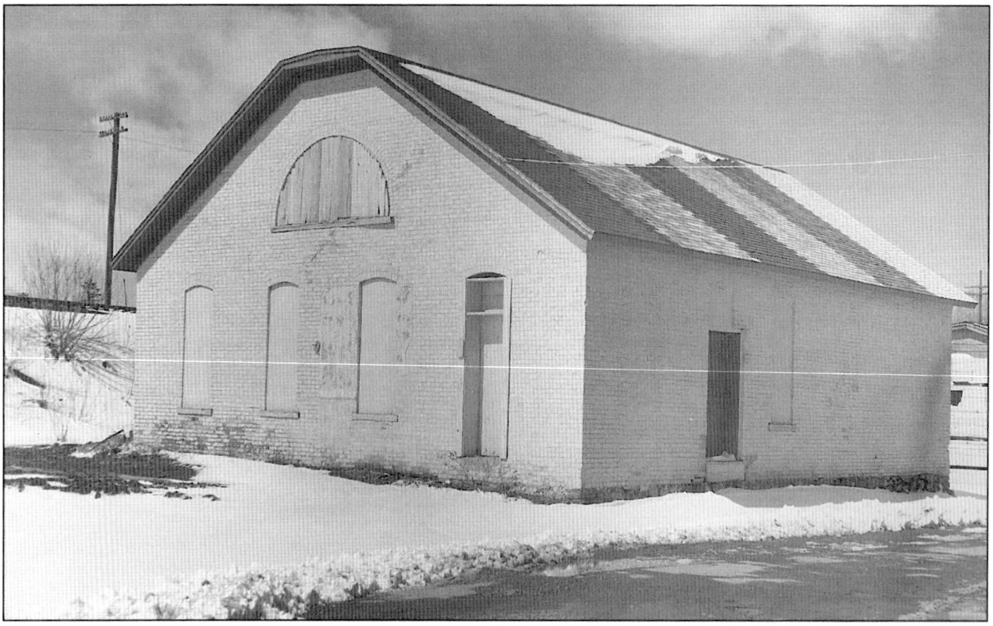

East Aurora's first electric light current was produced in this building on Elm Street south of Oakwood Avenue.Three men—Henry H. Persons, H.W. Richardson, and R.F. Whaley—met to form a company to furnish electric light to the village of East Aurora. On January 10, 1891, the plant was ready for use. This enterprise was an experiment, but it was such a success that within a year the capacity of the plant was doubled. This meant that 1,800 lights could be used. In June 1903, the business was moved to Mill Street.

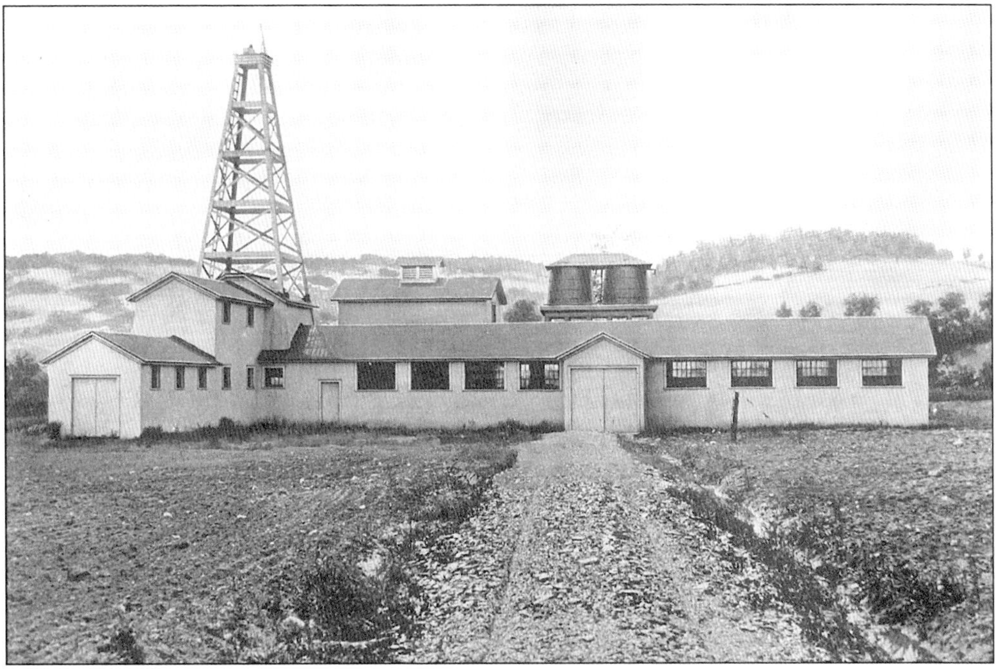

The Narenta Mineral Springs Company was on the south side of Jewett-Holmwood Road between Grover and Davis Roads. This photograph was taken in 1911. The company's motto was, "The source of the greatest natural laxative spring water that has ever been discovered."

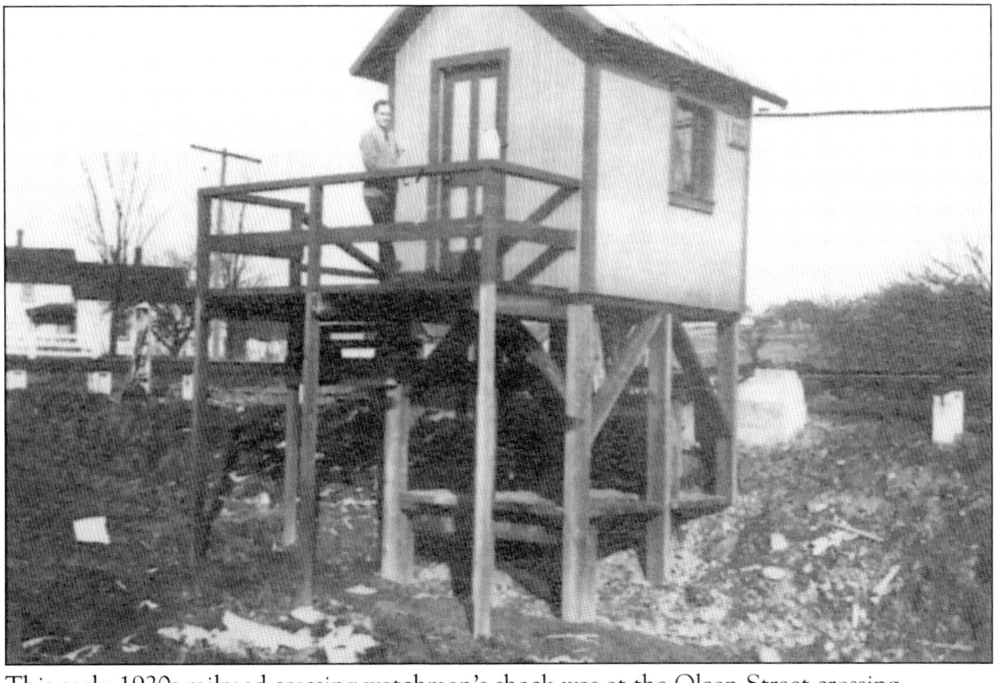

This early-1920s railroad crossing watchman's shack was at the Olean Street crossing.

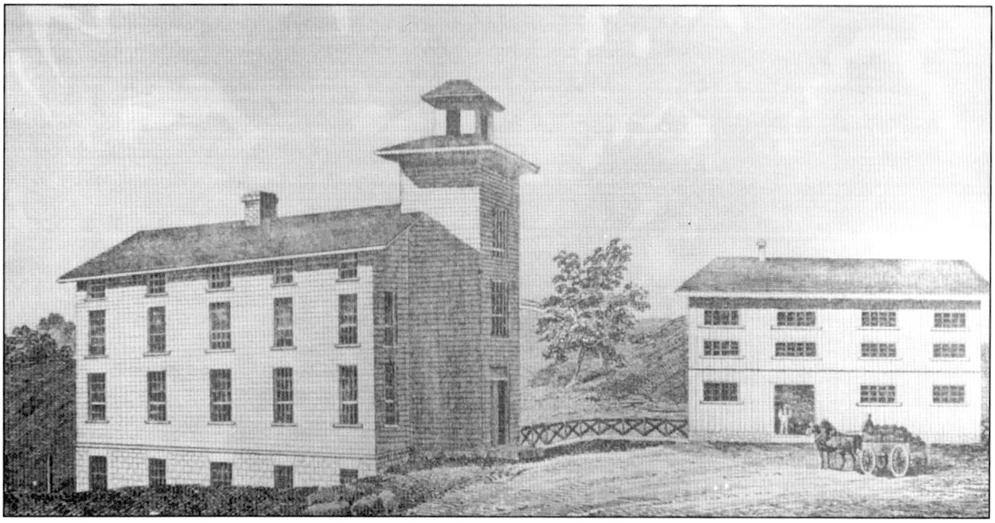

Joseph S. Bartlett had a carding and fulling mill, the Bartlett Woolen Mill, on Cazenovia Creek. The mill burned in 1865, and his sons John P. Bartlett, O. Allen Bartlett, and George Tory built a new factory in 1866. The four-story woolen mill stood on Mill Street near the present disposal plant. These men made their own dyes and manufactured yarn and blankets. One hundred pounds of wool and 60,000 pounds of yarn were produced annually. The business closed in 1882.

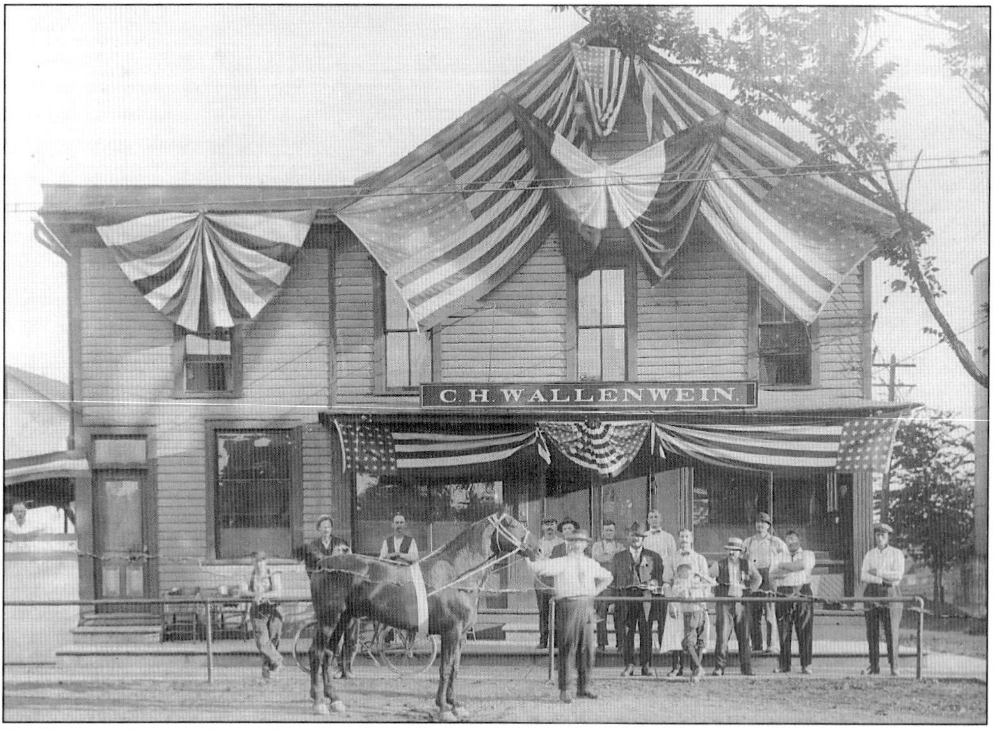

Wallenwein's on Oakwood Avenue is seen here as it appeared during Old Home Week in 1916. Charles Wallenwein owned this hotel, restaurant, and tavern. He was the local distributor for Lang's Beer. The beer was brought from Buffalo to the bottling works, which were attached to the store.

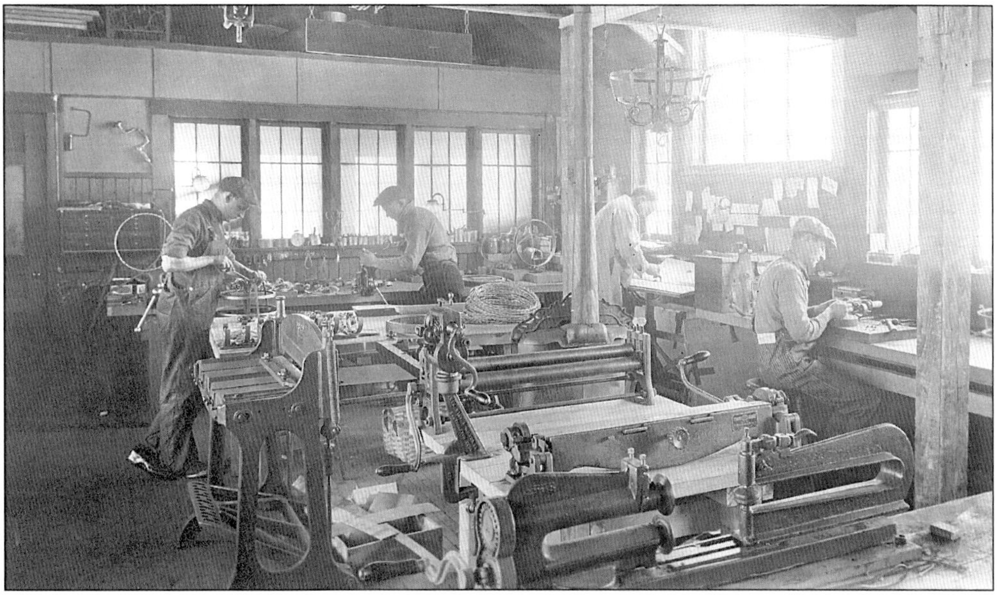

Victor Toothaker's shop at 70 Church Street is shown in 1920. Toothaker worked in the Roycroft Copper Shop as early as 1912. He designed the lighting fixtures for the Grove Park Inn in Asheville, North Carolina. The workers, from left to right, are ? Burton, unidentified, ? Varley. Seated at the bench is Henry Unverdorf. Fisher Toy Manufacturing began operations in this building in 1930.

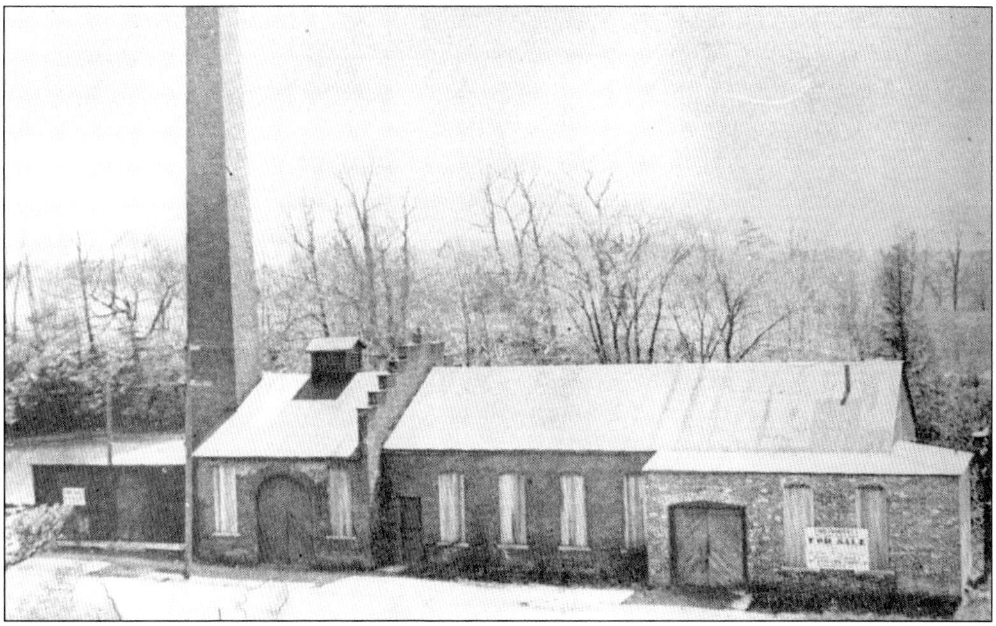

In June 1903, a new electric power plant was built on Mill Street. Two water wheels were installed along with two boilers for use when the water was low. The plant's three dynamos, the marble switchboard, and all the equipment made it one of the most modern plants in this section. The plant ran successfully until 1918, when it was sold to Dr. George Stevenson, who operated it until January 26, 1922. Stevenson then sold it to the Depew and Lancaster Light, Power, and Conduit Company.

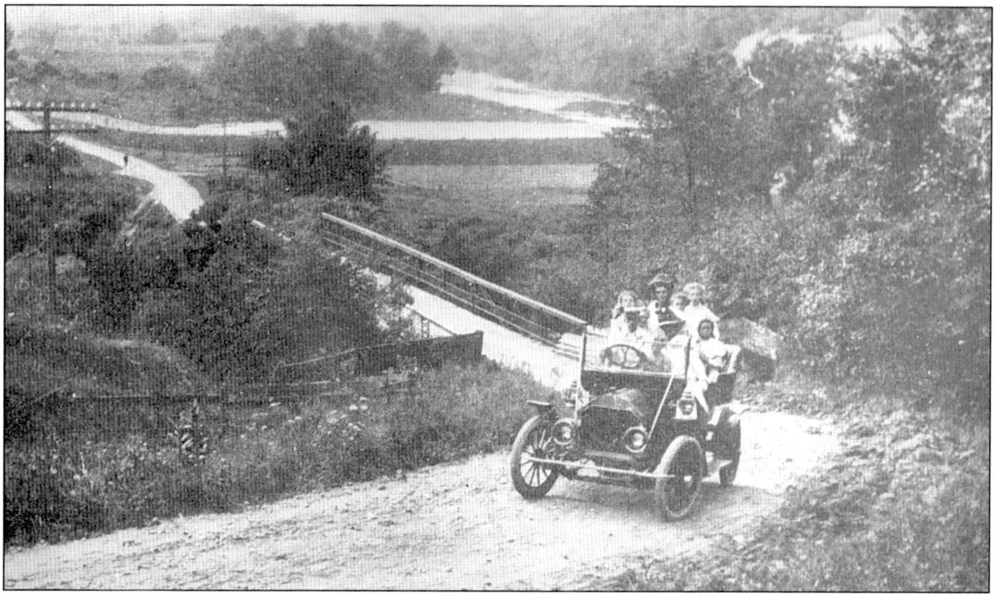

This 1909 Regal four-cylinder touring car, shown climbing Reed Hill near East Aurora, was carrying ten passengers.

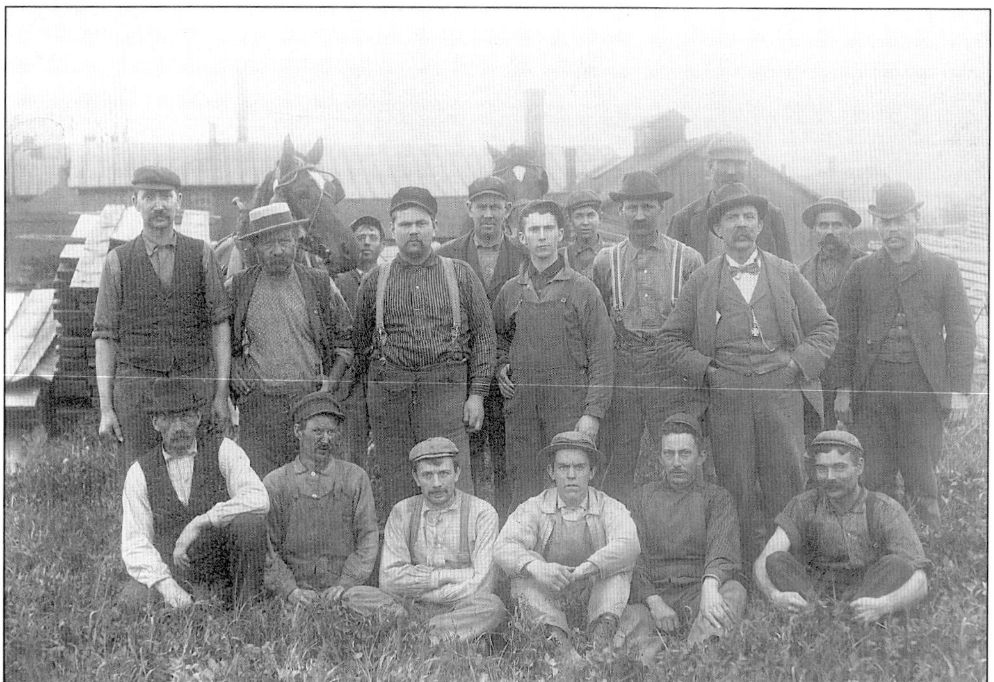

The workers standing in front of the large S.H. Peek and Son Foundry and Planing Mill are, from left to right, Gus Ensinger, ? Gasmire, Charles Criwe, William Regan, Frank Regan (foreman), ? Burnap, ? Essex, Luther Regan, Howard McMillan, Fred Billington, and Charles Dahlman. The picture was taken between 1910 and 1915 in front of the mill, which faced King Street.

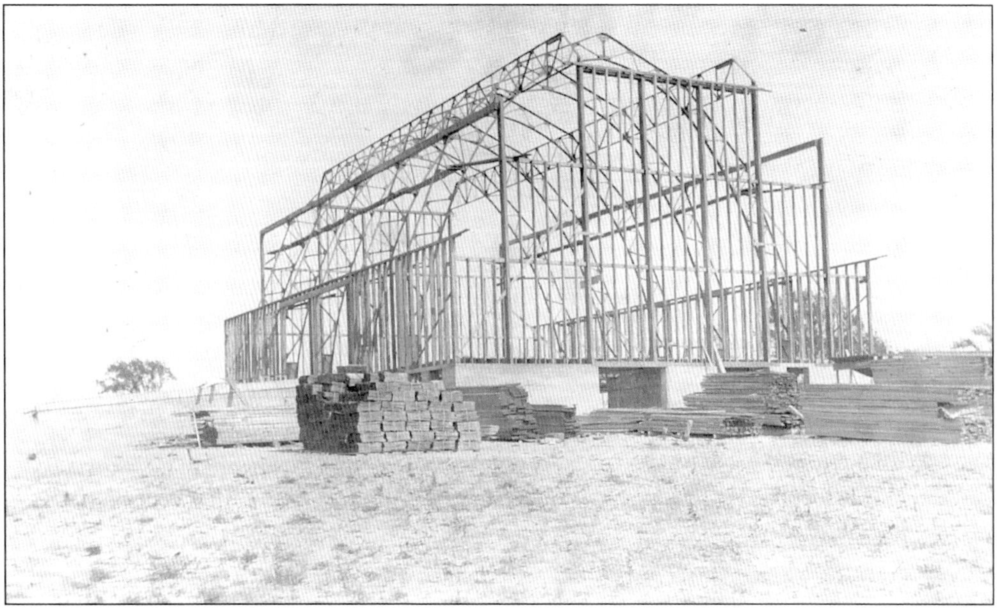

The Clement barn, on Beech Road, is seen here under construction. Steel was used to make the main arches and the five uprights. This frame was then covered with wood.

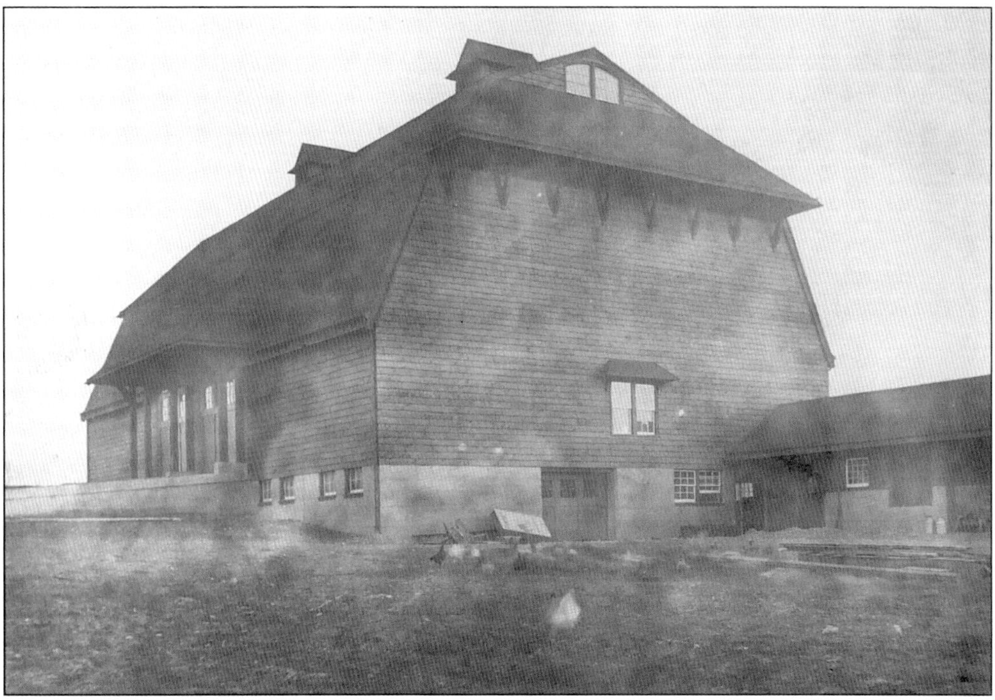

This view of the Clement Barn shows it as it looked *c.* 1912. The Elmhurst Special Milk Company was started by the Clement family. This dairy met the high quality standards required for certified milk, and it was medically recommended. Standards for milk production and distribution were improved because of this pioneer venture. Horse-drawn wagons and the milk-commuter trains delivered milk. The Elmhurst Company was in operation until 1932.

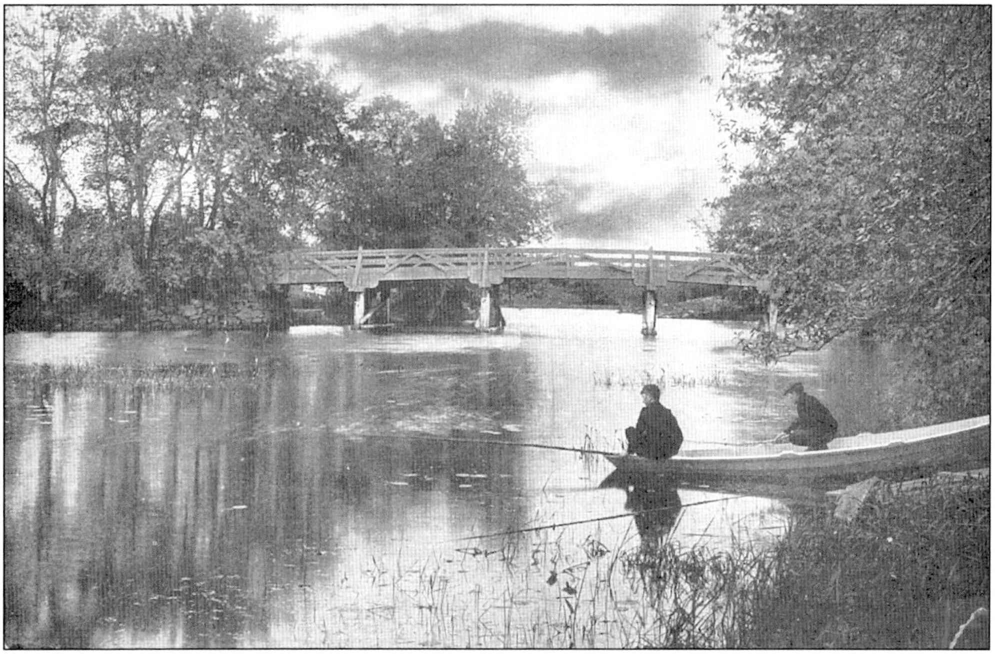

Butlin's Bridge spanned the east branch of Cazenovia Creek south of South Street and west of Olean Street. Butlin bought this bridge when a new one was built in Buffalo. He moved it to his pasture so his herd could cross the creek to graze.

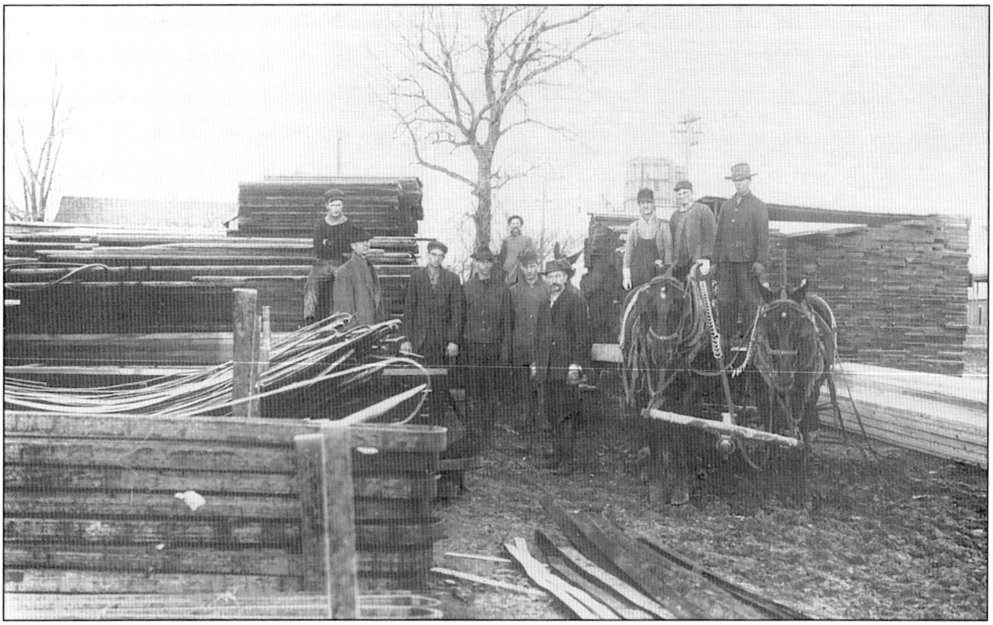

This photograph shows the crew of the Zink Lumber Company in East Aurora. The company was founded by Albert Otto August Zink sometime before 1914. This company was the central lumber supplier for East Aurora. Shortly after World War I, Zink sold the business to his nephew, Wallace Zapf. The company was the forerunner of Tenny Lumber. After selling the lumber business, Zink entered the automobile and tractor sales business, still under the name of Zink Lumber Company. (Courtesy of A. Louis Zink, grandson.)

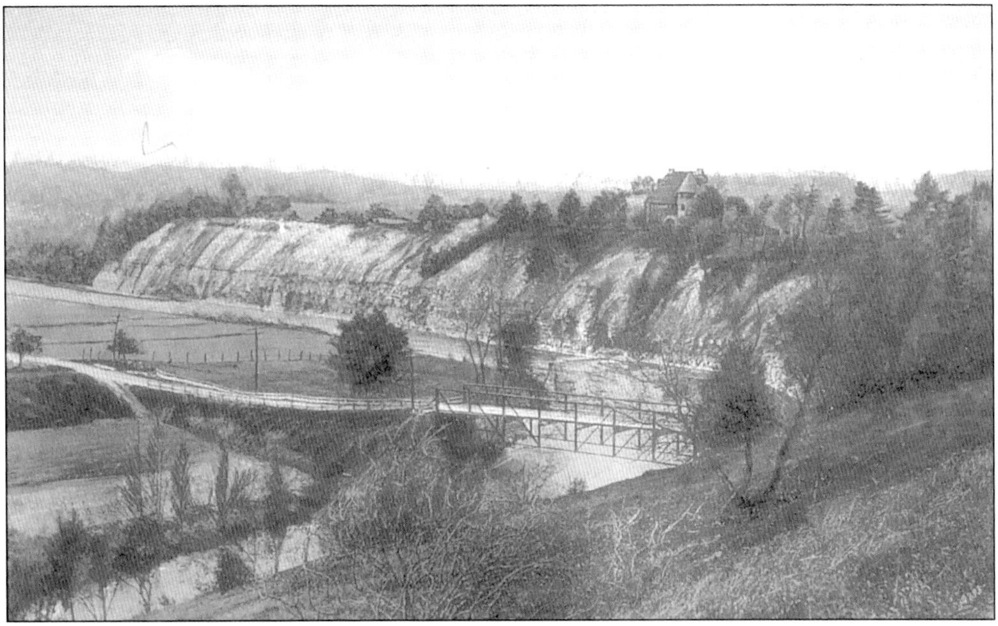

This scene on a penny postcard shows Cazenovia Creek and the Cornwall house known as Rushing Waters. The bridge and road in the foreground are now Route 20A.

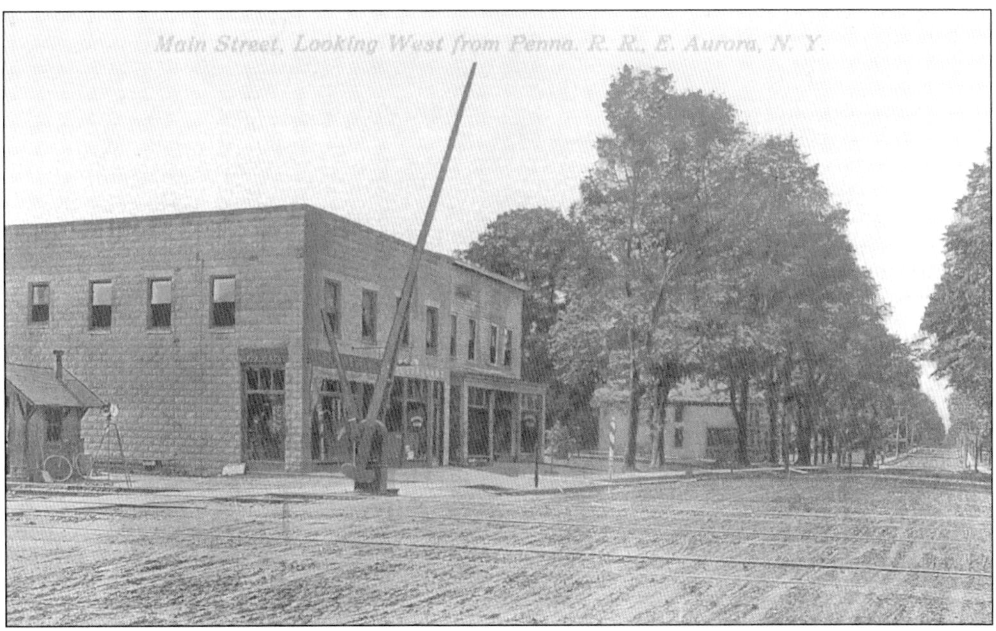

These gates were addressed in the September 3, 1903 edition of the *East Aurora Advertiser*: "Some time ago we were promised gates at the Main Street crossing of the Pennsylvania RR. As has been announced, the standards were erected but were not completed—they were left ajar. They are still in the same condition and we have about concluded that they were intended for ornaments instead of for use. What fine ornaments they make. They are so artistic."

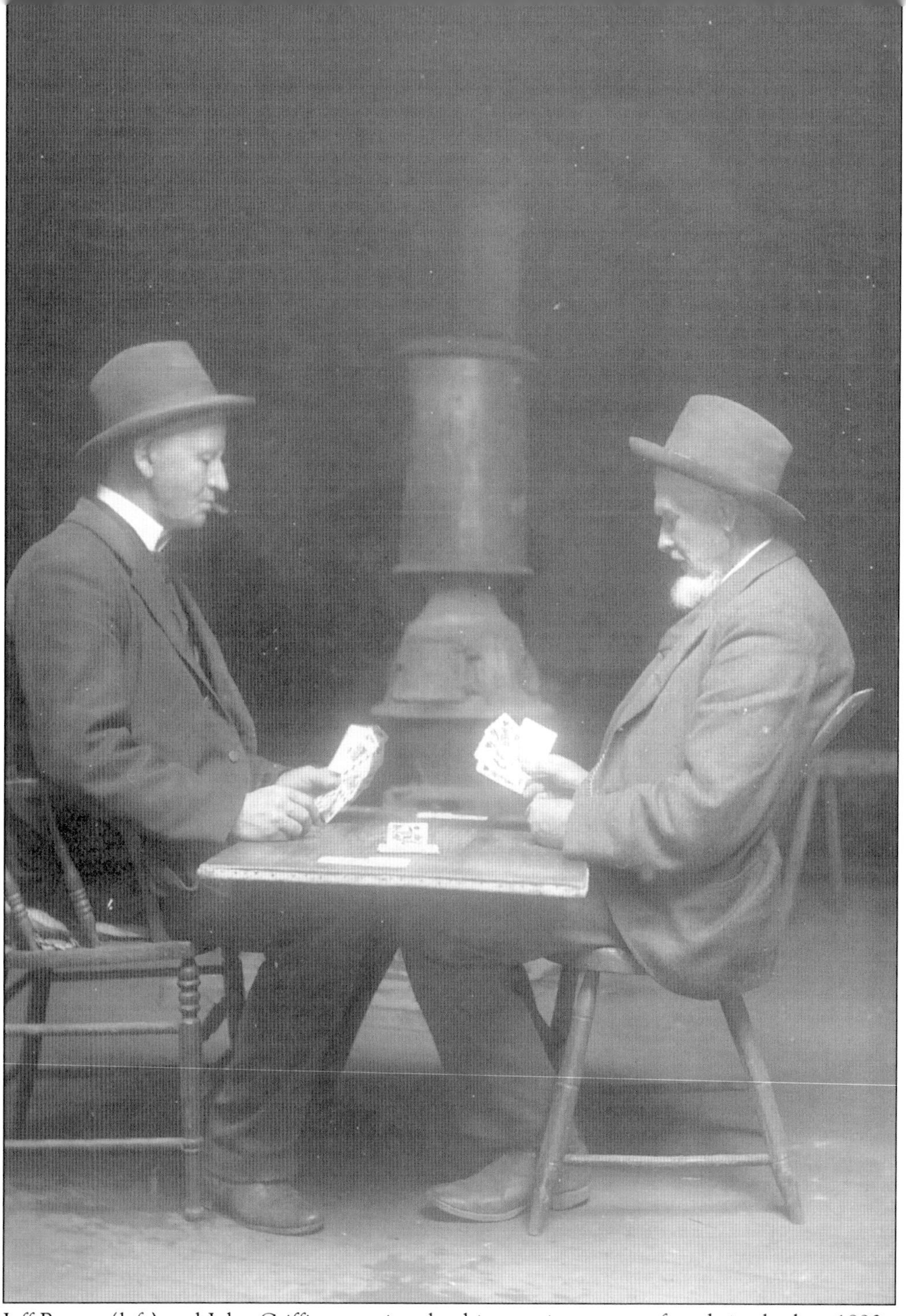

Jeff Rogers (left) and John Griffin seem involved in a serious game of cards in the late 1890s. They have the privacy of a room over Roger's carriage shop at 765 East Main Street. The wood-burning stove must have been a source of comfort on cold winter days. Griffin was father of Leander and grandfather of George, Albert, and Louise. Why do we get the impression these gentlemen are posing for this picture? After 1920, Kelver Auto occupied this property.

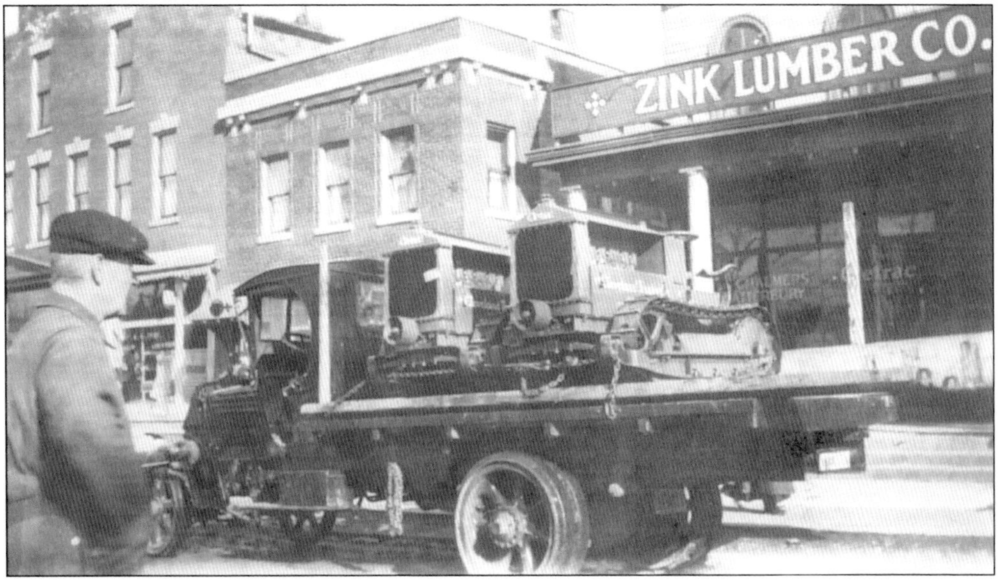

Albert Otto August Zink sold Maxwell, Chalmers, and Atterbury automobiles and Celtrac tank-type tractors around 1915. The business was on Main Street in the former Maple Leaf Hotel. The Independent Order of Odd Fellows building is second to the left. (Courtesy of A. Louis Zink, grandson.)

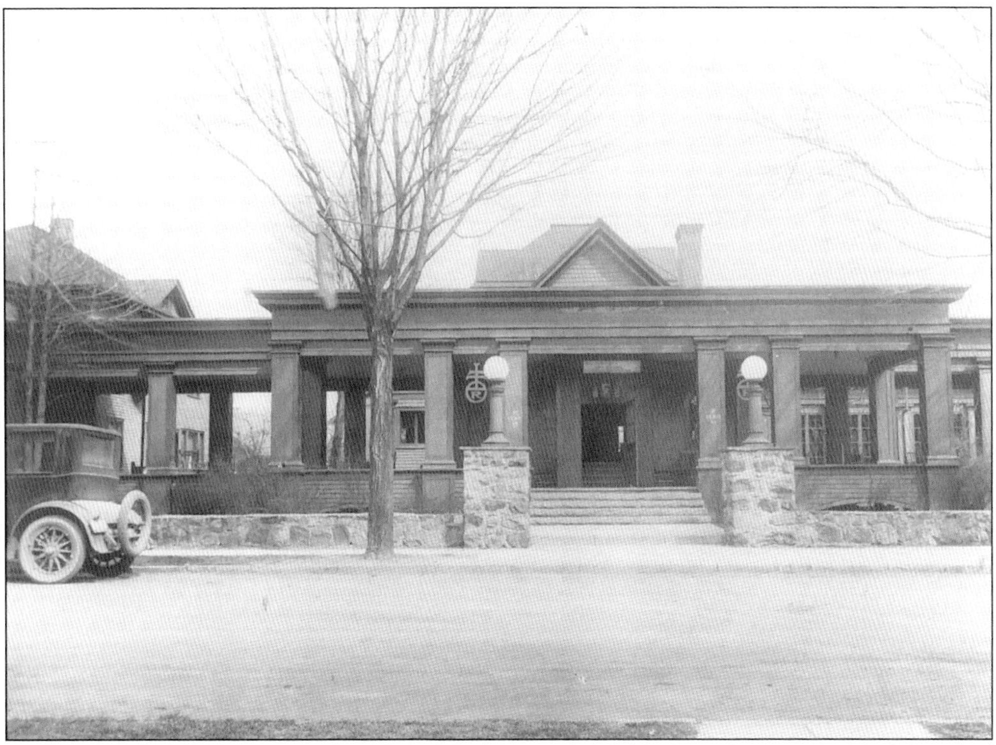

Shown is the Roycroft Inn at the turn of the century and the peristyle connecting the special guesthouse with the inn. After many years, living separate lives, the two buildings were reconnected in 2000. (Courtesy of the Roycroft Inn.)

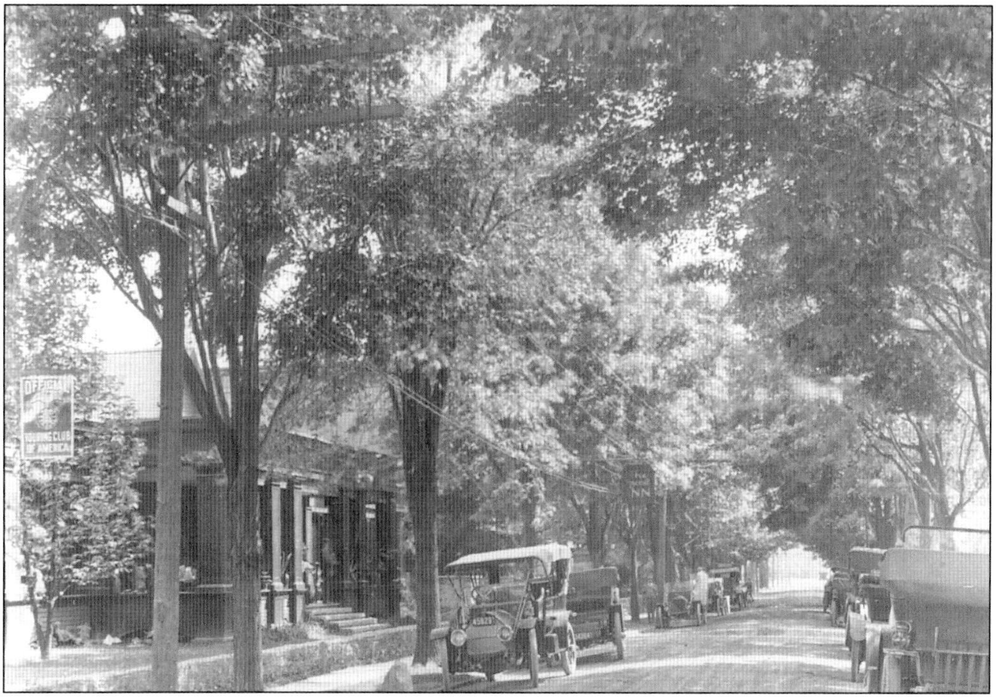

In this *c.* 1911 view of South Grove Street, horses and automobiles shared the unpaved road. (Courtesy of the Roycroft Inn.)

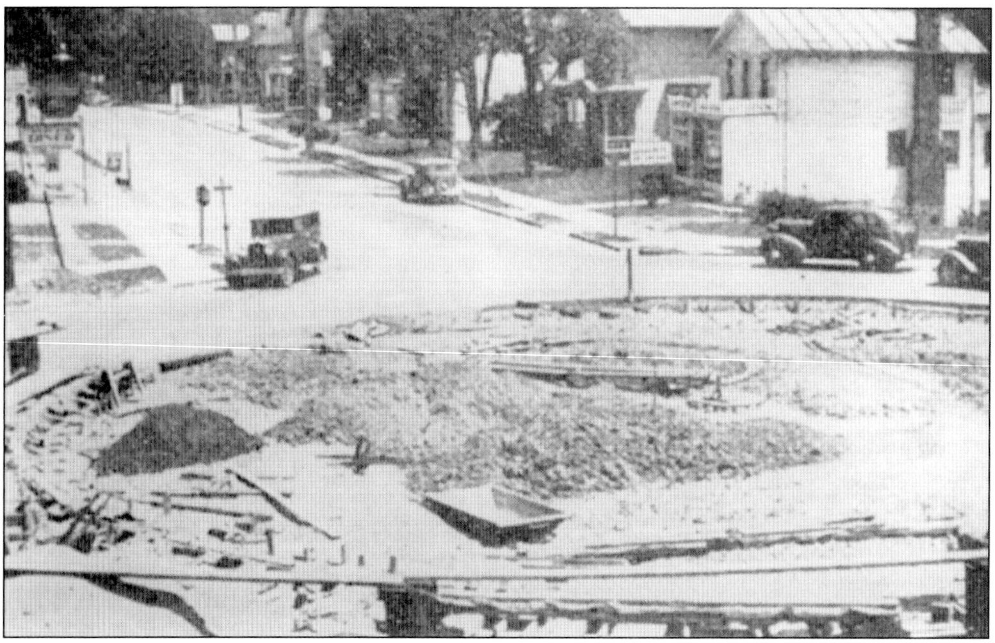

On May 19, 1936, the *East Aurora Advertiser* reported, "Traffic Circle Replaces Triangles at Willink Square" How's that for geometry? This was a Works Progress Administration (WPA) Project. An 80-foot circle replaced the triangle and eliminated confusing traffic hazards in the village. With this change, converging traffic from Main Street, Route 16 from Buffalo, Route 20 from Orchard Park and traffic from Knox Road moved smoothly around the circle.

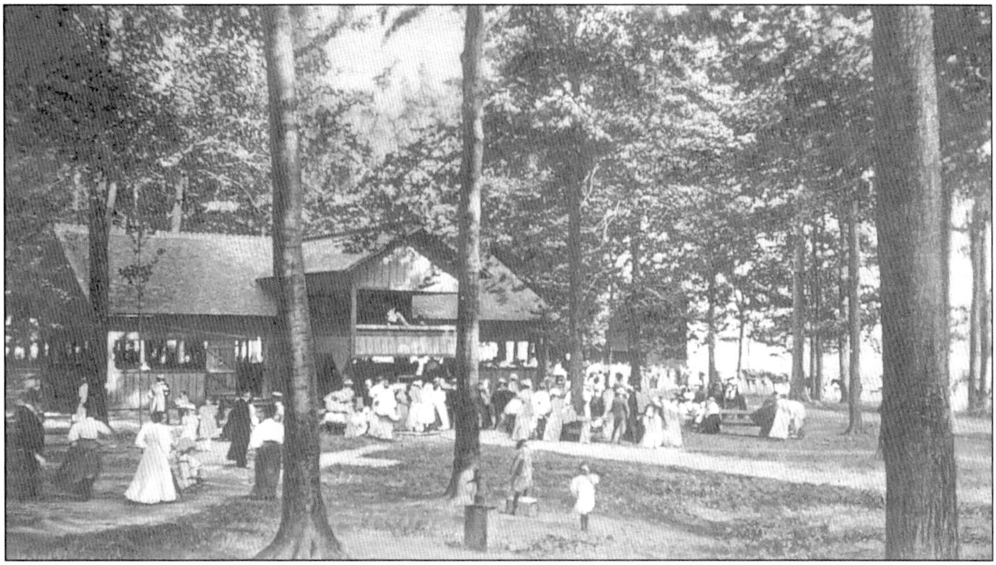

Hamlin Park, in the village, provided many recreational facilities. There was the Roycroft Pavilion, tennis courts, and picnic tables, a football field, and a baseball field, which was the home for the Mercury baseball team from 1908 to 1910. In 1900, Cicero J. Hamlin and his wife gave land for Hamlin Park to the village of East Aurora. The property had formerly been known as Holmes Grove. The deed stated that the village was to expend the amount of $100 per year to improve the park. Failure to do so would cause the land to revert to Hamlin or his heirs. Hamlin Park remains a center for many community activities.

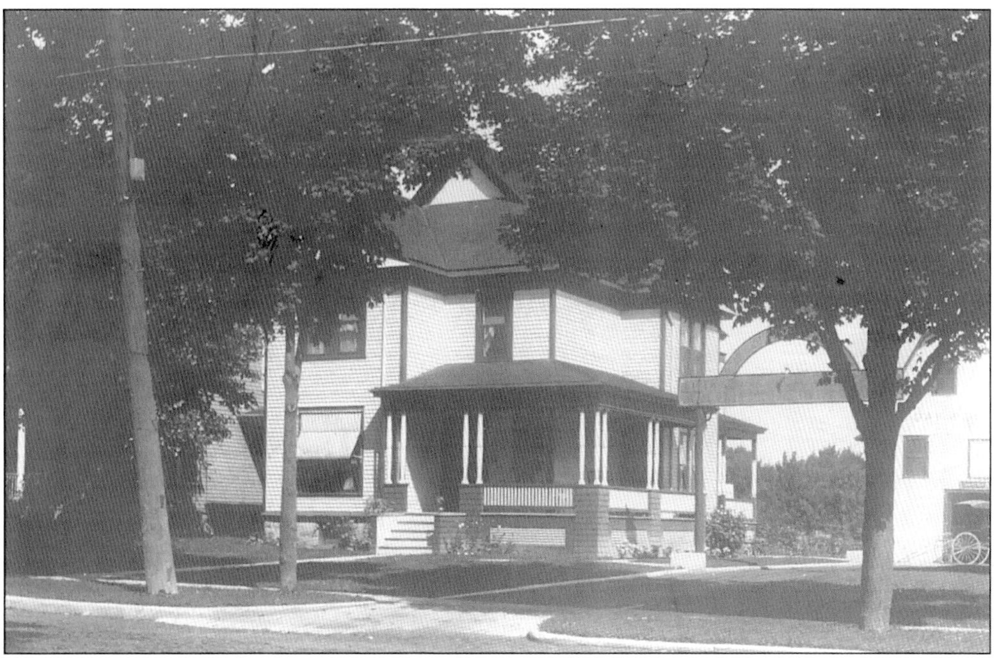

At the right side of this photograph is the Oakwood Livery Stable at the end of Sycamore Street.

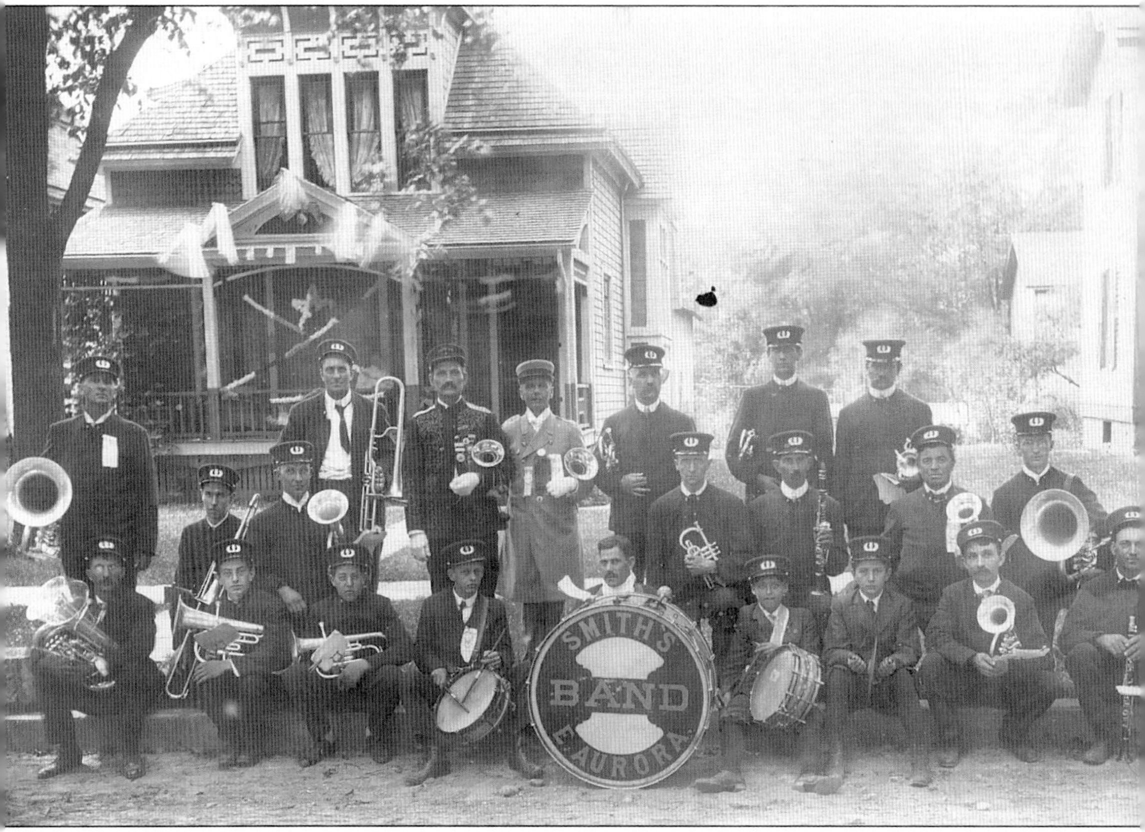

In 1894, Ezra Smith wanted to have a band of his own and asked Frank Spooner and Frank Kelsey to help assemble a group of players. Both men were excellent cornet players and owned fine, silver-plated instruments. Ezra Smith equipped the band with a complete set of the best silver-plated instruments. He also furnished uniforms with red caps and coats and either powder-blue or navy pants. He engaged Pate M. D'anna to teach the players, and the band became quite proficient, playing engagements all over western New York. They had a bandwagon, which required four horses to draw. The driver, Denny Pratt, kept the wagon at his farm or at Fred Green's barn. The wagon seated 18 to 20 men and carried instruments in the back compartment. This photograph, taken in Batavia, includes, from left to right, the following: (front row) Frank Durstein, Emmett Fritz, Sayles Buffum, Robert Haines, Herbert Buffum, Walter Whiting, Phil Fritz, Frank Higgins, and Charles Baker; (middle row) William Crandell, Lester Heller, Arthur Bass, Roy Wheeler, Frank Wright, Frank Hatch, and David Baker; (back row) Len Ernst, Henry Heller, Clarence Lamb, Frank Spooner, Louis Priafert, and Will Heller. The group was disbanded *c.* 1910.